"Brilliantly relatable, ho~~...~~
immortalized his incredi~~...~~
inspire ~~...~~

**Mark Beaumont, long-distance cyclist,
broadcaster and author**

"Inspiring AND useful – Leigh's insights on the
mental aspect of preparing for a big challenge are
amazing; I wish I'd read them years ago. There's
so much to learn from here, about achieving
athletic goals and life goals."

Sean Conway, adventurer and author

"This is a great read for anyone with an interest in
cycling or adventures. However, for those with an
interest in sport science, psychology or team dynamics,
Timmis book is so much more. It offers a brilliant case
study of just what it takes and just how many people
need to be involved in order to take on a credible world
record attempt."

**Dr Josephine Perry, sport psychologist
and author of *The 10 Pillars of Success***

"An awesome story that shows what goes on
'under the hood' of a high-performance athlete.
Leigh is an inspiration."

Jamie McDonald, adventurer and author

"I turned the pages as quickly as Leigh turned the
pedals. This tale of mental and physical endurance is
both jaw-dropping and inspirational."

Steve Silk, journalist and author

"A truly incredible achievement, and a fascinating insight into elite sporting performance – what it takes, and what it gives. Leigh brings his experience of an exploration of the world by bike and distils lessons from that, alongside the learnings of taking on something as all-consuming and ambitious as this challenge, and brings us along with him on a record-breaking ride."

Leon McCarron, adventurer and author

"Leigh is an exceptional human being and he writes with honesty and humour. This book is both a fascinating story and a profound inspiration."

Lord Burlington, Chancellor of the University of Derby

"A bonkers, fast-paced, and adrenaline-fuelled adventure. This is a fascinating insight into the world of ultra-endurance cycling. A great read, but rather him than me!"

Simon Parker, travel writer and broadcaster

"A compelling story of sport and self. Leigh's honest account taps into the importance and value of mental strength, proving there's more to athletes than physical fitness."

Mike Carter, journalist and author

"*Leigh Timmis' bravery is doubly impressive; not only did he take on a gruelling record attempt, but he faced up to his own inner demons and vulnerabilities.*"

Alastair Humphries, adventurer and author

"*This is a spirited, candid book, about aiming high and keeping going. It's impressive that anyone can sustain such a wild pace across an entire continent, but Leigh has much more to reckon with before the physical start line appears. His enthusiasm is captivating, even when the inner battles are hard won. He writes with great affection for the teammates who steered him and, with their help, finds the best in himself. It reminded me that mindsets are built, not bestowed; that faith in yourself can be the greatest challenge of them all. A fascinating, behind-the-scenes dive into how, and indeed why, world records get smashed. A banging adventure tale too.*"

Stephen Fabes, author and doctor

"*Wowsers. Talk about grit-on-wheels. I'm in awe of Leigh's willingness to push himself to the edge, in pursuit of a deeper understanding of himself and the demons that haunt us all. A beautifully written, immersive and truly gripping read.*"

Anna McNuff, author and adventurer

THE RACE OF TRUTH

An Hachette UK Company
www.hachette.co.uk

Summersdale Publishers Ltd
Part of Octopus Publishing Group Limited
Carmelite House
50 Victoria Embankment
LONDON
EC4Y 0DZ
UK

www.summersdale.com

Printed and bound by CPI Group (UK) Ltd, Croydon, CR0 4YY

ISBN: 978-1-83799-140-2

LEIGH TIMMIS

THE RACE OF TRUTH

A RECORD-BREAKING BIKE RIDE ACROSS EUROPE

summersdale

To all those who have mustered the courage to stand on the start line, this book is dedicated to your journey ahead and the possibilities that await.

CONTENTS

PROLOGUE

My body slammed hard onto the asphalt. Stones ricocheted across dusty potholes as the bike clattered to a standstill. Ten days and 8 hours into the record attempt, I lay on the road, broken and defeated, with one thought repeating in my mind – *No more, just no more, I've got no more.*

Kerr ran over, video camera still recording, and helped me to my feet. I said nothing and turned my back. Walking away slowly with my head down, I half stumbled to the motorhome. I had one foot on the step to climb in when Jahna stopped me.

"Leigh, what are you doing?" she shouted from the physio table.

"I just need to sleep," I moaned.

"Not like that," she shot back, "look at the state of you."

Blood ran down my left leg. My jersey and shorts were torn, my right knee bruised and furrowed. The 30 minutes of sleep I was desperately craving were about to be replaced by a painful session on the physio table. Jahna, always amazing, pulled the grit out of my lacerations, cleaning and disinfecting the grazes, while I forced myself to eat in silence. Distant.

Why on earth have I put myself in this situation?

I never thought it was going to be this way. This was just the latest in a series of extreme decisions I'd made in the wake of my diagnosis with depression. An adventure across Iceland by motorbike, chasing the ski season to New Zealand and Canada, bartending around the world and ultimately, a seven-year circumnavigation of the planet by bicycle. Even after all that, I still needed another challenge.

This was it; the ultimate "Race of Truth", man against the clock. I'd decided to dedicate every possible second of my life to breaking it. This was going to be my definitive performance. I'd set the bar higher than anyone had ever expected, to prove myself once and for all. No second place. Winner takes all.

Those delusions of grandeur seemed a distant memory as Jahna dusted me down and I dragged myself up from the physio couch. My body was good to go but, as I'd learned again and again, the head matters more than the legs.

The end of the break arrived without respite and the meticulously planned yet relentless strategy continued. GPS files loaded, evidence video recorded, equipment checks completed and Jem's usual line, "Ready to roll out?" With a deep sigh I shook my head but lifted a leg over the saddle and clipped into the pedals.

"Just get on that wind, mate, just tap it out and you'll be alreet," Jem encouraged, understanding how tired I was, knowing my temptation to stop. I gave a weak push to get the bike rolling, startled by the sharp pain of torn skin snagging on Lycra and the pressure of swelling bruises.

"Smile, yeah?" Jem shouted after me as the bike began to move. "Smile…" I threw a forced "smile" back at him. "Good lad!" he praised.

How much longer can I last out here? For the whole morning I'd been cycling with negative thoughts spiralling through my mind: *I'm too tired for this. I need to rest. I can't do it.* After falling off the bike, they were only joined by more. *Look at the state of your riding – terrible. You are your own worst nightmare. You can't keep going like this, you're going to crash again and get yourself killed.* I cycled despondently, listening to the internal monologue I'd become familiar with over the last year, certain that I just wasn't good enough.

It took the team 25 minutes to pack up and get back on the road. When they pulled alongside me, the electric window slowly buzzed down. I looked around into the dark cabin of the motorhome and, as my eyes adjusted from the bright daylight, I saw Jem's bearded face beaming at me.

His shout changed everything: "Eh, mucka! What's the view like from the balcony?"

Jem knew exactly what he'd said and why he'd said it. It was a personal quote that Phil and I had hooked our psychological interventions on. The balcony was a metaphor. I stood upon it – or, at least, Future Me stood upon it. The

Leigh who had finished the attempt. When I faced my toughest challenges, I could look up to the balcony, and I could ask for advice, for how to push on through. After all, there was only one person to whom I needed to justify the completion time, and that was myself. Jem's line spurred me to shift focus.

A sneer turned into a smirk and I nodded my head. "You bastard," I shouted, as the smile continued to grow. I eased off the pedals and the gap between the bike and the support vehicle slowly grew as I looked at my situation through different eyes.

All morning I'd had the tailwind I'd been waiting for, praying for, the kind of tailwind that makes or breaks records, but I'd wasted it trundling along in self-pity, thinking about how tired I was and how difficult the challenge had become. I'd lost focus, becoming so wrapped up in adversity that I forgot the whole reason I'd put myself out here. I was looking at all the things that were going wrong instead of looking at what I could control.

What would I shout to myself from the balcony right now?

In the end, the pain, the fatigue, the tiredness wouldn't matter; they would all fade with time. What mattered was that I gave everything I could, knowing that I could look back on whatever I achieved without regrets.

This wasn't about breaking a record; this was about life.

PART ONE:
HOW TO BUILD AN ATHLETE

LIVE TO RIDE...

ONE

LIVE TO RIDE, RIDE TO LIVE

On 22 April 2017, I woke in silence under canvas. A drained bottle of beer and an empty packet of Bakewell tarts lay discarded on the grass outside, the remains of my solitary celebration of the last night on the road. I unzipped my tent and peered out to look up and down the bluebell-lined footpath where I'd wild camped. Sunrise cast dappled light through the canopy onto the springtime colours of rural Derbyshire. The roar of my camping stove disturbed the quiet as coffee spluttered through my well-travelled moka pot. The smell of the crisp air and dirt mixed with the aroma of Arabica beans. There I stood, wearing a hoodie and boxer shorts, gazing over a familiar landscape that I hadn't seen in seven years – home.

Turning on a smartphone that I'd been given a month before, notifications pinged relentlessly. "Around the world in seven years... on a bike," read the BBC News headline. "Leigh Timmis: The man who cycled the world," the title of the BBC video. "Why you're wrong about Iran – and 14 other things I learnt cycling around the world for seven years," printed the *Telegraph*. My adventure was international news. I completed my morning routine for the last time, packed my tent and pedalled my heavy, worn-out bicycle along the bumpy woodland path, back to the road.

On my handlebar, a torn paper map with my route marked in fluorescent highlighter pen guided me down increasingly recognizable roads for my last few minutes alone. Helmet-free, wearing beach-bum sunglasses, I cruised along in grubby, ill-fitting clothes donated by strangers on my expedition. I looked down at the bike I called Dolly, the steadfast companion who had accompanied me through every country and encounter. Memories of all the roads those wheels had rolled along replayed in my head.

In a small village just outside the city, a gathering of 30 or so cyclists had formed to meet me. My dad, stepdad and the school friends I'd cycled with as a teenager were all there, and the entourage was completed by a local cycling club called Cycle Mickleover. Overwhelmed, I struggled to know what to say to everyone. An old friend passed me a hip flask and I took a swig of whisky. Excited conversation surrounded me but I withdrew into a bubble of memories as we set off to ride the final miles into my hometown together. Pedals, wheels and thoughts cycled simultaneously.

"Nothing ever happens in Derby" stated a graffitied mural on the pedestrianized high street through the city centre where I grew up. Derby is considered by many to be the birthplace of the factory system that set Britain's Industrial Revolution in motion. The original Silk Mill still sits opposite the cathedral that towers above the single-storey skyline in the old heart of the industrial city. The factories and offices of Rolls Royce and British Rail employed most of its residents, including my dad. As a teenager in the 90s, it was the only world that I knew; I studied engineering and took work placements in the nicotine-stained, prefabricated buildings of Derby's industrial estates.

The bike was my escape.

When I was 14 years old, mountain biking took a hold of me and three friends. The relatively new sport had the chilled-out feel of the surfing community; we wore baggy shorts and skateboard shoes, we had long hair and listened to Green Day, Nirvana and the Foo Fighters. On any given day, at least one of us had scabs on our knees and elbows from a fall and we all built a collection of scars on our shins, shaped by the teeth on our pedals. We escaped the classroom's stark white walls into the world of our imagination; designing bikes, dreaming up our perfect build from exotic components and talking about trails we'd ride that evening.

After school, I used to ride 5 miles to the other side of town where the four of us met up. We sat on the floor around the TV and watched mountain bike videos of our heroes, before copying their tricks and jumps in the University of Derby car park. When the campus security guards chased us away, we sprinted to the woods at the top of the golf course, where we thundered down dusty trails, our hearts racing. I was hooked.

There was one video called *Dirt* that we rewound and played again and again. It starred the best British mountain bikers of the time popping wheelies across the countryside and hanging off their bikes as they skidded through gates. The film wasn't about their achievements, winning races or endorsing brands. It wasn't really about bikes. It was about four friends hanging out and having fun. They were rock stars to me and I wanted to be just like them. They coined the phrase "Live to ride, ride to live" and I lived by it too.

Responsibilities and pressures didn't matter then – everything else in life was just the stuff in between biking. Life was great, I was fulfilled, and I had a purpose. When I was on the bike, I was myself, in my own space, at my own pace. I wasn't trying to live up to the expectations of others; I could shut out the rest of the world to be in a place where I was in control. The future looked exciting from the saddle.

On long summer days, my friends and I challenged ourselves to ride as far as we could, choosing a route and just pedalling and pedalling. It felt as though we rode to distant places, even though we were only a few miles out of town.

As we grew braver, we took our bikes further, catching the train north to ride in the Peak District, where we disappeared for days with only a paper Ordnance Survey map and a jam sandwich. We rode the rocky trails across sandstone edges, under the wings of paragliders and past crowds of rock climbers. The smooth roads we cycled circumnavigated reservoirs where dinghies sailed before we dived through gates and hammered our bikes down technical, rocky tracks. It was as though life was simplified by those rides, the rudimental bikes that we built ourselves connecting us directly to the earth. We felt every contour on the map through our legs and lungs and the descents rattled our eyes in their sockets. The wind and rain froze us on hilltops when we packed too few clothes and the sun burned us when we stayed out in it too long, absorbed in the moment. We relied on our own skills to navigate the trails and to make repairs when things went wrong. Young, far from home and only connected to the city by a train timetable and the nearest phone box, we felt adventurous and alive.

The bike expanded my horizon beyond the city, into the National Park and countryside surrounding it. I never imagined it would take me out of England and around the globe.

———————————————

I cycled ahead of the other cyclists, distracted by my thoughts. I had believed that at the conclusion of my epic cycle adventure, I would return as a changed man to a home that remained the same. But the grim city that I had left seven years before felt clean and optimistic as the cycling club guided me past new architecture and an imposing gold, silver and bronze velodrome.

I rode quickly past the historic landmarks I recognized in my hometown, anxious to find what awaited me at the finish. There she was. On the opposite side of a cobbled square I saw the tiny figure of my mum. She stood alone in front of the applauding crowd. Naturally shy, she would never have chosen to stand there; no doubt the media had asked her to be more visible. Wearing jeans and a thin jumper, she was the mum who had encouraged me to be myself, the mum who had picked me up when I fell, the mum who was always there. Among the insanity and noise of the moment, nothing else mattered. I was just a son reunited with his mother for the first time in years. It was just as I had imagined.

Through the darkest times cycling the world, I'd been motivated by the thought that, no matter how difficult, I would overcome any challenge I faced and one day this moment would come; I would return home and I would hug my mum again. That thought had brought tears to my eyes so many times before and yet I worried I wouldn't feel the emotion when it really happened. As I cycled across the square, tears streamed down my face. Camera crews from the local media gathered around us. I embraced Mum and whispered in her ear, "I love you so much, I can't believe what I've done." After years of being the stranger in places that I hadn't known, I belonged.

My hands trembled and my heart pounded, overwhelmed with the most incredible elation. An adventure that had begun in Derby seven years before and wandered 70,000 km (44,000 miles), through 51 countries on a budget of only five pounds a day, had come full circle. Champagne corks popped, speeches were made, and I tried my best to string a few words together that would summarize the moment for the interviews that followed.

I'd cycled around the world.

Crowds dispersed and calm descended. I sat beside Dolly, just as I had done in distant forests, mountains and deserts, but now I was in the garden of a pub in my hometown, surrounded by friends and family. It was surreal; I'd achieved more than I ever expected even in my wildest imagination. My life had been painted with a million vibrant colours from the experiences, characters and landscapes of an impossibly varied world that I'd viewed from the saddle of a bike.

"Cheers!" we shouted. Pint glasses clinked and beer flowed. We laughed and hugged and celebrated.

"So, what's next?" asked my dad.

_____

I arrived home with nothing but a bike, a tent, the essentials for survival, and a maxed-out credit card. At a time when friends had houses, cars, high-paying jobs and children, I moved into the spare room at my mum and stepdad's house. I'd been around the world and ended up back in the place where I grew up; at 35 years old, the adventure was over and I was faced with the "real world".

Two days later, my younger sister also returned to Derby from New Zealand. Emma and I had a strong childhood bond, reinforced in the stench of a tent we'd shared for months across multiple adventures; unbreakable. She had run across Africa twice and had an ultra-endurance world record herself; there were a lot of similarities between us. Living together as a family again was like looking into the past. Childhood and adulthood existed in parallel. I told her I wouldn't have cycled around the world without the lessons we learned at a very young age and she agreed; it was the same for her and her achievements.

When I was six and Emma was four, Dad wanted to build his own house, so our family moved to a self-build scheme in Derby. Oakwood would become Europe's largest housing estate. In a cut-out from a weekly magazine of the time, there's a photo of me and the other children in the bucket of a tractor surrounded by our proud families, in front of the houses they built themselves. The parents had full-time jobs and so, for two years, our weekends and evenings were spent building. Emma and I grew up on a muddy construction site. I remember pushing toy cars through tunnels dug in piles of sand, jumping on heaps of fibreglass insulation, running in and out of half-finished houses, riding my BMX bike around the gardens and making jumps out of bricks and scaffolding boards. The sound of hammering nails over static on the radio, the smell of cut timber and the view of overcast skies through roofing joists. We must have moved in while finishing the interior because I remember the bare floorboards of a bedroom shared with Emma.

Dad was a man who followed convention. When the house was built, he started an Open University degree and his evenings and weekends continued to be occupied for years to come. In a world that valued education, employment, promotion and security on the housing ladder, he fulfilled society's expectations and then some. Personally, I questioned whether the sacrifices he made for his achievements were worth it. Dad always seemed to be too busy to do anything with us and would say so as he refocused on his work.

I wanted our childhood to be like the ones I saw on television: when the father arrives home, he embraces his children and they share stories of their day. However, when *my* dad arrived home, he vented his frustration at the other "idiot road users" on us and when I tried to share my stories and experiences with him he'd say, "We don't need a running commentary on everything you do." My friends at school seemed to have great relationships with their dads, and I felt sad coming home from friends' houses, whose dads would play football with us or go out to collect conkers. I'd pull at Dad, working on his computer, and ask if he could play but he would plainly tell me, "Not now, can't you see I'm busy?"

He seemed to struggle to contain his emotions and his anger permeates my childhood memories. One day, I remember my sister and I were bickering in the back of the car as he drove, so he slammed the brakes on so hard that our seat belts locked and our heads were thrown forwards as the car skidded down the road, he then turned around and shouted at us, with an incomparable fury. At the other end of the scale I don't remember Dad telling me he was proud of me or that I'd done well – rather, there was always something more that I should achieve. He grew into a figure of authority, who I found it difficult to talk to, not knowing if I would provoke an emotional response. I stepped on eggshells around him, but some of them turned out to be landmines. He would regularly get angry at me and shout.

It seemed as though Dad didn't have time for us; he had the ability to build a house but making a home was seemingly a bigger challenge.

I resented some of Dad's behaviour towards me as a kid. I feel that he left emotional gaps in my upbringing that manifested in my own behaviours, but I can't hold it against him. He fulfilled his important role, he brought in the money to afford the childhood Emma and I had with Mum. Everybody has their own battle to fight and I'm sure he was trying his best. A traveller once told me that the characteristics we don't like in others are actually what we don't like in ourselves. For a long time, I tried not to make the mistakes that I'd seen my dad make but I often found myself walking in his footsteps. Looking back, it's clear that what angered me about Dad was often a reflection of my own behaviour. Although it seemed to be that our relationship wasn't always healthy, I felt that it added momentum to my life; I was trying to live up to what I believed were Dad's expectations of me, but I never felt that I did. Even as an adult, the child within me was still looking to prove himself and every time it felt as though Dad pushed me away, he pushed me to achieve more.

One year, on holiday from primary school, Emma and I spent a week on our grandparents' farm, 3 hours away on the south coast of England. Farm life was wild; we were free-range children. We raced up and down the long garden of the small white bungalow, past the shepherd's hut and under the apple trees, taking it in turns to push each other in a wheelbarrow. We played in the dusty kennels, shot air rifles and foraged for fruits and eggs in the garden. As we walked the dogs through the woods, we heard the roar of the elephants from Marwell Zoo; life in the countryside was an adventure.

Towards the end of the week, we snuck out of sight and stood alone on the gravel driveway. Emma asked why I thought we were there for so long without Mum and Dad. I clearly remember feeling like the big brother as I explained my conclusion to the question I'd also been contemplating. I told her that I thought we were either getting a new brother or sister, or that Mum and Dad were splitting up.

When we returned to Derby, our parents told us they were getting divorced. I spent night after night crying myself to sleep or sobbing in my bunk bed as Mum and Dad yelled at each other and slammed doors downstairs.

Emma and I moved out with Mum into a small house that she finished with second-hand furniture, less than a mile away from the self-build street. Us kids had the two largest rooms in the house and Mum's room was tiny; barely big enough for a single bed and a wardrobe. We called it the "cat flap". At this time I started spending more time outside. There was a small green space beside our house where I towed Emma on her roller skates, tied to my bike with a skipping rope. I'd outgrown my BMX and Mum or Dad bought me a heavy, sluggish mountain bike, which I tinkered with in the garage, learning how to index the gears, sharpen the brakes and fix punctures. After the divorce, riding the bike was a place where I could be myself – an element of my life that was totally under my control. In a way, I could express myself through the bike; sprinting or cruising, I rode at my speed.

Getting into bikes also helped keep me occupied, which was useful because Mum was growing busier all the time. I don't know what the employment options were as a single mother with two kids to feed but Mum made a brave decision. She created an opportunity from the experience she had and decided to expand a cleaning company she'd started.

Mum showed us an ability to radically change our lives for the better. As a child, she was abused by her parents and was told she had to move out as soon as she was old enough. It was a history that Emma and I were protected from – it was never spoken of. Mum overcame her malevolent upbringing and created a loving home, raising Emma and me with warmth and kindness. It must have been difficult creating something that you have never experienced, but she did it. Mum says that she always wanted to raise her children to feel loved, and she did exactly that.

Mum remarried a few years later and just before Emma and I became teenagers we moved in with our stepdad, Al. For a man who didn't want to have children, he handled it incredibly well. He was a tall financial adviser with "milk bottle glasses" and he wore leather gloves to drive, which we called his "murdering gloves". Al and I stayed awake into the early hours to watch Formula One when the races were on the other side of the world and he had a Sega Master System, on which he let me play "Alex Kidd in Miracle World". Al didn't want to be "Dad" but he was always there for us, as a friend and as a role model.

As young children, we still saw Dad on alternate weekends and every Thursday evening, when he walked us round to his house after work. It was the same every week: he'd feed us tuna, pasta and mayonnaise, and watch us do our homework. I didn't understand why, if you only saw your children so rarely, you wouldn't make those moments memorable. When I left school, I lived with Dad for a couple of years because I knew he wouldn't treat me like a parent. We were like ships that passed in the night, which was better than the inevitable arguments that would ensue when we collided.

Al knew the importance of family and compassion. When he was young, his parents were loving and caring and always said, "I love you" to each other before they left the home. On one rare occasion when they had an argument, his dad slammed the door as he left the house without saying those important words. Later that day, he was involved in an industrial accident at the Rover car plant where he worked. He died from his injuries, in hospital, a week later.

As our stepdad, Al showed Emma and I a masculinity that was founded in reason and emotional intelligence and he opened his life to us completely. Every day he told us he loved us and that he was proud of us, and he was there when we needed support.

Al's philosophy was that you had to look after yourself before you could look after others and Mum's was similar. She always said that she didn't mind what Emma and I did when we grew up, as long as we were happy. Those beliefs were clear in their actions when they raised us, and things were the same over 25 years later when they took me in after cycling the world. Their support underpinned everything I've achieved and allowed me to take opportunities that changed the course of my life.

Steve Reynolds, the organizer of my escorted ride into Derby, had introduced himself on the day I returned and invited me for dinner when the dust had settled. A week later, I took Steve up on his invitation. Arriving at his home, I walked across the vast brick-paved driveway, looking up at the enormous L-shaped building towering above me, climbed the steps and knocked on the front door. I stood, sweating, in cycling shorts so old that they were becoming transparent, a charity cycling jersey and old cycling shoes with Velcro fasteners that no longer worked, holding a change of clothes in a backpack.

Steve opened the door. "Hi Leigh, welcome, it's great to see you. You cycled here?"

"Erm, yeah," I replied, ashamed that my old bike was the only transport I owned. "So, how many houses is this?"

"Just one," Steve laughed. "Come through to the kitchen."

"Oh, wow!"

Steve was in his late 50s and the owner of a successful mobile technology company he'd built from scratch. He welcomed me into his family home just like every other stranger I'd met around the world and we bonded over a love of bikes. We laughed while comparing stories of cycling up the iconic Stelvio mountain pass in Italy, which he'd done on an 8 kg racing bike and I'd done on a 40 kg touring bike. We realized we shared similar experiences but through very different methods. Steve invited me to join Cycle Mickleover, the bike club he organized. I'd never cycled with a road club before and the thought of riding in a peloton, a tightly-bunched group of cyclists, at speed, intimidated me. I wondered whether I could even keep up. I was a cycle adventurer who travelled at leisure. In my panniers I carried food, drink and a tent so I could stop whenever I wanted to.

The following week, I found my old eight-speed aluminium road bike in Mum's shed, pumped the tyres up, oiled the chain and joined their Sunday club ride. I straddled my cheap bike in the pub car park, surrounded by thousands of pounds' worth of top-of-the-range racers. Everyone had carbon frames and wheels, with brands and components that I'd never heard of. It looked like rocket ship technology to me. The cyclists, wrapped in aerodynamic fabrics, spoke in terms of drag coefficients, power meters, FTPs and MMPs, bikes for climbing, aero bikes and electronic gears. It meant nothing to me. I'd been passionate about mountain biking and touring but I realized that I knew nothing about road cycling. The most high-tech gadget I had was a magnet on the front wheel with a wire up to the LCD display on my handlebars that told me my speed, distance and the time of day. I was out of touch.

I held on for my life as the bike rattled over the potholed roads of Derbyshire on narrow tyres with a crowd of other cyclists all around me. They felt too close and I worried that I couldn't move to avoid any obstacles ahead. *What do I do if they brake suddenly? How am I supposed to see the holes in the road ahead?* With guidance, I started to figure out how road cycling worked and I enjoyed chatting to the other cyclists as we swapped places in the group, zooming down Derbyshire's country lanes to the soundtrack of clicking gear shifts. Fifty miles later, back at the pub we started at, I felt good and I'd built some confidence. I started to think this was something I could get into. I asked when the next ride was.

With a couple of rides under my belt, I learned group riding etiquette and realized that there was nothing to fear. I could hold the pace and enjoyed cruising in the middle of the pack, sheltered from the wind at 20 miles per hour. Everyone looked after each other.

When I got to know the intimidating group of expert-looking, Lycra-clad "speed demons" with expensive bikes, they turned out to be human beings, some of the best I'd met. On cold, wet, miserable mornings, when I was tempted to stay in bed, it was knowing that my friends would be waiting in the pub car park to cycle together that encouraged me to go out. Each person had their own motivations for cycling. For some, the club ride was an escape from stresses that they experienced through the week, some were losing weight, some trained to race and, to others, the club was their social life. Club rides weren't just about cycling; they were about a group of people getting outside, exercising, catching up with friends and seeing new horizons together. The bike club changed lives.

At that time, I saw returning to Derby as the end of my cycling adventure, but Steve saw it as just the beginning. He introduced me to a local bike shop and convinced them to lend me a good-quality bike. Riding a top-of-the-range, carbon-fibre Cannondale Super Six, I led a 100-mile (161 km) charity ride out of the city, on the way to Skegness. At the end, we visited the Derbyshire Children's Holiday Centre – that I'd raised £12,000 for while cycling around the world – and celebrated with dinner and drinks on the seafront. A group of us cycled back to Derby the following day, completing 200 miles (322 km) in two days. It was the furthest I'd ridden in

48 hours. I continued to ride the borrowed bike through the summer, and with the help of the bike club, I began to realize that in seven years of cycling around the world I'd built an impressive foundation of fitness. I saw the potential that Steve had seen but at that time it wasn't important; I didn't know where to direct it and I had bigger things to worry about, establishing a life for myself in Derby.

As Steve and I spent more time cycling together with the club, I opened up to him about the overwhelming opportunities I'd received since I'd arrived home. I'd been offered a television interview with BBC News, a guest slot on a daytime TV show, photoshoots for magazines and newspaper articles, speaking engagements for businesses, a National Geographic event, and an invitation to present a TEDx talk. I had no idea where to begin unpacking seven years of experiences and presenting them in a way that anyone could comprehend, let alone how to act on TV or in front of a live audience.

Motivated purely by generosity, Steve and his family took me under their collective wing, offered to assist me and, through the summer of 2017, helped me get my career on track. Steve showed me how my experiences from cycling around the world applied to business and personal challenges that everybody could understand. His daughters, Hayleigh and Shelley, created a visual brand for me, taught me about storytelling and how to present on stage. Steve's wife, Gill, supported me through every panic and concern; she let me bounce ideas off her and shared her own experiences to guide me. I spent an increasing amount of time at their house, sometimes staying over to run through talks and new content. They even had me doing fashion parades in new clothes and cycling gear.

As I spent more and more time with them, it felt as though I was all but adopted into Steve's family. We hung out in his garden, drinking gin and tonic in the drifting smoke of the barbecue, playing games, and sharing stories in the sun. We spent evenings catching up on culture that I'd missed while I was away, calling the seven years I'd spent cycling around the world "The Blackout" because I had no general knowledge from the time. That summer became synonymous with Marvel movies and the *Guardians of the Galaxy* soundtrack. I joined the family for dinner in restaurants that I previously thought were too good for me and his daughters dressed me so I didn't look like I lived in a tent anymore. They raised my self-esteem and my confidence began to grow.

Steve's family believed in me and they wanted to help me reach my potential. After I'd lived for so long with one foot out the door, always ready to leave, they made me feel settled.

With their support, I sat on the red sofas of BBC News and talked about the extremes of life on the road. I attended photo shoots and interviews for cycling and lifestyle magazines. Shelley accompanied me at the TEDx event, where I stood on stage wearing borrowed clothes and shoes, praying that I wouldn't forget what we'd scripted. With cameras and lights pointing at me, I delivered a talk that I was proud of and I began sharing my lessons and experiences at corporate and educational speaking events.

Nevertheless, as the summer began ticking away, I found myself drifting without a purpose. I was financially treading water with income from low-fee speaking events at schools and bike clubs, living half the week at Steve's house and the other half at Mum's. Steve showed me that I could create a life from what I loved, not only in speaking but in cycle tour leading or brand ambassadorial roles, I just had to decide what I wanted to do. I had fantastic opportunities but there was something missing. I was still looking for that elusive "What's next?"

The more audiences I spoke to about cycling around the world, the more I began to doubt that I had achieved something of value. Once the awe of where I'd been and how far I'd cycled had worn off, my answers to some questions seemed disappointing.

"So, how much money do you get for cycling around the world?" I'd be asked.

"No, you don't get any money. But I'm rich in experiences," I'd laugh.

"Oh. Okay. What about a certificate?"

"No, nothing like that either."

"So, why did you do it?"

Why did I do it? At the time, I believed I'd spent seven years learning about the world and my place in it. I'd learned different languages and overcome great adversity. So much time alone on the bike had been almost meditative, I thought I'd learned a lot about myself. I was regularly asked if I was going back to work now that I'd finished my holiday. *Had it all been a selfish pursuit: personal gain but no social value?* I didn't have lessons about team building or peak performance to share at corporate events. I couldn't endorse giving up work to pursue a dream.

My reflections reminded me of a decision I'd made long ago. Before I cycled around the world, I went to see a talk by an adventurer who had walked across the Sahara Desert. For 45 minutes he showed slides and spoke of his adventures as though he had just returned. Afterwards I found out that he'd finished his challenge almost ten years earlier. From that moment I decided I couldn't be like that; I never wanted to live my whole life based on one achievement. Around the world would only be my first challenge and I didn't want to do the same kind of adventure again – I'd proved I could do that. I needed something completely new.

I wanted to be the guy who cycled the world *and...*

One bright morning, I sat in the sunlight that poured through the Velux windows in Steve's lounge with my feet up on the reclined cream leather sofa. As I flicked through the pages of a cycling magazine, I read an article about the world record for the fastest crossing of Europe by bike – a 6,500-km (4,000-mile) transcontinental time trial.

Three cyclists had attempted to break the record that year and none had done so. In July, Iain Findlay set off from Russia, heading to Portugal and at the same time, Jonas Deichmann set off in the opposite direction. After a week, Findlay abandoned his effort due to stomach problems and, although Deichmann reached Ufa a couple of days quicker than the existing record, his attempt wasn't verified on the Guinness website. The magazine article reported that Sean Conway, one of the UK's premier adventurers, had recently abandoned an attempt due to a torn muscle. It piqued my interest.

It wasn't the first time I'd considered something like this. In the first month of cycling around the world I met a brightly dressed, excitable Australian guy carrying a ukulele, called Sebastian Terry. He told me the story of his best friend who had tragically died at a young age and it had caused Seb to question whether, if he was to die tomorrow, he would be happy with the life he'd lived. To that end, he'd written his bucket list and was travelling the world, ticking off his "100 things". I met him on number 36 – walk across a country – after he'd spent five months completing number 46 – learning French. He laughed as he explained that after completing his walk, he was flying to the United States to conduct a wedding and deliver a baby, ticking off two more. When I explained to him that I was going to be spending years on a bike and I wondered whether there were other things I could do at the same time, he'd suggested breaking a world record. A seed had been planted.

As I read the article about the record for the fastest cycle across Europe it looked achievable at that very moment. James McLaren's 2016 record still stood at 29 days, 18 hours and 25 minutes. After some quick calculations, knowing that the route was about 4,000 miles, I guessed that would be about 225 km (140 miles) a day. I could beat that. Definitely. Without a doubt. I could knock hours, probably days, off it. I shouted through Steve's house, "I've found it, this is what I'm going to do, I could do it tomorrow, I should fly out there now!" Steve and I looked through the record guidelines together.

"From the lighthouse in Cabo da Roca, Portugal, to Ufa Railway Terminal, Russia. Any route may be followed. The same bicycle must be used throughout the entire attempt. The journey must be tracked by an accurate, professional GPS device. During the attempt, the challenger is not allowed the aid of drafting. No distinction will be made between supported and unsupported journeys. The clock starts from the moment the participant crosses the starting line and does not stop until they reach their goal."

In cycling, the individual time trial is called the "Race of Truth" because the result depends solely on one cyclist's ability; no slipstream from other cyclists and no group cycling to benefit from; just the cyclist and the road. To me, this was the ultimate test, cycling between the geographical borders of a continent – from the coast of Portugal to the Ural Mountains, 1,000 miles inside the Russian border, against the clock.

Steve tapped the screen with conviction, pointing out one sentence that changed my approach to the attempt more than anything else: "No distinction will be made between supported and unsupported journeys."

"Yeah, but I don't need support, I know I could break that record right now," I told him.

"Which way will you achieve your best result?" he asked.

"Well, with a support team, for sure but—" I began to reply before he cut me off.

"And which way can you best mitigate failure?" Steve pressed me again.

"Yeah, a team would help but—"

"Then that is the way you will do it."

Without Steve, I wouldn't have even considered going fully supported; there were too many obstacles. In comparison to going unsupported it was extremely expensive, it would take much longer to prepare and it would require much greater effort to coordinate. At that time, I was a chancer; I was carefree and took risks. The only times I had done things without compromise were in matters of life or death. In those situations, I made certain that there was no room for error but at home I let my standards slip. Steve changed that. He focused my attention away from what I *could* achieve and on to what I *wanted* to achieve. Through the summer, I'd grown. I was no longer the same person who was content to subsist on five pounds a day, living out of pannier bags as I had around the world. He showed me that there was a best way to do everything and that the best way was the only way. In breaking a world record, I was going to discover just what I could do. Steve convinced me to commit to an ethos of *no compromise*.

I was interested to know how Sean Conway had created his strategy, which had been on course to break the record, so I phoned him to chat about it. His answer reflected how everybody was approaching transcontinental cycling records at the time. Sean told me that he had the route of the previous fastest challenger and knew where he had stopped every night. His plan was to go a few miles further every day and, by the end, he would knock a few hours off the record. While that approach might get a world record certificate, copying others didn't seem like the best way of doing things. With Steve's *no compromise* hat on, I questioned how, by doing the same thing again, I would differentiate myself from everyone else and how I would find out what I was truly capable of. I intended to make my own mark on the world. Steve and I put a plan together to turn the traditional approach on its head.

I was an outsider, coming in with fresh eyes, unaccustomed to the world of ultra-endurance cycle racing. I would bring innovation to a record that had previously been tackled by spending more time in the saddle to cycle more miles. The ultimate uncompromising method was to pull together a team of experts who would use science and technology. Professional support throughout preparation as well as on the road would improve my performance through training, analyze the challenge to find every marginal gain, build an evidence-based strategy, and mitigate risk of failure on the road.

I looked at the demands of the attempt and previous reasons for failure, and designed a team based on the best solutions to the problems. I would require a coach, a nutritionist and a physiotherapist to optimize my physical performance and a driver and a mechanic to join them on the road.

An unsupported effort would cost about £2,000 plus a bike. To put together an attempt with a preparation team in the UK, a support team on the road and all necessary equipment, flights, visas and vehicles would need about £50,000. Seven years spent living in a tent were less than ideal foundations for financing and managing a complex world record project. Evenings at Steve's house expanded into using his company's office space by day, as he helped me to develop a business mind.

Every day I learned something new and every day I asked questions. In the same way that I didn't know about cycling aerodynamics, power or heart rate, I also didn't know about memorandums of understanding, letters of engagement or non-disclosure agreements. We put together a 16-page project outline detailing our objectives, the record and our approach, the performance team, our visibility and awareness campaign and sponsorship opportunities.

While cycling the world I'd fundraised for the Derbyshire Children's Holiday Centre because I believed that, even on a global project, I should help my local community. After explaining to Steve that I'd struggled with anxiety and depression in my twenties, he asked why I hadn't raised money for a mental health charity. The honest answer was that I was afraid of talking about it. When I left in 2010, there was a huge stigma attached to mental health and I feared being judged. Although this attitude hadn't disappeared completely, during the time I'd spent out of the UK, society's understanding of mental health had progressed. Steve urged me to talk about my own struggle and to involve a mental health charity in the world record. I partnered with MQ Mental Health Research, whose active scientific research into the causes of mental illness reflected my scientific approach to the record.

Steve mentored me and his experience directed me throughout the course of the project. I took on everything he taught me because I wanted to be like him; to have complete financial freedom, to be the one who people turned to for support, to be confident in my convictions. As a role model 22 years older than me, Steve was less like a friend and more like a father. I'd never consciously looked for father figures in my life, but our relationship naturally grew that way. Since I was young, I'd suppressed or tried to eliminate many of my own characteristics that I negatively associated with Dad and maybe I was looking for someone to fill those gaps.

Steve could be fiercely harsh with his words but I knew he wanted the best for me, respected me and was proud of me – he told me as much. Steve's honesty and direct nature changed me, fast. Looking over my emails he would ask "Why are you writing like it's a letter to the Queen? Give it here," and show me how to write for business. When I missed a call with a potential sponsor he was stern. "You don't get a second chance to make a first impression," he told me, "you've ruined it." I didn't make the same mistake twice. Steve only aligned himself with success and so, with him by my side, I believed I could do anything.

My decision to attempt the record was made, but I had to prove to myself that I was being realistic. On a warm Saturday morning, less than five months after returning from cycling the world, my alarm went off before dawn and I loaded my jersey pockets with spares and snacks. I closed the door and began cycling my borrowed bike just after sunrise. By 2 p.m., I was eating fish and chips on the beach at Skegness before I turned around and completed the return journey. I cycled 200 miles (322 km) in just under 12 hours, doubling the furthest I'd ever ridden in a day. Knowing it was possible marked a major milestone; I'd been told about club cyclists completing this ride before but until I did, it held a mythical status. Now, 200 miles was confirmed as a distance I could ride in a day, I knew what it took and what it felt like. I was elated. I wasn't sure whether I could get up and do the same thing the following day but there was time to work on that.

In a surge of enthusiasm, I bought a GPS unit and a heart rate monitor and declared the ultimate statement of intent: I shaved my legs. I was no longer an adventurer; I was an athlete.

On 8 September 2017, a week after my ride to Skegness, I submitted an application to *Guinness World Records* with a proposed start date of 11 June 2018.

The clock was ticking.

TWO
BROTHERS IN ARMS

Dust kicks up into the warm air as deep-treaded mountain bike tyres thunder downhill, speeding between trees. My heart beats hard and fast, adrenaline pumps through my body as I dab the brakes and my feet slip on the pedals. Bright sunbeams dapple the trail under a dense green canopy, catching my eyes as I jump in and out of the shade. The chain clatters and gears clunk, changing quickly, tyres struggling to grip over tree roots. I'm in the zone – no past, no future, only the moment. This is life on a knife edge; clip a rock and I'm over the handlebars, brake too late and I hit a tree, misjudge a jump and my wheels are destroyed. Pow, pow, pow, my legs burn as I fight gravity up a short, steep ascent before whoosh, a sweeping turn drops down through a tunnel of trees. Descending faster and faster, the world becomes a blur. Focus. Focuuuuus... I tell myself. Wheels hit the take-off ramp, suspension compresses and the bike leaves the ground. I'm flying.

Time. Slows. Down.

The clicking of the freewheel and the wind whistling past my ears are my only connections with the world as I stare hard at the landing spot. Touch down. *I rail the bike through the final high-speed turns and skid to a standstill. Four of us stand in a line, sweating and gasping. The blood pulsing through my veins is the only sound in the still of the woods. "That was mega,"* I shout and high-five my best mates. "Again?"

The childhood memories were clear as yesterday. Campus security checked me in and I drove into the car park at the University of Derby, where my friends and I used to practise the tricks of our heroes before using them in the woods. Exchanging the thrill of the trails for the sterile classroom, my 14-year-old self would never have seen this coming. Neither would my round-the-world self, for that matter. Cycling had always meant freedom.

I walked into Blends, the busy student coffee shop, ordered a small, black Americano with an extra shot, and took a seat at a circular table in a cosy corner under the stairs. Opposite me sat Dr Mark Faghy, a couple of inches shorter than me, with stacked arms and pecs. Built like a human triangle; he clearly lifted weights. Wearing a tight, stripy blue and white T-shirt, he reminded me of a Jean Paul Gaultier perfume bottle, only paler.

A doctor of physiology, Mark's award-winning work focused on clinical and academic research into performance physiology and physical activity. He was a consultant for numerous hospitals and premiership football clubs, and he led the university's new £10.8 million elite sports facility called the Human Performance Unit (HPU).

Mark and I were introduced through the university business school, where I'd been delivering guest lectures about cycling the world. As we sat in the comfortable surroundings of Blends, I told him about the vivid flashback I'd just had in the car park and how those childhood experiences had taken me around the world. He talked about an upcoming project of his that saw him travelling to South America to work with an international football team, about looking forward to getting married in just under a year, and what seemed like his obsession with visiting the gym early every morning before lectures began. Time disappeared quickly in conversation with Mark – he already felt like an old friend, before I explained my vision for an attempt on the world record.

Mark would later tell me that from the moment I spoke of innovating techniques and approaching the project with a different perspective, he was invested. From his point of view, a Derby boy using the local university to significantly break a world record would help establish the HPU and put the sports department in good stead for years to come. But the thing that personally interested Mark was that he was always looking for opportunities to pioneer new approaches and the way I was talking was the way that he worked.

Mark was hooked on the idea of developing a new, healthy methodology and turning heads while we did it. He spoke enthusiastically about the opportunities this kind of project opened up, the value that science would bring and the case studies that would come out of this unique endeavour. From our first meeting I knew he was the perfect man for the job. Mark came back to me a few days later, confirming that the University of Derby would sponsor the scientific aspect of the project and he would head up the team as my performance manager.

We agreed to meet over coffee on a weekly basis to map out how the project would look, drawing up the finer details and targets. The June start date that I'd set to optimize weather and daylight hours on the road gave us a 22-week training window if we began early in January. That time would be broken down into six-week blocks, and at the end of each we'd run a test to measure improvements and recalibrate my training. As Mark described the testing protocols he'd be using, the vision that I'd previously only dreamed of started to take shape. I'd seen videos of professional athletes connected to scientific monitoring systems, their faces covered by breath analysis masks and having blood samples taken, and I saw myself in that iconic way. Aligning myself with the professionals I aspired to be was surreal; part of me wondered how this could be happening when six months ago I lived in a tent. Yet, it was everything I wanted it to be.

I described to Mark the two other experts that I believed were necessary to complete the team; a nutritionist and a physiotherapist. Mark asked, "Who have you got as your psychologist?"

"A psychologist?" I questioned. "Why do I need psychology?" I believed that this was a purely physical challenge; that an efficient heart and lungs powering strong legs was all it would take to go as fast as possible across Europe.

"You could be the fastest cyclist in the world when you stand on the start line, but it means nothing if your mind isn't strong enough to get you to the finish line," Mark told me. I had no idea at the time that one sentence would have so much impact on my life.

At our second meeting in Blends, Mark introduced me to his friend and colleague, sport, exercise and performance psychologist, Dr Phil Clarke. Phil drank what looked like dirty dish water – a cup of milk with a splash of hot water that had possibly seen a single dunk of a teabag. The first thing Phil told me about was his experience of running the length of Ireland – 16 marathons in 13 days. I looked him up and down in disbelief; about 6 inches taller than me and built like a rugby player, with a ginger beard and dishevelled hair, he reminded me of the Honey Monster from the Sugar Puffs cereal advert when I was a kid.

Clocking the look in my eyes, he clarified, "Oh, it was a few years ago, so it was – I was a bit slimmer back then," in his

Irish brogue. In talking about the run, Phil barely mentioned physical exertion; his experience had been one of mental and logistical challenges. He told me of the struggles that he went through, adapting the strategy when his running partner was injured; dealing with uneven impacts on his legs due to the camber of the road; the daily struggle of motivation to keep going when the end seemed so distant; and the uplifting experience of the final day with his friends and family at the finish line. "Not many people in the world, when they have given everything, can put their left foot in front of their right foot and continue on," he told me. Phil didn't just see the world through the eyes of a psychologist, he lived it.

Phil specialized in performance under pressure. I was fascinated by his stories of professional darts players choking at the oche, physically unable to release their grip on the dart in championship-deciding situations, but was perplexed by how pressure would affect someone's performance like that. I was certain it could never happen to me; I believed the body and mind were separate, in fact, cycling was so natural to me that I didn't need to bring my mind to it. Psychology seemed like the least important aspect of the project, but I acknowledged the weight that Mark gave it and went along with it.

In a brief conversation about the record attempt, Phil explained what he considered the most important psychological factors that we had to prepare for. He had two priorities: how I would mentally deal with long days in the saddle and how I would react when things went wrong. My confidence and success would be in knowing what lay ahead; he told me we needed to get to the start line, "with no stone left unturned."

In managing my expectations, Phil prepared me for the worst, telling me that even with the best intentions, we wouldn't reach perfection. As our first ultra-endurance event, mistakes would be made and things were going to hit me that I couldn't anticipate. Our psychology sessions wouldn't begin until a couple of weeks into physical training, but in preparation, Phil asked me to write down my biggest fears and my strongest motivations for taking on this challenge.

As we chatted, Mark and Phil explained that my development wouldn't be a matter of adding training into the day-to-day routine that I already had; it would require a whole lifestyle change. In any science experiment there had to be control in order to obtain meaningful results, and this "life experiment" was no different. Every aspect of my life would be stripped down, analyzed and quantified in the finest detail. I would become aware of what my body could achieve, how my mind worked, how to fuel myself and how to maintain my condition. In analyzing my lifestyle completely, we would be able to make purposeful changes that would deliver my peak performance.

I'd never expected this level of analysis. I'd imagined having a coach who I might meet once a week, a dietitian to suggest the right foods and an occasional sports massage. The project had stepped up a gear. At that point, I was excited to become a lab rat under the supervision of expert scientists. Although the discipline was a total contrast to my carefree travelling lifestyle, the total immersion in a project was exactly the same. My life would be dedicated entirely to one sole purpose again. I had no idea what I was getting myself into.

It made sense that, as well as preparing together, Mark and Phil would join me on the road for the attempt. This would ensure that the road team was made up of people I trusted, who knew the project inside out, and who could raise my spirits. They got the all-clear from the university and their families. Mark would have a chat with the in-house physios at the HPU to get someone on board and Phil would make a call to a dietitian he had studied with. The team was coming together and everything seemed perfect.

I felt privileged that two of the most well-respected experts in their fields had joined me but, at the time, I didn't realize that they would become two of my best friends too – there for me in the lab, the lecture theatres, and at the end of the phone when I needed to talk. Just as it had been in the same place 20 years before with the best mates I used to mountain bike with, Mark, Phil and I became like brothers.

The three of us laughed as we looked ahead to the journey of three guys in their pursuit of an extraordinary achievement. However, Mark and Phil weren't there to make me feel good about myself, they were there to challenge me. Our attempt had an achievable strategy and an impressive target. We were confident that we would be able to complete the challenge in less than 20 days, not only beating the world record but potentially taking an unprecedented nine days off it.

As Mark, Phil and I went our separate ways for the holidays, Phil shouted to me, "Enjoy Christmas and indulge as much as you like."

"That's right," Mark added, "when the break's over, the hard work *really* starts."

THREE

IT NEVER GETS EASIER, YOU JUST GET FASTER

The beauty of a science laboratory is simple; there is nowhere to hide. Sterile white walls and bleached work surfaces gleam under stark fluorescent lights. Silence and the smell of disinfectant fills the air. Devoid of clutter, only essential equipment is tolerated in the lab and every piece of apparatus has its specific place, purposely wheeled from storage to experiment on stainless steel trolleys. The laboratory in the Human Performance Unit at the University of Derby is like an operating theatre, but in place of the operating table sits the Lode Excalibur, a magnetically braked ergometer – an exceptionally precise static bike. The lab has one blue door and no windows. There are no distractions. There is no hiding from the truth.

On 9 January 2018, I stepped into the domain of scientific analysis and began a project unlike anything I had ever done before. Like a kid in a toy shop, I played with specialist equipment that was prepared on the countertops, throwing jokes at Mark and Phil that fell on deaf ears. One of Mark's masters students and a university technician joined us in the lab, both wearing latex gloves and plastic aprons over their matching blue tracksuits. It gave me an even greater sense of confidence to have four people working together, all there to get the best out of me, however, they spoke about me as a subject, as if I wasn't there. In the laboratory, a line was drawn: we were no longer buddies; I had become their case study. The monitors, the technical apparatus, the staff and even the terminology – it was exact, it was advanced, and it was all there to improve me. If I'd asked, they would have told me what it meant, but it would have taken years. This was the scientists' domain. My role was to follow instructions.

Our initial session would quantify my maximal physical capacity and everything on the way to it; the foundation that Mark and the science team had to build upon. My basic physical statistics were measured; height: 174 cm, weight: 75.0 kg, body fat percentage: 15 per cent. I provided a urine sample to measure my hydration and Excalibur was precisely adjusted to my proportions.

I wore a loose-fitting jersey and shorts, and mountain bike shoes that the local bike shop had given me for adventure cycling last September; the best clothing I owned but far removed from the sleek kit in the world of elite road cycling. I draped my towel over Excalibur's handlebars, sat on the saddle and clipped my shoes into the pedals, watching the scene around me. The masters student prepared the blood analysis equipment while the technician uploaded the test programme into the computer. Mark stood beside me, explaining the morning's procedure.

The incremental test would comprise a series of 3-minute intervals, separated by 1-minute rests, beginning at a low resistance and increasing with each new effort. At the end of each interval, blood would be taken from my finger and I would be asked to give my rate of perceived exertion (RPE); how hard I felt I was working. The computer would continuously monitor the quantities of oxygen I used and carbon dioxide that my body produced through a mask. I would cycle to the point of exhaustion, when I would be physically incapable of turning the pedals.

The team took baseline measurements of heart rate and blood lactate (a chemical marker of physical exertion) and Mark asked for my RPE before starting. He held up a laminated scale from six to 20, where six was defined as no exertion and 20 as maximum exertion, with increasing levels of difficulty in between.

"What happens at zero?" I asked.

"You stop existing," Mark replied.

"I'll go with six then."

I strapped the cold, plastic heart rate monitor around my chest and took a last drink of water before Mark secured the breath-by-breath analysis mask over my face.

"You look like Bane from *Batman*," Phil laughed.

"Luke, pshshsht, I am your father," I replied.

"That's *Star Wars*, you clown!"

Wires, tubes and radio frequencies connected my body to the computer, the system was calibrated, and the programme was fired up.

I spun the pedals and the test commenced. Three minutes passed quickly at a low resistance. The force against the pedals was then released and I freewheeled for a 1-minute break, before electromagnets inside Excalibur added another 35 watts of pedalling resistance and the next interval began. The trick was to get ahead of the machine. If resistance built up before I pedalled, I started on the back foot. If I spun the pedals at a high cadence, rotating them at a quick tempo, before the resistance kicked in, I was fine. *Easy.* Efforts at the beginning of the test felt good, pedals spinning comfortably, breathing under control, waiting for the sharp click; the prick in my finger to take a blood sample. Again, I gave a low number when asked about my exertion on the third interval. The fourth time the resistance was increased, sweat started to bead on my skin, I reached for the towel and wiped my face. Having already removed my jersey, I asked to turn on the fan. Cool air blasted in my face and a note was taken; for continuity, the fan would be switched on at precisely this moment in every subsequent incremental test – such was the scientists' microscopic attention to detail.

The masters student called Mark over to the machine where she was analyzing my blood lactate samples. They whispered to each other, pointing to numbers and shrugging their shoulders. "I'm getting some strange readings from your bloods. Have you had particularly low lactate levels before?" she turned to me and asked.

"I don't know," I shrugged in response, "this is the first time I've been tested." I guessed this meant something very good or very bad but there was no time to ask. I turned my attention back to the test.

In front of Excalibur stood a large computer screen that showed my physiological data in real time. In the top left of the monitor was a graph that displayed the power and duration of each step of the test. Another graph recorded the oxygen and carbon dioxide passing through the mask, plotting "shark fin" profiles that grew taller with each 3-minute effort and dropped on each rest. Beneath the graphs was a table of numerical values that gave a detailed breakdown of every variable. What I'd only ever considered to be natural sensations in my legs and lungs as I'd pedalled before, became quantifiable statistical data.

I tried to trick the machine by slowing my breathing, believing that I might be able to reduce my oxygen use, but there was no fooling it; I had as much control over my oxygen consumption as I did over the timer that counted down to the next interval. Any belief that my actions dictated the numbers was shattered. No matter what I tried, I was unmasked by the data. Sandstorms, scorching heat, deep snow, whatever I was exposed to around the world, I'd eaten that for breakfast, but this was showing a different vulnerability; this was personal. I'd been certain of myself since reading about the record; I'd convinced Steve that I could do it and I'd brought expert scientists on board but now I was laying it on the line. The truth would be revealed. No bravado, no excuses, only numbers. A hamster in a wheel. I was locked in.

Intensity built on the static bike and as I entered the final stages of the experiment the atmosphere changed in the lab; conversation became scarce as breathing took priority. On the sixth interval I gave an RPE value of 16 and on the seventh it went up to 18, described as "very hard" on the scale.

"You're making it look easy Leigh, you could do this all day." Mark encouraged me with calm statements, while diligently monitoring my statistics.

With each increase in resistance the pedals became more and more difficult to turn; I was stationary, yet felt as though I was dragging a heavier and heavier weight behind me. With the build-up of pain throughout my body, the clock began to torment me. Earlier in the test, each 3-minute interval had seemed to pass so quickly but, as I reached my limit, the timer seemed to count slower and those same 3 minutes felt longer and longer. Conversely, each 1-minute break seemed to disappear in an instant.

I didn't want to look as though I was out of my comfort zone in front of people I barely knew. Elsewhere in life, I'd become a master at masking emotions and my exterior betrayed my interior. However, there was little chance I could mask how difficult I was finding the test by this point. There was no doubt in my mind that Mark's positive language was more motivational than descriptive. Irrespective of the data, he would see from my face I was finding it far from easy. There was no hiding: the bike revealed the "real" me.

During the penultimate interval my heart raced and my legs burned, RPE 19. In the rest that followed, I began to question whether I'd underestimated the numbers and whether I could even turn the pedals with any extra resistance.

"Get that breathing under control, Leigh," I heard Phil shout as my gasps rattled through the mask.

I could stop now, this could all be over.

"Have you got anything left for the next effort?" asked Mark.

I turned my head but don't remember seeing him, just answering with a staccato, "Yeah," and a nod that shook sweat across the floor. I'd been asked to leave everything on the bike and that's what I intended to do.

"Okay, ten seconds, Leigh. Five, four, three…" I spun up the pedals and the resistance wound up in the ergometer.

After more than half an hour of relentlessly increasing resistance, my muscles felt ready to burst, sweat ran down my body, and condensation filled the inside of the mask. My heart rate was again rising and the monitor beeped on every pulse. My whole upper body expanded and contracted to get as much oxygen into my lungs as possible and, on every breath, air wheezed in and out of the mask valves.

Mark energized himself to inspire more from me: "Come on Leigh, leave it all on the bike, that's it, keep that cadence up, keep pushing." The technician, the student and Phil cheered me on too. It was the first time I had experienced the encouragement of everyone around me. It was intoxicating.

The hairs on the back of my neck stood up and goosebumps rose under the sweat running over my skin. Lungs gasping. Legs screaming out in agony. Vision reduced to bright blurs of colour. The crippling pain of lactic acid. RPE 20. Every signal from my body was crying out to stop but the words inside my head called out louder and stronger: *no compromise.*

This wasn't just for me; my actions represented everyone who believed in me. I pushed through the pain, pressing on the pedals as hard as I could, emptying the tank. The shouting disappeared beneath the ringing in my ears, as my arms pumped as well as my legs. Veins, muscles and bones protruded under my skin. Contorted face, eyes closed with gritted teeth and giving everything, the pedals gradually turned slower and slower until Mark shouted, "Aaaaand stop."

Silence. Emptiness. Dripping with sweat and out of energy, I opened my eyes and my awareness returned to the laboratory. The test was complete and the results were saved. "Keep spinning your legs, Leigh," came a distant shout from Mark, I pushed the pedals and the resistance in Excalibur slackened off. Feeling faint and nauseous, the mask was removed from my face, and I slurped water from the nearest bottle. With my heart rate dropping, I began to regain control of my breathing and a strange thought crossed my mind; even after all that, *could I have pushed on a bit longer?*

A few hours after the incremental test, I received an email from Mark. The data revealed a very good baseline. I already had the physical capacity of an elite cyclist. *Phew*. Relief was quickly replaced by excitement. Attached were spreadsheets that integrated data from the test, a preliminary long-term training calendar and a schedule for the first six weeks. It was the blueprint for how my life was going to be; my path to improvement.

Like his organization of the laboratory, my schedule had meticulous attention to detail with heart rate, power, duration and cadence for each session, all clearly organized and colour coded. The intensity of each workout was represented on a colour scale, like the temperatures of a weather forecast; recovery rides were blue, endurance rides green, tempo rides orange and high intensity interval sessions were red.

Before Christmas, I'd ridden frequent, long duration, low intensity rides in the belief that I needed to build up my cycling miles and top up with intervals and efforts in the few weeks before the event. I expected the early months of training to be green every day. I counted the colours; the weeks were dominated by red; three interval sessions a week, separated by empty "rest" days. The schedule was the complete opposite of how I expected to prepare for a long-distance event.

It was hard to believe that these short, intense sessions would prepare me to ride hundreds of miles a day across a continent. The schedule had me training for a fraction of the time ultra-endurance cyclists were recording on social media. It felt wrong – Mark's approach seemed too far removed from logic or convention. He reassured me that the protocol he'd prescribed was relative to my capacity and would progress rapidly to develop a big endurance base. Training indoors allowed us to control and measure every variable and mitigated the dangers of long rides outdoors in bad conditions.

This was a key theme of Mark and Phil's approach; science brought a core value of working smarter rather than harder or longer. Our targets were always SMARTER: Specific, Measurable, Achievable, Realistic, Time-bound, Enjoyable and Recorded. If our attempt for the Fastest Cycle Across Europe was a stick of rock, you could break it at any point and SMARTER would be written straight through the middle.

Showing me the incremental test data, Mark explained that each six-week phase of training would focus on improving my capacity at a specific power output. His objective was to increase my sustainable power, in turn giving my body a wider range of "physical gears" to use on the record attempt. The "smarter" way to achieve this was through short, high-power intervals on an indoor trainer called a Wattbike where there were no external factors to affect me.

———————————

I appreciated the safety of Mark's indoor training programme as I de-iced my car in the dark at 7 a.m. on a Monday in January and climbed across the passenger seat because the driver-side door had frozen shut. My pale hands froze on the steering wheel as the fan noisily blasted cold air to clear the clouds of breath that fogged up the windscreen. The car had just about warmed up as I parked at the university and carried my gym bag into the Human Performance Unit.

"Welcome to your new pain cave," said the same technician I'd met in the test, as he showed me into the gym. The double doors automatically opened into the vast room kitted out with cutting-edge sports analysis technology. The air-conditioned space still held the rubbery and metallic smells of new sports equipment.

Walking in, I looked back at a wall of mirrors, in front of which stood strength training apparatus, a rack of free weights, kettle bells, jumping blocks and gym balls. On the far side of the room, before a glass wall that looked out on to playing fields, was a 30-metre indoor running track and long jump pit with gait analysis and timing traps. To my right was the locked blue door to the laboratory that I knew well from the previous week's incremental test.

A man driving a ride-on floor cleaner passed me as I walked across the vast, central space and looked up at the high ceiling where a rack held motion capture cameras for technique analysis. I spun around in awe as I wandered over to the Wattbike, where I prepared my bottles and GPS, and stripped down to cycling clothes. In my mind I was the main man; the around-the-world cyclist, training for a world record, with access to the best sports equipment available. There was nothing I couldn't do.

I hit play on a pumped-up gym playlist that squeaked through a feeble speaker beside me and programmed the morning's training session into my bike computer. I was to complete six high-power efforts, or intervals, each lasting 5 minutes. Between each effort was a 3-minute recovery period. The session would last just over an hour including warm up. Looking at the programme, I thought it would be easy and decided I'd stop by at Blends for a bite to eat afterwards. I crunched my mountain bike shoes into the pedals and warmed up.

Beep, beep, beeeeeeep! The countdown sounded and I turned up the resistance on the Wattbike. The music disappeared beneath the whirr of the air brake and my heart rate shot up. *Jesus wept – that's difficult.* The first interval was a shocking 5 minutes of suffering but I hit the target and sustained it. I reduced the resistance for the recovery break and the music reappeared over the noise. My heart rate came down as I spun my legs. The next two intervals followed suit until I began to crack. Recovery time started disappearing too quickly and I was still breathless as the countdown beeped for the next effort. *Are you kidding?* I thought. *How the hell am I going to get through another 25 minutes of this?!*

In the fourth interval, I couldn't force my legs to pedal at Mark's specified power. Pushing the pedals as hard as possible and approaching my maximum heart rate, readings began their slow descent, along with my morale. I felt as though I had no control. In my head I quickly went from being the main man to the pain man; the around-the-world cyclist, training for a world record, where the best sports equipment was breaking me and there was nothing I could do about it.

Through the fifth and sixth intervals I gave up hope of hitting the target. My legs were like jelly as I tried everything that would normally help on the road; sitting in the saddle then standing up, spinning the pedals quickly then grinding each rotation slowly. My pulse thundered in my ears and sweat dripped into a puddle beneath the Wattbike. I gave it my all but I was cooked. If Mark was there, I would have called him over to see that his session was wrong and I would have looked for permission to get off the bike but, alone in my new pain cave, I had to answer to myself. Motivated to prove the scientists wrong, I would continue to the end. I'd pedal myself into the ground and take the data back to them as proof of their error. Naively, I'd never contemplated failure in training. I believed there had to be a logical explanation as to why I hadn't achieved my goal. Something had to be wrong – it couldn't be me.

After I showered and the pain had washed from my legs, I visited Mark in his office. I showed him the disappointing data I'd logged from the session and told him, "Mark, clearly *you* have made a mistake in your calculations, look, there's no way I can do what you've given me. Why don't you check over your maths and when you put together something I can do, I'll smash it out in the gym."

Mark looked at the data. "You're capable of achieving what I've set you, Leigh, and the proof is in the results from the incremental test," he told me. "What you've hit is a mental obstacle and *you* have to find a way over it."

The shame of my declaration, *why don't you check over your maths… I'll smash it*, washed over me.

"Imagine this," he continued. "There's a hunter-gatherer, doing his thing, running across his territory, foraging and occasionally sprinting as he chases his prey. Mid-sprint, he thinks he's running his fastest but, at that instant, a lion bursts out from the long grass and races towards him. He kinda becomes superhuman, launching into another gear and finding extra momentum to dodge the attack. He had speed and strength in reserve. Human beings still have the same physiological capacities, and if you want to make adaptations, you've got to tap into your reserve gear."

How am I supposed to find more power when I already feel like I'm working at maximum effort? I thought. I was disappointed in myself and frustrated by a training programme I had believed was going to be easy, which now seemed too difficult.

Phil phoned me that evening. We hadn't begun psychology training, but he wanted to chat about my first Wattbike session. I told him it was awful, that I'd failed because I couldn't hit the targets on the plan that Mark had given me. Phil asked what I had done when I couldn't sustain my power and saw my targets slipping away.

"I just struggled through to the end," I told him.

"That's why I know you'll get this record, because you didn't stop," he replied.

Relief washed over me; my numbers weren't ideal but my determination was on point. I'd always thought that "A for effort" meant "you're a loser but I'll phrase it nicely" but it was the effort, not the numbers, that had got me to the end of the session. Maybe psychology would come in useful for my record attempt after all.

In our brief phone call, Phil shared his first pieces of advice with me to help overcome the mental obstacle that

Mark had said I was up against. "The next time you're training, I want you to control the controllables." He told me to look at what I could control and focus everything on that. In each repetition I was to give all my effort and energy, holding nothing in reserve, treating every interval as if it was the last. In recovery between the efforts, I was to spin my legs as though the pedals were made of glass, controlling my breathing to be as fresh as possible for the next rep. Phil summed it up for me, "Call it being either 100 per cent on or 100 per cent off. Through training I need you to start finding comfort in the uncomfortable."

On the wall in Steve's office is a signed picture of former professional road cyclist Jens Voigt, quoting his famous catchphrase "Shut up, legs." When I went back to the HPU two days later to attempt the same session for a second time, I repeated that quote to myself over and over, as reassurance that the pain was only in my mind and that I could push through it. I went at the session as hard as I could, leaving it all on the Wattbike. But I failed. I returned again and again, knowing that I was the only person standing in my way. I wouldn't stop until I proved to myself that I could do it. In the second week of training, on my fifth attempt, I hit the target on all six intervals. I was elated. I did it again next time round.

The following week, my target of six intervals became eight. When I achieved that, it was increased to ten. I followed every detail of Mark's training schedule. I didn't skip a session because I was tired or because I didn't feel like training. I was in the HPU every day I was supposed to be, putting in the effort and logging the results.

At the end of Phase One of physical training, Mark scheduled a second incremental test at the lab. The results were outstanding; my maximum power and cycling efficiency had both increased significantly. Using the most recent data, Mark recalibrated my training schedule to account for the improvements and to focus on making further advancements. Due to the precise, controlled nature of indoor interval training, it was easy to adapt my sessions, and I began to understand the benefits of Mark's scientific approach over traditional distance-based outdoor training. I realized that I could achieve much more than I had expected.

FOUR

WHAT'S YOUR WHY?

The atrium of the University of Derby main campus resembles an airport departure lounge; right-angles and circles of steel-framed architecture support walls of windows under a high glass roof. Bright shafts of sunlight cut through the air of the vast blue, grey and white space. Stationery shops, convenience stores and student support centres line the ground floor under a long, sweeping ramp that leads into aromatic clouds of coffee and fast food from Starbucks, Subway and the food court. Giant banners hang from the roof, declaring accolades and endorsements from governing bodies. Revolving doors spin life into the vast space, bustling with the chatter and movement of tight-jeaned students; everyone is going somewhere.

A blast of heated air warmed me as I sauntered in from the bitter winter and met Phil for our first psychology session. We walked up the ramp, along the balcony and through glass double doors into a 300-seat lecture theatre, where we pulled together two chairs and a desk in front of the empty auditorium and began to chat.

Before meeting Phil, I thought that a sports psychologist was a motivational quote-shouting cheerleader, as opposed to professional counsellors, who were "real" psychologists. Phil did occasionally fire one-liners at me but I quickly realized that these alone didn't make a difference. It was the months committed to developing psychological strategies that created performance-defining moments.

As he began to describe his process, Phil explained that performance psychology wasn't just for sport; the techniques he would show me could be used to achieve any goal, from hitting work targets to personal aspirations. The same skills could even be applied to chatting up girls at the bar. I asked if Phil could make girls want to meet *me* at the bar. "I'm a psychologist, I can't perform miracles, lad!" he laughed.

Phil's objectives were for me to confidently overcome the psychological roadblocks I would encounter on the attempt: boredom, pain control and emotional regulation. "What am I going to need emotional regulation for on the road? I'm not going to fall in love out there, I'm riding a bike!" I laughed back at him.

"All right then…" he replied, raising his eyebrows, "so, let's go through those fears and motivations for this challenge that I asked you to write up last month."

I hadn't done it. In fact, I'd purposely avoided doing it. I knew I wouldn't like what I found. Phil reiterated what Mark had told me before Christmas – how being the fastest cyclist in the world when standing on the start line meant nothing if my mind wasn't strong enough to get me to the finish line. He explained that the mind was like a muscle and it could be trained but, just like training the body, there was no quick fix. Psychological interventions needed to be uniquely personalized to the individual, there was no "one size fits all" approach. The development of my psychological strength, motivation and mental wellbeing required commitment to building self-awareness, implementing new routines and developing an enhanced mindset. I needed to put as much effort into managing my thoughts and emotions as I was with training my body. Up to now I had pushed that advice aside.

I can be told something a million times, but it turns out I have to learn my lessons for myself. In the enveloping shame at failing to even acknowledge the start of the psychological journey, I began to recognize the truth I'd long been avoiding.

In a philosophical conversation in the oasis town of Kashgar on the edge of the Taklamakan desert, a French hitchhiker once told me that life serves us lessons like dishes in a restaurant. If you don't learn your lesson from the first course, the dish is served again but spicier. If you still don't learn, the dish will be served again and again, spicier and spicier, until you do learn.

As the years passed cycling around the world, people

started asking pertinent questions. When I stopped to teach English for a year in Taiwan, I got to know the owner of the school and once a month we had brunch together. He asked me about the behaviour that he'd observed; why I self-sabotaged my relationships and why I was always moving on. Before that, a good friend from Australia had asked what I was running from and when I was going to stop cycling. I always had a smart answer that I'd read in a book: my time in the saddle in the pursuit of experiences gave me a better exchange rate than the time spent behind a desk in pursuit of money.

Nothing else mattered when the wheels were spinning. Cycling around the world, I never had to deal with problems for long. Experiencing a bad day, disagreement or misunderstanding, I would cycle on knowing that tomorrow would bring a new place or new people; the bike constantly avoided obstacles, my "roadblocks". Apparently, I was the only person who didn't see that whenever I had the opportunity to settle, I made another rash decision to leave. Travel was my great escape.

Returning home seven years on, once again, I faced the routine daily challenges and pressures. Before I'd left, I had looked at adventurous heroes of mine who pushed the limits of cycling, sailed the oceans and scaled mountains, and believed that with such tenacity, daily life wouldn't faze them. In part, that was what I was looking for; I wanted to be unfazed by life. Now I'd proved that I had the resolve of those adventurers yet, faced with the same everyday pressures, I reacted the same way I had before. I became overwhelmed, stressed, anxious and depressed. It seemed nothing had changed. Along came the world record article, the next escape, an even higher accolade perfectly disguised as the next way to prove myself. I could ride my way out of my problems again.

The incremental test results confirmed that I'd been blessed with naturally strong legs, but the way I'd responded to the first training session showed that I was held back by a troubled mind. Every time I had to confront my mental health, I'd turned to the strength of my legs to avoid it. Due to the scientific nature of the world record project, no stone would be left unturned and, in order to use those legs, I was forced to face the aspect of my life that I'd hidden from. There was no denying that I would have to look within and face my demons. This time, my body and mind were inseparable. I realized that life is not straightforward, it's complex, contradictory and non-linear. Just because I'd found what I was good at, didn't mean it was the answer to everything.

"We're not reinventing the wheel," Phil told me, "you are the wheel."

I was going to have to go through my experiences all over again, relive the hardships, understand the thought processes and behaviours that informed my character, and implement the actions I'd neglected in counselling. I didn't go into the project as a blank canvas; I needed to figure out what made me who I was, break it down and rebuild myself stronger. While physical training could progress rapidly, psychologically I had to look back to go forward.

Achieving the world record would come down to winning the battle in my mind.

The spiciest dish had been served.

"If you have a strong enough *why*, your *how* will find itself. So, what's your why?" asked Phil.

I was certain that I knew the answer. "To break a world record," I declared.

Phil paused. "I'm going to need you to dig a little deeper than that. Is there anything else?"

"Okay, it's not actually the certificate, it's about the respect everyone will give me for that achievement. They'll see what I'm capable of, right?"

Phil looked me in the eye. "If I took your certificate away, would it make the achievement meaningless? What if nobody respected what you did, does that mean it was a waste of time? Your motivators need to be intrinsic, things that don't rely on anything or anybody other than yourself."

Phil described the type of testing situation I would encounter on the road. He asked me to imagine the 14th or 15th day of the attempt and I'm exhausted. I wake up in the comfortable bed of the motorhome, it's cosy inside. My body aches as I pull myself up from the mattress. My legs are so sore that I struggle to walk. I'm hungry but can't stomach the idea of eating. Outside, it's raining and there's a headwind. I've got to ride for 14, 15, maybe 16 hours in those conditions, on busy roads, with nothing but my own thoughts. I've got to get back on the same saddle I've been sitting on, day in, day out for the last two weeks, on saddle sores where layers of skin have peeled off and what's left is blistered.

"Now, if I tell you I'll give you a certificate to do that, you'll tell me to get lost," Phil said, "and you won't care about the respect of other people because they don't understand the pain that you are going through. So, what's going to make you get on that bike and stay on it all day?"

I felt vulnerable. I couldn't give Phil a deep answer. I questioned whether I was doing this just to impress others, and whether I had any truly intrinsic motivators. Phil coaxed a list of personal reasons out of me, including not letting others down, needing a goal, wanting to make a living from what I love, fulfilling the "live to ride, ride to live" dreams I had as a kid, to see what I was capable of, and to take what I had learned from cycling around the world to a new level.

Phil described those motivations as the layers of an onion; when challenges on the road tore each one back, another would be revealed. But I needed to find the core – a motivator so strong that it would endure the most demanding ordeals.

Phil's words forced me to look into the toughest challenges of my past. I stepped into the dark memories I'd locked away and escaped over ten years before. I'd forgotten a lot of the details, as though my memory had been switched off through the trauma of depression, but Phil found the thread and began to pull.

In my early 20s, I'd pursued success in the way that seemed to work for everyone else. It appeared to follow a simple prescription: get a good qualification, a good job, earn good money and respect, then you're doing well. To do that, I gave up the thing I loved, cycling, because it didn't achieve any of those things, it just made me happy. At the time, I didn't realize that there could be things in my life just for enjoyment. I believed everything had to tick a box on the path to success.

Through the summer after graduation, the people around me changed dramatically. When my friends moved away from Newcastle, where we studied, I stayed and moved into a small room that I rented in the attic conversion of a three-storey house. I went from living with three of my best friends to living with seven people I didn't know. I rarely saw my housemates and we didn't have anything in common. After three years at university, starting out in self-employment was also a challenge and, although I got on with the film-makers I worked with, I didn't feel intellectual enough or have strong enough opinions to join in their conversation. In my mind I wasn't "one of them". I lived 3 hours away from my family in Derby and I rarely made the journey down to visit. I felt alone.

I swept those "weak" emotions under the carpet; I was a man who knew what was important to achieve if I wanted to prosper. The box-ticking exercise had worked well at university and I graduated in 2005 with a first-class degree in Media Production. Tick. So, I took the same box-ticking exercise and applied it to "real life". I established myself as a freelance film-maker. Tick. I worked on feature films, short films and music videos with the film community. Tick. I facilitated the government's creative learning initiatives. Tick. I earned plenty of money. Tick. I had the respect of my peers. Tick. I made my life appear fantastic from the outside; I laughed and joked and acted carefree. However, I was good at masking my true feelings and, in reality, I couldn't find joy on the path that everyone else followed. I neglected the essential things that were important to me and, through the ensuing series of choices I made, gradually things started to unravel.

I believed that I would become happier with greater success, so I dedicated every waking hour to a job that my heart wasn't in. I dragged myself out of bed with a motivation to get more work so that I earned more money. I accepted every job I was offered and ended up struggling to keep all the plates spinning. My mind was always full of the endless things I had to do: workshops to run, corporate jobs to complete, commitments to fulfil with the film community, new work to pitch for, upcoming courses to plan, and I was still figuring out how to run a business. I was overwhelmed and thought I had to do everything at once. I regularly pulled all-nighters, hunched over the desk in my tiny attic room, staring into a small beige monitor. I felt like I carried the weight of the world on my shoulders, I had nobody to turn to for support and I feared the repercussions of failure. I couldn't share this with the other film-makers in the community for the fear that they'd think I was weak and wouldn't want to work with me. It was an unsustainable way of living and the cracks began to show.

I started to disappoint clients. Working on projects late at night before early morning deadlines, I encountered problems that I didn't have solutions to. Realizing that I couldn't complete jobs on time, I panicked. My heart beat loudly in my chest, my palms sweated, and my mind became a whirlwind of concerned thoughts. *What am I going to do? How am I going to explain this? What are they going to think of me?* I had nobody to share my concerns with and I started to doubt whether I had the skills to do my job properly.

Overwhelmed and unable to resolve the problems, I struggled to sleep. The sun came up and I got out of bed, already drained, wondering how I was going to get through the day. I delivered projects late and I let people down. I had prided myself on perfectionism; it wasn't in my character to deliver anything incomplete. I saw myself as a total failure.

I continued to accept more work as it was the only way I knew, and as my pressures and worries built up over months, I felt increasingly down. At this time, I received a phone call from the local cinema where I facilitated workshops, asking if I would deliver a talk about animation to a group of 100 secondary schoolchildren. Then, public speaking made me nervous and self-conscious and I avoided it at all costs but because the speaker had called in sick at the last minute, I felt as though I couldn't let the cinema down. I stood on the stage in front of the silver screen, showing movie clips to explain the origins and the magic of animation. At that moment, things went into freefall.

I expected awe and excitement from the children, but they didn't seem to care. I asked them questions but not one of them put their hand up to answer; they didn't respond to anything I did. It happened over and over. I questioned what I was doing wrong. I doubted myself and felt uncomfortable. I wondered if they were all judging me. The stress and frustration built up inside me until I reached my breaking point.

"Are you even interested in what I'm talking about?" I shouted at the audience, throwing my script on the stage. "Do you want to be here? Come on! What the hell is the point of me even doing this?"

The auditorium went deadly silent as the audience looked at me, shocked. A second later and I was as stunned as them. I couldn't believe the way I'd reacted. When I finished the presentation, the room emptied until the only person left was the cinema manager, who had been stood at the back the whole time. My heart sank. In a meeting afterwards, I explained what I was going through. She told me that I clearly had too great a workload and that the cinema would help by taking away that burden. It was the last time I worked there.

I'd sunk into my lowest time and my then girlfriend tried everything she could to bring me happiness. She woke me up by playing piano, she wrote me a card of all the things she loved about me, she invited me to house parties and we went to clubs and concerts together. Often, I would leave the party or nightclub unannounced, halfway through the night, to wander alone through the rainy streets, beating myself up because the happiness of others only amplified my own sadness. I didn't believe I brought anything to the group – I had nothing to contribute, nothing to talk to them about. I pushed her and everyone else away. I thought that nobody understood what I was going through; they couldn't appreciate the difficulties I was dealing with. I felt more isolated when I was surrounded by people than I did when I was alone.

A year after graduating, I propped open the skylight in my cramped attic room, the solemn lyrics of Elliott Smith singing out of tinny computer speakers on my desk. Looking out over the skyline of a city where I was certain everyone was living fulfilled lives, I was solitary, in a place where I no longer felt I belonged. I sat on my bed and cried. The carefree days of my childhood were gone and there was no chance I could be happy again.

I tore off a piece of paper and, as tears ran down my face, I scrawled a note.

I don't feel worth anything. No matter how much I have succeeded, it seems worthless and trivial and like I waste my life doing these things while everyone else is happy. I can't let others be happy – I ruin my relationships by making others feel so bad, like I do, by belittling what they do and pointing out their bad points and their worthlessness. I can't have a good time. I'm not doing as much as others. I'm afraid. I'm such a dependant, I need someone else to hold my hand through everything. I rarely make friends, just meet other people's friends. I never make the first move; I always need to know that someone's done it before. I can't sleep and I lie awake with a heartbeat that is absolutely insane – fast, hard, massive.

As I wrote these lines, I hated myself. I absolutely hated myself. And I couldn't live with it any more. With that thought, I scribbled at the top of the page, "Why I need counselling."

My doctor booked me an initial session with a therapist. I followed an informally dressed lady in her 50s into a spacious room, where sunlight flooded in through large windows. She closed the door gently behind us, sat on a comfortable armchair and gestured for me to take a seat, too. To the side of us was a wooden coffee table, under one of the windows, a tidily organized desk and a filing cabinet, and plants were dotted around the room. It was nothing like my expectations of lying on a black leather couch while a psychologist in a suit analyzed me and scribbled notes on a clipboard. It was calm, we just chatted. I opened up about everything that was happening in my unravelling life; losing work, pushing people away, my feelings of futility and questioning what the point of life was if achieving the success that everyone expected of me only led to emptiness.

It was a relief to talk about everything that I'd bottled up inside. The world didn't end because I spoke about what I'd thought of as my weaknesses; in fact it felt refreshing. When she explained that I was struggling with depression and anxiety, I felt unexpectedly pleased because there was a reason for the way that I was feeling and there was a solution. I started going to sessions with my counsellor once every two weeks.

I was happy to talk about my problems but I avoided self-analysis and looking into the parts of myself that would be painful to change. Instead I turned the conversation to textbook examples. We discussed philosophical theories that I'd read about like John Keats' concept of negative capability and the feminization of masculinity in a deindustrialized world. Although my counsellor asked me to take time to consider these issues in myself and my family, I didn't have the bravery to look within. It was the same with the homework she gave me. I left each session with something to consider about my own life, that we could discuss next time. I left with a diagram of Maslow's hierarchy of needs, which proposes five tiers of human needs that need to be met on the path to becoming all that one can be, but I didn't consider the parts that I'd neglected in my own life. After another session, I took a page about family scripts that explained why people and families repeat patterns of behaviour through generations, in relationships, in health and problem solving, but again I didn't apply them to my own life. And after another session, I was set the task to think about relaxing and leaving everything; to have nothing at all on my mind. It became another one of the things I didn't bother to do.

However, one question that she asked hit me hard and I have remembered it ever since. "When you look to your future, what colour do you see?"

I replied that the future hadn't been made yet, it didn't exist, there was just empty time waiting to be filled. If I had to give emptiness a colour, it would be black.

My future was empty and black.

Although we shared so many similarities, one thing was vastly different between my sister and me; while I got confused between making myself or others happy, Emma did exactly what Mum had told us. She pursued her own happiness. When she left school, Emma knew that she didn't want to go to university, she wanted to see the world. At 18 years old, she bought a backpack, a Lonely Planet guide and a ticket to South East Asia. Travel seemed such an incredibly audacious idea to me, radically different to anything we'd experienced before. When I thought moving to Newcastle Upon Tyne was brave, she spoke of visiting exotic countries I'd never heard of – Cambodia, Vietnam, Thailand and Laos. I rarely heard from Emma through the years that she travelled. When she occasionally returned between adventures, her backpack was scuffed and had new flags of the countries she'd visited sewn on to it. She had new piercings and tattoos on her tanned skin, she wore brightly coloured summer clothes, and everything she pulled from her bag smelled of incense and tiger balm. She played me pirated CDs she'd bought on the tourist trails and described busy streets of neon lights and watching fire dancers under palm trees on the beaches. Emma was alive; her bright green eyes and contagious smile brought positive energy into every room that she walked into.

I wished to be like Emma. I felt as though I was the sibling who worked hard and everything I did had to be towards a socially valued achievement or "success", which only brought me pain. The colour of Emma's life was tangible and, although I'd taken a step in the right direction, I still wasn't finding the same after four months of counselling.

If my little sister could do it, I could do it. The spark of an idea came to mind. In September 2006 at 24 years old, I applied for a working holiday visa for New Zealand in an impetuous act of defiance. Screw it. I'd travel.

"Did you decide to travel to fulfil the expectations of others?" Phil asked.

"No," I told him. "It felt as though throughout adult life I'd accepted being content but never truly happy. I'd blocked out the idea that I could lead my best life through fear of losing what I had. In a state of depression, I had nothing to lose and I took that risk."

Phil put it more succinctly. "So, after asking yourself *why* for so long, you began to ask *why not*?"

That response was important. It was my own. It wasn't something that others expected of me. The way I reacted to my life hitting rock bottom taught me lessons about myself that no mountaintop could. I'd created an opportunity to stop following convention and to instead live by my own beliefs. To discover what lengths I could go to. To find out what I could overcome and to achieve what nobody believed was possible. It was like a dictionary definition of the person I wanted to become.

"So, when everything is going against you on the record attempt, what do you want to do?"

"I want to find out if I can act the way that *I* want to act. I want to respond in the way that *I* feel is right, not anyone else." I was discovering a motivation based on nothing but my own positive expectations of myself, a motivation strong enough to get me through anything. It was the core of the onion.

"I want to define who I am," I told Phil.

That was my *why*.

FIVE

I DON'T SLEEP, I DREAM

Cycling around the world, I met cyclists, travellers and adventurers on the road, who taught me how to cook with simple, cheap ingredients and maximize the equipment and supplies I carried. They pointed me towards secret natural treasures that only locals knew about and showed me places to wild camp, hidden in forests and scrubland.

My saddlebag lifestyle became primitive, almost animal; I put up my tent in the wilderness, fell asleep at sunset and woke with the sunrise. Every morning I followed a routine, cooking a breakfast of oats and coffee while packing my tent quickly to avoid being found in my hidden camping spot. My equipment was organized into specific bags so I could find the gear I needed quickly, whether I needed to eat, sleep, change clothes or fix a mechanical problem. Every time I had to pedal across a mountain range, the weight of the bike forced me to reconsider how much I really needed to carry. I stripped life back to the bare essentials until I lived in total simplicity. The road changed my priorities and the 28-year-old who left England concerned with hair products and brands of clothing, grew into his 30s with a shaved head, wearing second-hand clothes. My habits were optimized for survival.

Returning home, I expanded out of my panniers into the relative luxury of Mum's spare room. In the seven years I'd been away, Mum and Al had been optimizing their lifestyle too. Their four-bedroom family house I used to stay in when visiting from university had been downsized to a two-bedroom bungalow. My parents were winding down. Al had retired and Mum only worked a few hours a week, making time to spend with her friends and to volunteer at a local hospice. They were still as supportive as they always had been although not to the same extent as when we were young. Mum loved having me back in the nest; having desperately wanted to raise a close family, it must have been difficult for her to see her children go away for so long. Every few months I'd sent my diaries home from cycling the world for Mum to read, hoping that she could experience some of those adventures through my eyes. I'd opened up to Mum about my struggles with depression before I went travelling and it allowed her to share her own experiences of mental ill health with me, too. We trusted each other and knew first-hand the difficulties each other had faced. Our similar experiences brought us close. Our family dynamic from decades ago quickly resumed; we enjoyed spending time together, cooking, gardening, taking walks and chatting openly.

When I told Mum that I was going to attempt the record, she was pleased that I'd found my next challenge. Although she was concerned that I would be sacrificing financial income to achieve it, I don't think it came as a surprise. After all, my sister had a world record already. Mum would do anything she could to make sure the project was a success for me, she didn't mind that I wheeled expensive bikes through her house and she cooked and cleaned for me to save me time wherever she could. However, she told me how glad she was that I'd met Steve because she didn't have the knowledge or experience to help me grow in the way he could. Although moving back in with Mum and Al in my thirties created frustrations for all of us, it was a nourishing environment of love and trust. In my return home, survival mode was switched off and I reverted to old ways.

Those old ways came with old habits and old feelings. When I returned to the world of responsibilities, pressures, finances and deadlines, I reacted in exactly the same way I had in my 20s. I began running late for meetings, forgetting to do essential tasks and working long into the night. I was still to find sponsors for the record. I also had an important one-man show coming up that would fund my personal life for a few months, which I had to write and sell tickets for. I felt anxious and drained and I was losing confidence that I could pull any of this off. They were all-too-familiar feelings.

Ironically, the world record attempt, which I hoped would raise awareness and funds for mental health research, was having a negative impact on my own well-being. With the project in full swing, I was losing control of my life and the way things were going I wouldn't make it to the start line, let alone challenge the world record. It was time to face my demons.

Phil and I completed a performance profile to determine the psychological qualities crucial to the project. The page-long list of characteristics I prioritized included perseverance, mental toughness, self-belief, pain management, planning, leadership and negotiation. There was room to improve all of these but as Phil and I compared my behavioural strengths and weaknesses, it was clear that my fundamental daily habits were holding me back the most. We had to build a record breaker from the ground up and that meant, for the first phase of psychology training, we went back to basics. Phil helped me implement the lifestyle of a professional athlete which optimized the use of my time and effort. As with every aspect of the world record, our intention was not to work harder or longer, but to work smarter.

Late for another psychology meeting, dishevelled and scruffily dressed, slurping coffee and chewing a chocolate bar, I rushed into the dimly lit student bar, pulled up a stool and spewed the contents of my backpack over the table in front of Phil. He looked up from his laptop, unperturbed, and welcomed me. "Y'all right there pal, what's going on, so?"

Phil looked at the mess I'd instantly created, my laptop dumped in front of me, its sleeve discarded beside it, covered by my paper diary, a couple of notebooks, some scraps of paper, my coat and the chocolate bar wrapper. My poor time management and organization had manifested themselves on the table.

"There's no secret to this, lad. There's no magic dust I can sprinkle over you." Phil shook his head. He told me that achieving excellence was going to come down to hard work and implementing habits and routines to maximize my potential. He outlined three instructions that were the foundations of an elite athlete's lifestyle.

Be the best at skills that require no talent. Phil explained that "talent", my elite physical capacity on the bike, took thousands of hours of purposeful practice to achieve. Yet there were many daily tasks that I could be excellent at without dedicating time or training. For example, being in the right place on time, dressing appropriately, having the right equipment prepared for the gym or having a plan as to what I would achieve on a daily basis. Finding these basic tasks in my everyday routine and becoming efficient at them would streamline my life, saving time and energy that I could commit to achieving my goal.

Control the controllables. Phil reiterated what he'd told me on the phone after I failed to hit Mark's targets in my first training session. Just as there was no certainty that I would generate the desired numbers on the Wattbike, similarly, it wasn't for me to decide which companies did or did not sponsor the record attempt. Instead of concentrating on the outcomes of tasks, Phil asked me to focus on the effort I put into them, as this was something I could influence. In every aspect of life, just as in the gym, there would be things that concerned me that I had no influence over, and it was my responsibility to channel my attention onto the things that I could control.

Be where your feet are. Steve regularly compared me to a kitten chasing any string that was shaken in front of it; I was continually distracted by things that were unrelated to the task at hand. Phil made it clear that if my feet were at a meeting, but my mind was on other things, I might as well not be there at all. I had to change; in the gym I had to be completely focused on training; at my desk I had to concentrate on my work. To help with straying thoughts, Phil suggested keeping a to-do list on my phone and whenever something came to mind, I had to write a memo, park it, and continue with my work. Wherever I was and whatever I was doing, if I wanted to be the best, I had to apply myself completely.

"That's classic bullshit bingo, mate! I just got a full house!" I laughed to Phil. Bullshit bingo was something we both laughed about, describing meaningless motivational quotes that appeared in our social media feeds and the repeated lines I'd heard him say. I often used humour to mask my own discomfort but this time Phil didn't laugh. He nodded, acknowledging what I meant but emphasized that it was only worth continuing our sessions with these simple rules in place.

Phil asked to look at my desktop. I hesitantly turned my computer to face him. The screen was a jumble of icons: folders, documents, photos, shortcuts, screenshots and downloads, disorganized and overlapping each other. He turned his computer to face me; an empty desktop and only five or six folders neatly organized down the left-hand side. Phil told me to organize a system of logical folders and subfolders with simple names and subjects, and to save my documents in the appropriate place. I could use any method that worked for me with only one prerequisite: I had to be able to find any document quickly and easily.

My space at home was as disorganized as my computer; the spare room that I stayed in at Mum's house was a dumping ground. On one side of the room was a small dressing table from which I managed the project, with a chair that could be half pulled out before hitting the bed that took up most of the floor. On the other side, the narrow space next to the wall was piled full of bags and boxes of bike cleaning fluids and components I was testing. My training bike leaned against the wall behind the door, and a heap of folders, papers, books and boxes made a daily migration from the bed to the floor so I could sleep, and back again in the morning so I could work. I spent more time looking for documents and equipment than I did using them.

We implemented a system of filing to streamline my physical space, as we had with my computer desktop. My lifestyle was divided into three "zones" that were not to overlap. These working, relaxing and sleeping areas were each assigned a separate space. My table, bike and the university became work zones, the lounge in Mum's and Steve's homes were relaxing zones and my bed was my sleeping zone. Wherever I was, I had to be fully committed to achieving what that space was intended for.

The efficiency of this system was improved further. I had a habit of gathering my cycling gear in the minutes before leaving for training. Every day there was something different holding me back; clothes were still dirty, shoes were misplaced, drinks bottles going mouldy, or the sensor from my heart rate monitor would be lost. Phil told me to put a box beside the front door with a list of everything I needed for the gym taped to it. The evening before training, I was to fill the box with every item on the list and if something wasn't clean or ready, I had time to prepare it. Just like my saddlebag life on the road, training mornings would become streamlined routines that ran on time: wake, eat, pick up the box on the way out of the door, work out.

Next, Phil turned his attention to my tiny diary illustrated with pictures of vintage bikes. It was full of appointments, notes and scribbles, rarely time-based and never allowing for travel. Some commitments were on my computer, some on paper. There was no order and no prioritization, just pages of things to do. I couldn't see the wood for the trees.

His solution was simple. We got rid of the disorganized scribbled notes, opened a digital calendar and implemented a colour-coded system, similar to the one Mark had applied in my training schedule. Red engagements could not be moved – they had to specify start and finish times, and they had to account for travel and contingency for the unexpected. Every morning, I was to schedule five things from my phone's to-do list as flexible green tasks, to be completed around the fixed appointments.

While organizing my daily schedule, Phil insisted that I allocate 1 hour of downtime every day and that it was categorized red, i.e. non-negotiable. It was hard for me to justify; I was already at full capacity with work and Phil was asking me to take an hour out. He reminded me of the advice he'd given when striving for my physical best: in order to push the pedals at my maximum power through each interval, I had to relax fully on each recovery. The same applied here; quality rest would improve my capacity to work.

The idea of focussing on rest and sleep to become more productive seemed counter-intuitive. I grew up in a world where sleep wasn't important; I woke early as a teenager to do a paper round before school and, as a film-maker, I worked on animations long into the night. This seemed natural to me in a society where working more hours led to more success. The ultra-endurance cycling world pushed this attitude even further, with racing legends famously completing epic challenges such as the Transcontinental and the Race Across America, on half an hour of sleep every day or so. In my opinion, sleep was wasted time.

"You *need* to get eight hours of quality sleep a night or, honestly mate, you're compromising all the effort you're putting into training," Phil said.

"You can't be serious, man? Eight hours? On top of an hour's downtime?" I argued. I'd taken on everything Phil had suggested to this point. However, now I was forced to push back. "Do you know how much work I've got on at the moment? I've got a to-do list longer than my arm and you're asking me to sleep through my schedule."

"Look, the hard workouts you're doing create the potential to improve your performance but it's only during recovery that your body adapts and becomes stronger. And it's the same with your cognitive performance, your mind. You'll be much more productive when you're awake. There are loads of white papers to evidence it."

"No matter how good all that sleep makes me, I can't believe it can make up for, like, three hours of extra working time every day."

"It will. Sleep is the most powerful performance-enhancing drug and so few people make the most of it. Honestly, do you need me to show you the evidence?"

"Yes, actually I do." Our conversation ended abruptly; I was so frustrated. I had so much to do and it felt like in that one session, Phil had added loads more to my workload and taken away my time to do it. I felt like nobody understood what I was going through. At least I'd got that point across to Phil, I was sure I'd called his bluff and there was no way he was going to dig out a bunch of reports for me.

Two days later, Phil handed me a stack of peer-reviewed papers, published in scientific journals, referencing the positive impacts of sleep on physical and cognitive performance. I didn't even read them; if sleep meant so much to Phil that he produced that amount of evidence, then he was serious. We immediately implemented a rigid sleep strategy.

Achieving good-quality sleep relied on building a routine and sticking to it so at the age of 36, I was given a bedtime. I was to be in bed at 10 p.m. and awake at 6.30 a.m. Every evening at 9 p.m., an alarm sounded, at which point I had to move all incomplete tasks to the next morning and relax in my hour of downtime. Everyone learned about my bedtime; no matter where I was, when the alarm went off, in a Pavlovian response I packed my things and headed for the door. My life was ruled by alarms and routine and, like every other aspect of this science experiment, the details were logged and monitored.

I began to sleep longer and deeper and by reviewing my notes, I started to see how diet, exercise and other variables impacted my sleep. I wasn't perfect – sometimes urgent deadlines forced me to stay awake longer and in the early days, my old habits of working late were hard to override. I grew frustrated lying awake in bed thinking about the work I had to do. But when I stuck to my sleep schedule, I reported a lower rate of perceived exertion for the same physical efforts, I was more positive and focused, and my mind was less likely to wander. Increasing my sleep improved my physical and psychological performance significantly.

———————————————————

It wasn't easy to adjust my lifestyle with Phil's new habits and it certainly didn't happen overnight. They required commitment and repetition, and I often overlooked them, relegating them down my list of priorities when busy. I knew all Phil's instructions would have a positive impact on my productivity, yet at the same time I felt compelled to push against them. In my impulsive early 20s, I'd argued with friends and family about their rigidity in being organized, which I saw as a restriction on my autonomy to go with the flow. It seemed that, even as an adult, I still had the same childish knee-jerk reaction, even though I knew the discipline would enable me to achieve much more.

After living in a tent for seven years, it took time to familiarize myself with new ways of working. When I left the UK to cycle around the world smartphones were a new concept but when I returned, everyone had one. It was as though the world had moved on and I'd remained the same for seven years. Steve gave me one of his old phones and I started to use it straight away. The new level of planning helped me break down the work I needed to do each day, reducing the habits I'd developed of procrastinating and not acknowledging what had to be done. However, there were areas of Phil's advice that I neglected. In many ways, I still disagreed with Phil's prescription. I wanted to become a better cyclist; I didn't care about being tidy or organized. Steve kept me on the right track, focussing my time on the urgent jobs I needed to complete, but I felt I lacked the tools to do this myself, and that my head was a jumble of things to do without priority. "Being where my feet are" and "controlling the controllables" were still difficult for me. I began to realize that a lot of the thoughts I had and the pressures I put on myself weren't things I could control; rather expectations I had or that I believed others had of me.

Looking back through my own experiences of poor mental health and my habits in my 20s, I can now see striking correlations. When I was disorganized, and my sleep was erratic and short, anxious thoughts ran around my head as I struggled with depression. Cycling around the world, what little I owned was organized and I slept with the sun's daily cycle, camping wild, falling asleep shortly after sunset and waking with sunrise. These were the happiest years of my life. It would be an oversimplification to conclude that my routines were the only factor in this, nonetheless, it is difficult to imagine that life on the road would have been so enjoyable without them. As my new habits clicked into place and I repeated them over the first phase of psychology training, many of the routines I'd created in my saddlebag lifestyle were adapted to help me become more effective in a more "normal" way of living back home.

After six weeks, Phil and I reviewed the changes we'd made. I hadn't achieved everything but he reassured me that that was okay; developing a lifestyle was an ongoing process and I had made progress in every area we'd identified. Implementing an elite athlete's lifestyle improved the basic skills that had been limiting my potential and created a more productive environment, without having to learn anything new. Excellence on the bike could only be built on this high-performance lifestyle. Becoming a record-breaker wasn't just about cycling, it had to be at the front of my mind in every decision I made and in every daily action. It was all-encompassing. It was obsession.

SIX

THE NUTRITIONIST

Growing up, my sister and I accused Mum of incinerating our dinner. Mum still argues that she cooked everything thoroughly to ensure she didn't kill her babies with food poisoning. In her defence, she was recently divorced and alone with two young children to look after, running her business from before we woke up to after we'd gone to bed. It's only from discussing those memories with Mum years later that I learned "back-to-front dinner" with dessert first wasn't necessarily a treat, it was because she'd been too busy to get food on the table. I don't know how she found the time to feed us at all, let alone keep the meals home-cooked with fresh ingredients. When I was a teenager, Mum came home from work one day and was awestruck to find I'd heated up a tin of soup on my own. From that point through to adulthood, my cooking ability was shaped by little more than necessity; at university I was limited by budget, when self-employed I was limited by time and when cycling around the world, I was limited to one pot and whatever I could find or pronounce in local markets.

Steve's family called me a human dustbin. I never gave myself the time to create gastronomic masterpieces but food was intrinsic to some of my favourite memories. The smell of fresh coffee and oats outside my tent in the cold morning air, perfectly cooked pasta served on the back of a small yacht, the crisp taste of a cold bottle of pilsner among hot, dusty mountains. I appreciated good food and drink but, as with sleep, it never took top priority – it kept me alive.

In training for the world record, "food" became "fuel" and every detail was controlled. I was training my body for its ultimate athletic performance and, as I was told at the time, you wouldn't buy a Ferrari and run it on cheap fuel. Iain Findlay's attempt the previous year had failed due to what looked like food poisoning in Lithuania and it was important to mitigate this risk for our attempt to be successful. Mark, Phil and I had a conference call with the nutritionist who joined the team, to discuss our approach to fuelling and begin to form a plan.

Jonathan didn't like his name shortened to Jon. He explained the complexity of extreme fuelling for an ultra-endurance event; that the human body can absorb a maximum of 90 grams of carbohydrate per hour and we would need to build my tolerance to this through training. We would be testing a range of foods to see what I enjoyed and what would fuel me best. He was researching supplements we could use such as caffeine and energy drinks, as well as exotic substances I'd never heard of;

beta-alanine, sodium bicarbonate and creatine. Jonathan was making enquiries into nutrition brands that would potentially sponsor the project. He told me that he would develop my fuel schedule by modelling the nutritional highs and lows I would encounter, analyzing how we could utilize fuelling to maximize each situation and establishing control in my diet to minimize errors.

To create the basis for his plan, Jonathan asked me to log everything I ate, just as we'd quantified my physiology and psychology. The nutritional aspect of preparation was filled with great promise and just like the first day in the Human Performance Unit, I knew I was embarking on an exciting adventure into another specialist field of elite sports. I began recording my meals and took my first steps into the world of sports nutrition.

A month into the project, Jonathan visited me, Mark and Phil in the laboratory of the HPU at the University of Derby. Looking like a bodybuilder, his woollen jumper hugging every contour, he stood imposingly before me and spoke with authority. The shame of doing PE in my pants and vest washed over me as I stood wearing only ill-fitting, grey underwear when he unexpectedly asked to examine me. Cold steel tongs clamped the pale skin on six areas of my body under the green tint of fluorescent light. According to the skin callipers, with a body mass of 71 kg, my fat percentage was 12 per cent. The optimum was 8–10 per cent. To achieve this, Jonathan's objective was to reduce my body fat through calorie deficit; a meal plan that provided fewer calories than my body required per day.

My training diet was broken down into three plans, each tailored to three levels of daily demand: low/moderate, high and very high energy expenditure. The plans were given to me with technical, graphical summaries which looked fantastic but meant nothing to me. Beneath the scientific breakdown was the bit I understood, an itemized list of the quantities of foods I could eat for each plan. They were accompanied with the guidance: "Try and have them spread out evenly over the day and in any order you wish for now. Aiming for a modest weight loss to improve body composition." There was also a page of recipes.

I compared the notes of the meals I'd been recording myself with details from Jonathan. Where I'd logged a breakfast of "oats and milk", the scientist detailed "oat flakes, rolled, 80 g" with "milk, skimmed, pasteurized, average 200 g". Accuracy was everything when quantifying what I was consuming, as measurement would bring improvement. Every variable was to be recorded in detail, for example the type of coffee, brand and brewing process, how close to sleeping I drank it and any effect on sleep. I had embarked on a diet that was purely focused on physical performance; food had become science. Until now, I'd been consuming all and recording little. Jonathan turned this around.

In streamlining my lifestyle, Phil and I had looked at every opportunity to multitask and identified dinner as a perfect time to combine socializing, family time and nutrition. Mum jumped at the chance to cook with me – it was a rare opportunity for us to spend time together through my busy schedule and for us to connect as we had when she baked with me and Emma as children. On top of these personal reasons, Mum wanted to learn more about sports nutrition. While I was away, she'd taken up running to lose weight and found success with a Couch to 5K programme. Following that, she'd decided to set herself the target of a 10 k running event. Through the course of training, weight had dropped off her; she looked great, she'd found a new hobby and created a new friendship circle. Learning about nutrition was another step on her own journey as well as mine.

In our eagerness to begin an exciting adventure into sports fuelling, Mum and I began cooking from the page of recipes that Jonathan had given me. The quantities were monstrous, but we persevered with a Peanut Satay Curry that sounded delicious. Three large cauldrons of orange curry sat bubbling on the hob, infusing the kitchen air with nuts and spices. It seemed far too much, so I sent a picture to Jonathan. He replied that we weren't using that recipe and that he hadn't told me to cook it, I was not to eat it. I was frustrated, *why would he send recipes that I wasn't even going to use*? Our culinary adventure ended before it even began, the list of tasty recipes that Mum and I were excited to explore were filed away and we stopped spending that time together as meal preparation fell into a basic, repetitive routine. Kilograms of satay curry were bagged up to put in the freezer and I began eating only from the three itemized diets that he specified.

Every day started with a delicious berry smoothie but that was the highlight of my nutritional regime. Ingredients were carbohydrate heavy to provide a source of energy and to improve my performance and recovery. Even in comparison to my one-pot camping dinners, there didn't seem to be any standout meals to be created by combining the prescription of potato, muesli, quinoa and oats. When asked what kinds of foods I enjoyed, I'd written a list including lasagne, meatballs, roast dinners, jacket potatoes, chilli, pasta bake and fish. With the limited ingredients I was allowed, and no room for deviation, I was unsure how to make an interesting meal and I was concerned that I was going to get hungry. Jonathan's solution was to "ride the wave of the crave". He explained that hunger was just a craving and that, if ignored, the feeling would disappear after 20 minutes. He wasn't concerned by how monotonous and dull the ingredients were.

With the three-option meal plan, my intake was under strict control. I had no idea how many calories I was consuming or how many I was expending – all I had to do was follow the plan. It was based on Mark's energy expenditure data from the incremental tests, so I trusted it. As well as keeping a detailed record of everything I ate, I kept a log of my body weight to ensure that the diet was working. Every morning before breakfast, I stood on a digital scale in Mum's kitchen. Wearing only my underwear and with shaved lower legs, my thighs looking like a pair of hairy "Wookie shorts", I could only apologize on the days she walked in. I tracked the data and obsessed over graphs, becoming infatuated with getting down to the holy grail of 8 per cent body fat.

The plan worked rapidly and effectively; within a month I was down to 66.8 kg, a loss of 4.2 kg. I can't deny that I felt rewarded for my hunger when I saw definition in my leg muscles that were becoming "ripped" and other "useless" parts of my body becoming thin. Friends and family saw things differently. On club rides, those I cycled with pointed out that they could see my ribs through my Lycra jersey or that I looked like a "lollipop head" on a skeletal body. Sleeves on tight-fitting casual clothes were now baggy, and Steve's mum ordered me to stop losing weight. However, in my eyes, I was beginning to resemble a Tour de France cyclist, the imagery of my heroes.

Rapid weight loss came at a price as my energy and motivation dropped. Through training, I developed a greater physical strength than I'd ever had before and yet I was always tired, dragging my body around. I began feeling down and withdrawn. I was disappointed that Jonathan hadn't fulfilled the promise of this exciting adventure into sports nutrition and I was left deflated. Although the physiological and psychological aspects of training were difficult, I was always learning from Mark and Phil. In those other areas of the project there was balance; I trained hard through the week and Mark acknowledged the benefit of a café ride with friends at the weekend, I worked hard seven days a week and Phil enforced downtime to relax. But the nutrition programme was dictated and relentless. I began obsessing with details, following the nutrition plan to the gram. Everything was prescribed and if it wasn't prescribed, it wasn't beneficial. Like my pursuit of "success" in film-making, nutrition had become all about the end goal of weight loss, and not about enjoying the journey. I looked forward to days when long rides were scheduled because it meant I would be on a meal plan which allowed me to eat pasta and tomato sauce. I looked forward to such simple foods. I looked forward to sauce.

On the evenings when I worked at Steve's house, I ate with his family. On the controlled diet I began taking my own food. While the family had delicious smelling chicken and chorizo with chips or pulled pork burgers, I had a small plate of new potatoes, a chicken breast and a side salad. They were shocked at how little I was eating and how beige every meal was. They offered me what they were eating but I refused – I wasn't willing to compromise any aspect of my training.

The nutritionist lived far from Derby and, as it was impossible for him to attend meetings with the team, I tried to maintain regular phone contact. We established this from the beginning with a call every Saturday morning but as the weeks passed it became harder to contact him and communication ended up becoming short voice messages he sent through WhatsApp in reply to my emails. Unlike Mark and Phil, who explained their processes in layman's terms, with stories and metaphor, I began to feel like an idiot when I listened to Jonathan's messages. He spoke in scientific terms that I didn't understand and his instructions were sent without explanations. I felt out of my depth. I didn't have basic knowledge like whether measurements were dry weight or cooked weight and it took weeks until he told me vegetable and salad portions were "free" so I could eat as much of those as I liked. As contact with the nutritionist decreased further, I felt the project was a burden to him and I dreaded messaging him.

Due to the skin callipers Jonathan used, he was the only person who could consistently measure my fat percentage and, without current data, the team and I were working in the dark. It was the same with his dietary plan; I needed autonomy with my diet to fit in with my schedule, but Jonathan told me that deviating from the three-meal plan would sacrifice control. I asked if I could read research on the approach we were using, so I wasn't following his instructions blindly, but I never received any. Without guidelines or knowledge of food science, it was impossible for me to select the right option from menus if I was eating out or to diversify my food options at home.

Eight weeks after starting the nutrition programme and still on the same calorie deficit plan, I failed to hit the training targets that I had done before. Mark observed my reduced power, raised heart rate and increased RPE in training sessions. I was turning up late and instead of celebrating my progress or caring if I achieved my goals, I was apathetic. While the other experts on the team were aiming to increase my power, the nutritionist was aiming to reduce my weight and the two objectives were pulling in opposing directions.

When Mark asked if everything was all right, I explained the difficulty I was having with my energy and mood, and that I wasn't getting the information I needed from the nutritionist. Mark told me to leave it with him, he'd have a word. However, he didn't receive any responses from Jonathan either, so he overruled the nutrition plan, telling me to increase all food measurements by 5 per cent. I had faith in Mark's judgement. Not only was he leading the science team with my performance as his top priority but he was also present and could see the detrimental effect of the diet first-hand.

As well as compromising my training, I was concerned

that we weren't prepared for the upcoming test rides. The nutritionist hadn't followed through with his initial promises of testing a range of foods I'd enjoy and he hadn't made any enquiries to nutrition brands about sponsorship. He hadn't experimented with the exotic supplements he'd suggested, except a multivitamin to replace nutrients that were missing from my diet. He hadn't trialled any recipes that would work on the road or increased my tolerance to the high carbohydrate levels required. I felt as though my needs, and the needs of the project, were being compromised.

Nevertheless, I continued to dedicate myself to his plan in the belief that, as a qualified nutrition expert, his process would deliver positive results. The problem was not his working methods but his lack of communication. For our team to thrive, we all had to work towards the same goal and share information, as the sum of our parts was greater than our individual skills.

Throughout this time, struggling with a restricted diet and a regimented lifestyle, Steve thought I was going to quit. The discipline was so far removed from the carefree life of the man who had cycled the world. One evening, I was invited to join friends from Cycle Mickleover at an event that I love. The Bustler Market is a monthly street food party in the centre of town with an open-air atmosphere. Fairy lights are strung above festival-like crowds, who dance and chat between food trucks and drinks vendors, and the air is full of wonderful smells and sounds. It's the kind of event where you meet someone you know at every turn and everybody wanted to know how the world record preparation was going. But this time I didn't want to speak to them, they wouldn't understand. I isolated myself from my friends and sat alone at the end of a wooden bench. Steve tried to get me to join in, to order something to eat or have a drink with them but, yet again, on the strict diet, there was nothing I could eat at the market and so I left the party without saying goodbye and drove home.

SEVEN

THE MERRY-GO-ROUND OR THE ROLLERCOASTER

Financially, I was at rock bottom. I put everything into the record and had to beg, steal or borrow to make ends meet. I didn't have a job, so I kept all my expenses low by living on a shoestring budget. I wore old or borrowed clothes, didn't go out or spend time with any other friends except the cycle club, and hadn't been on a date since last summer. I lived out of my overdraft and only kept from going over its limit by delivering the school speaking events that put a few hundred pounds in my account each month. At the beginning of March, I presented the one-man show about cycling around the world to a sold-out audience at the Derby Guildhall, which put me back in the black. However, I knew that money would only last a couple of months and with total focus on the record preparation, I had no other work lined up. I didn't share quite how desperate my financial situation was with anyone. I knew Steve would tell me to prioritize getting out of my overdraft, which would sacrifice time I could give to the project, and I knew Mum would want to help but she didn't have money to give to me. I was grateful to be staying with Mum and Al, who didn't expect me to pay for rent or food, but that came with another sacrifice. After 13 years of independent living, seven of which had been the wild freedom of travelling, my fun, spontaneous lifestyle was changed. The invitations to random parties, the adventures in exotic countries and meeting travellers who understood me, all became a distant memory. Every day I had to commit to my training routines and navigate an unfamiliar business world, I was starving myself and I felt constantly stressed. Everything that I'd sacrificed in the pursuit of this project got on top of me. I felt that I was giving away too much in pursuit of something I could have just gone out and achieved on a whim.

The record attempt's budget looked scarily like my own. Steve and I had sent a project outline to dozens of potential corporate sponsors, yet it seemed as though nobody wanted to partner with us on the project. I was strung along in enthusiastic conversations about possible partnerships that were never committed to, companies came on board with great promises but delivered products that weren't fit for purpose and discussions with prospective sponsors approached perfect conclusions until communications went dead. One day, after a difficult training session in the morning, a frustrating afternoon of sponsorship rejections and an evening of mentorship from Steve, I'd had enough. I complained to him that the project was *too* difficult. I questioned whether it was all worth it; I could easily have gone back to an office to earn a salary, doing a job that I knew.

"Do you want to be on the merry-go-round, or do you want to be on the rollercoaster?" Steve asked me.

"I'm not sure I understand," I replied.

"Listen," he said. "Do you want to go around and around, doing the same thing every day, or do you want to experience the highs and lows of what's truly possible in life?"

As 2018's long winter and the frozen storms of "The Beast From The East" passed, my training schedule involved increased time outdoors. I needed to secure a bike for the world record and finding the right tool for the job was essential. A family-run cycling shop offered to lend me a bike to get me across Europe. They would build it immediately to get the wheels turning on my world record attempt and we could hone it through training.

The owner and I sat upstairs in his showroom, surrounded by expensive carbon-fibre bikes. As rain beat on the thin glass windowpanes of the old mill building, we discussed the fine balance of bike comfort and efficiency. The ideal bike would be lightweight, aerodynamic and deliver a direct power transfer. However, extended time spent in an uncomfortable position on a very rigid bike would cause fatigue and reduced power output. It was a difficult equation to balance. There wasn't an off-the-shelf answer but we could create the "Goldilocks" bike for my attempt by taking an aero bike with good handling and compliance, and making a few modifications. This was it, the moment I'd been preparing for when I daydreamed in class as a teenager; a bike built specifically for me, like a pro.

A couple of weeks later, I picked up my bike, a white, carbon-fibre Cervelo S3d. It was built around a frame that was one size too small for me, which allowed me to tuck my upper body into a more aerodynamic time trial position. We added clip-on aero extensions to the handlebars to give me that efficient body shape and to take the weight off my hands for a more comfortable position to use through long hours. We upgraded to electronic gears and disc brakes, to guarantee continued accuracy when fatigued and in adverse conditions. Short pedal cranks gave a more open hip angle, a power meter provided data analysis, and deep section carbon wheels brought improved aerodynamics with reduced weight. It was ready.

This bike couldn't have been further from the one I'd used to cycle around the world. Strangers used to struggle to pick Dolly up; quickly exhaling and shaking their head at the weight, an international language understood in every country. The world record bike could be picked up with a little finger. It blew my mind.

I pedalled away from the shop, across the toll bridge and along the river. A quick push on the pedals and the bike shot forwards, the steering was direct and responsive, and the brakes barely needed touching to bring me to a stop. I plotted the flattest route I could find and took off at warp speed. As my legs powered me along, my brain faced a dilemma. I needed to tuck down onto the aero extensions with arms stretched out in front. I had to leave the safety of the handlebars. A leap of faith. *How do I get myself into that position? How will I steer? How will the bike handle?* Cars sped past me at 60 miles per hour. *I'll have no brakes with my hands out there.* It was nerve-racking. *Okay, I've got to let go and just do it. Commit.* Nerves officially racked. *Go. Whoosh.*

In the aerodynamic position, the loud buffering of wind noise in my ears quietened under the thunderous rumbling of deep section carbon wheels on a smooth road and the subtle "zup" from the electronic gear shifters. I became accustomed to the position after a few rides and was able to thumb through screens on the GPS unit, analyzing my power and heart rate data to monitor and control my effort as I rode. In comparison to any other bike I'd ridden, this was a spaceship and I was taking this bad boy to another dimension.

I took the bike for a test ride down the lanes of Derbyshire with Steve and we stopped at a café for a chat. Sitting in the courtyard, soaking up the springtime sunshine, drinking fresh coffee and looking at our bikes, Steve asked if I'd had a professional bike fit. A bike fitter made small adjustments to a bike setup, which could literally be a few millimetres change in saddle, handlebar and shoe cleat position. These simple changes could lead to enormous improvements in comfort and power output. I told Steve the bike felt comfortable enough as it was and bike fits seemed expensive. He explained slight niggles he'd felt when he first got his bike, which had developed into aching muscles and could have led to injury in the long run. A bike fit would ensure the geometry of the world record bike was right for me. It didn't matter if I had the best bike in the world, a bike fit was the best upgrade that I could possibly buy. He put £150 in my hand and told me to book an appointment.

A week later, I spent 2 hours surrounded by walls of saddles, shoes and measuring equipment in the studio of Andy Brooke, president of the International Bike Fitting Institute. The challenge with bike fitting, as I was coming to realize about every aspect of the project and every walk of life for that matter, was that there was no single setup that worked for everybody. For that reason, the majority of the session was an assessment of me and my background. Andy asked about previous injuries, my cycling experience and the challenge I was taking on, before a physical assessment of my range of motion, flexibility and core stability. This all impacted how I held myself on the bike and highlighted asymmetries and imbalances that could be improved.

Sensors were stuck to the pivot points of my joints and a laser system collected data from the movement as I pedalled a static bike. Andy interpreted the output from behind a computer monitor, determining my ideal position and making a series of micro-adjustments to the bike. He set it specifically for me, guaranteeing as best he could the sustainability of my comfort, efficiency and aerodynamics.

Through his assessment, I explained that I was experiencing pain at the top of my left hamstring when training. Andy kept an eye on anything unusual through the assessment and identified discrepancies between the angles on my left and right sides. He explained that my hips seemed to be rotated unevenly, leading to an imbalance throughout my movement. Andy had adapted the setup as much as possible for me, however, due to the symmetrical nature of the bike, I would have to make some adaptations to my body to improve my position on it. He handed me the contact details of a chiropractor he knew who would help even out my hip rotation.

Unlike the shameful primary school PE lesson that I'd played out with the nutritionist, I remembered to take a pair of running shorts to wear during the chiropractor's assessment. I stood beside an electric heater in the dark, converted office, which reminded me of the industrial estates of my teenage work placements. "Any previous injuries?" asked the chiropractor, staring at the conspicuous bone protruding from my shoulder.

"Back in 2007, I had this dream of becoming a snow bum," I laughed. "I moved to New Zealand and, a couple of weeks after learning to snowboard, had this massive accident. When I came round, my left arm was totally limp, lifeless. Turned out my collarbone had broken and separated from my shoulder by two centimetres. It ended that dream, ha!"

I explained how the break was never fixed, just strapped down with tape. The chiropractor stood behind me and concluded that all my problems were stemming from that trauma. My shoulders were not correctly aligned and my upper back had twisted to compensate, which had led to my lower back counteracting in the opposite direction and my hips compensating further; my back was a series of S-bends.

He asked me to lie on his couch and commenced grabbing limbs and contorting me, my joints cracking as he pulled them. When he'd finished manhandling me, he laid me flat on the bed and yanked both my legs straight so that my feet lined up. "Much better, that's perfect. You're all aligned now, see?" he told me. I looked at him, puzzled; anybody could pull my legs to line up my feet. It felt like a trick, but I followed him to his card reader and parted with the best part of £100. "You're going to need at least eight weeks of this, so I'll book you in for next week, okay?" asked the chiropractor. I looked at him in disbelief and paid for that session, before walking out into the sobering air and wondering what just happened to my body and my wallet.

The next day I was working on a sponsorship proposal in Steve's office. "Have you ever been to see a chiropractor?" I asked him.

"Yes, why?" he replied.

"I went to see one yesterday, he pulled me around, cracked my joints and asked for a hundred quid. He's already booked me in for another eight weeks. There's no way I can afford that!"

"Don't go back to him, mate. You need to see a physio." Steve laughed and booked me an appointment with his. Who knows, if I'd stuck with it, maybe the chiropractor would have helped, but I felt uneasy about a clinician who prescribed eight weeks of treatment before even seeing my progress and, besides, Steve's suggestion of a physio sat better with me.

Beneath Strutt's Mill, an eighteenth-century cotton factory that dominates the surrounding rural skyline, is a small gym and Belper Life-Fitness Physio Clinic and Pilates Studio. I sank into a squidgy sofa in reception and waited to be called in to see the physiotherapist. Ruth Anness poked her head through the door, wearing leggings and a tracksuit top, her blonde hair tied up tight in a ponytail. "Hiya! Wanna come through?" she said in a chirpy southern accent, and I followed her away from the clanking of gym equipment and into the quiet treatment room.

Similarly to Andy's bike fit, Ruth carried out a full physio assessment, looking at alignment, range of movement and strength. In opposition to the diagnosis of the chiropractor, she found that my tension and imbalances weren't necessarily due to the broken collarbone but primarily because my body was compensating for a leg length discrepancy; my left leg was a centimetre longer than my right. Ruth systematically analyzed and worked through each muscle group with deep sports massage and acupuncture, as I held my breath and gritted my teeth. I'd imagined sports therapy would be a treat to look forward to after the intensity of training, but it wasn't the leisurely massage I'd enjoyed in spas or from friends.

Ruth became a sponsor of the project and an intrinsic member of the team. I visited her studio at the end of each week to make certain I was in optimum condition and she relayed information about my condition back to Mark and Phil, to ensure training was having a positive effect. Based on her observations, Ruth also prescribed a personalized mobility maintenance routine that I practised every morning to increase my range of motion, improve my muscular performance and reduce the potential of injury. This adapted every few weeks, to accommodate for changes in my body. As well as maintaining my form, stretching became a daily dose of relief from the stress of running the project. Unlike the extra sleep and downtime that Phil insisted on, I could justify half an hour of stretching to myself as it would enable me to physically go faster.

As an ex-professional athlete, Ruth understood the pressure I was under to achieve my peak condition. She knew the demand of full-time training and saw that I was struggling to stay on top of it while managing the business side of a world record attempt. Physio appointments became like counselling sessions; I lay on the treatment couch, with my face poked through its circular hole, and tried to take the conversation away from the admin that seemed to fill the other 23 hours of my day. Ruth explained making the same sacrifices that I was making now, when she was at the peak of her career as a pole-vaulter; it had been an all-encompassing lifestyle in the pursuit of excellence. She'd done the same again years later to establish her own physio studio while working full time in the NHS. I enjoyed my weekly catch-ups with Ruth and realized that all the successful people I was surrounding myself with had to make sacrifices to get to where they were.

When the bike shop, Andy and Ruth came on board to support the project, they became friends as well as sponsors. They helped ease the burden of the project and it took a turn for the better. The team was growing in expertise and the pressure on me to secure funding was reduced by their kind contributions.

I saw the sacrifices I made in my life in a different way, too. The sacrifice of earning money gave me the time I needed to make the project a reality. The sacrifice of nights out bought me the early mornings at the Human Performance Unit. The sacrifice of spontaneous adventures bought me routines that were necessary for growth. I had to give away the fun of those round-the-world experiences to make space to develop myself and to progress.

I understood Steve's question about the merry-go-round or the rollercoaster. Uncertainty and difficulty came with the rollercoaster, but it gave me the opportunity for great achievement and freedom to make my own mark on the world. The highs were all the outside world would see; the snapshot thrill of the descent collected from the gift shop on the way out; the expensive approach, the sponsorship, the team of experts. The lows on the rollercoaster were arduous struggles through hard graft, isolation and adversity, and only I could drag myself to the top. That was the reason Phil had put so much emphasis on finding my *why*. My motivation had to be strong enough to get me through all the sacrifices I needed to make and all the difficult lessons I needed to learn to realize my dream. It would have to keep me going when I wanted to take an easy way out and when I considered giving up.

It was incredibly difficult to constantly find the energy to keep pushing on but that was how deep I had to dig to achieve my vision. The rewards from the merry-go-round would never be worth the sacrifice. I committed to this realization and owned it.

I chose to ride the rollercoaster.

EIGHT

FREE YOUR MIND AND YOUR LEGS WILL FOLLOW

Mid-March and already half our preparation time was gone. Time was passing too quickly. Progress was rapid with the science team but I felt responsible for everything outside of scientific control. Around the world I'd only had to worry about myself. Now I was accountable for much more. I was concerned about strategies, border crossings, falling off, injury, weather, diversions, finding a vehicle, knowing my targets and limits, staying positive and still about financing the attempt. I bottled up my anxieties because, in my mind, others wouldn't understand and didn't need to be burdened by my troubles. Sharing them would make me look stupid and vulnerable. I still attached a stigma to mental health. I related it to social expectations of masculinity – having my "running commentary on everything" silenced by Dad and losing film work when I'd opened up about my personal problems after the cinema outburst. However, I needed to share what I was going through so I could move forwards.

Phil and I wrote out every worst-case scenario that we could imagine encountering on the road. In that brain dump, everything was out, and each problem had a name. As it had been in counselling, when my thoughts were shared, they appeared much smaller than the shadows they cast as anxious constructions of my imagination.

Establishing our intentions for the second phase of psychology training, Phil and I completed another performance profile. In determining which of my personal characteristics should be developed, I again focused on performance-based behaviours that I believed would solve the concerns I'd listed. Phil reminded me that although there were things I could control, more importantly, there were things that lay ahead that I had no control over – I'd already mentioned falling off, injury and weather. For these things I could only control my reaction. However, dealing with crisis moments, emotional regulation, and recognizing physical warning signs were all new to me. Phil had techniques that would help me manage them. Improving my physical and mental self-awareness were Phil's two major focus points in our second phase of psychology and he taught them to me through two processes: centring and Progressive Muscle Relaxation (PMR).

Bzzzzzzz. Bzzzzzzz. Bzzzzzzz. Every hour, on the hour, the alarm vibrated on my watch. I put down whatever I was working on, stood in a quiet place, feet shoulder-width apart, locked my hands on my chest and took deep breaths for 3 minutes. *Centring* was the tool I used to practise mindfulness, with the intention of bringing a calm mind to high-pressure situations. Phil explained that regular practice at this was the psychological equivalent of doing reps in the gym.

As well as calming the mind, Phil had prescribed centring so that I would become aware of my thought process and to begin taking control of it. While centring, I was to focus only on my breathing; if something came to mind, I should acknowledge it and let it go. Phil described building a wall in my mind to keep unwanted thoughts out, with an exit door to quickly evict any that did get in.

I stood beside my bike, against the wall at the end of my bed and started a 3-minute timer. What ensued was an unstoppable flood of memories and obligations that were at once bizarre, irrelevant and powerfully distracting. If my mind was supposed to have a wall around it with only an exit door, the fortress was stormed, the door burned and my mind was declared a colony of the Empire of the Irrational. I journaled the stream of thoughts.

Wind in high mountains. Kitchen noise distractions. What time target have the team set? Will I arrive at Steve's on time tonight? If people disturb me or ask what I'm doing,

what would I say, should I ignore them? Must call Elisa!
Cycling the Spanish coast listening to Anthony Robbins.
Kissing a French girl in Australia. I am a human balloon.
New York. Birdsong at my final wild camp at end of cycling
the world. I am not present. I've not achieved enough today.
I am getting nowhere.

I tried all kinds of visualizations to cut out the uncontrollable thoughts. The wall with a door hadn't worked, so I increased it to the caravanserai that I'd visited on the Silk Road, but they still got in. I imagined myself inside an impenetrable bubble, but it burst. And when I created what Phil called a "sanctuary", my mind put me in the donkey sanctuary in Skegness that Mum had fundraised for. I could not find peace.

I'd felt that conditioning my body through Mark's training schedule was as tough as training could get but conditioning my mind was even more difficult. I was frustrated by Phil's request for me to stop work every hour to listen to 3 minutes of nonsense racing around my brain. In our next weekly psychology review, I explained to Phil the trouble I was having and my concern that maybe it was just the way that my mind was; that I couldn't change it.

Phil briefly explained growth mindsets, that I wouldn't die the same person that I was born, and that I had the power to decide who I became. All behaviours are learned and I could develop the ability to understand and manage my thought process. If I wanted to change, I had to believe that in every situation I could either win or learn. There was no such thing as failure. His advice was to stop overthinking matters and focus only on the physicality of breathing. The pressure I was experiencing now was only going to be worse on the road.

Centring never became natural to me but, with an awareness of the turbulent thoughts cycling in my subconscious, I learned to put the brakes on when my mind began slipping down the rabbit hole. In the increasing stress of the project, rather than seeing the process as a burden, I found myself calming and for occasional moments, just *being*.

I ended each centring activity by visualizing myself outside the lighthouse at Cabo da Roca, the start line of the world record route. I knew how it would look from internet searches and every time I pictured it, I built a more vivid sensory picture in my mind; the seagulls squawking, the feeling of the coastal sun and salty wind on my skin. I imagined the adrenaline rush, waiting for the attempt to begin, and imagined using these centring skills to calm myself and to begin cycling with control.

———————

To recognize the physical signals my body was sending, Phil taught me Progressive Muscle Relaxation. Physical self-awareness was important for me to distinguish fatigue on the bike that I could cycle through, from injury that needed treatment. Through PMR, I would be able to locate muscular tension and release it through a breathing exercise. The 10-minute routine on an MP3 that Phil sent me was to be repeated twice a day, just before going to bed and once during the day.

I lay on my bed, pressed play, and a calming female voice began to narrate the activity from my mobile phone. "Know that anything you may need to think about, figure out or do soon, will go much more smoothly if you take this time now to just be here and relax." The opening line brought me peace. As I lay in bed, yet again worrying about how much had to be done, how little time there was and how I was going to make the project happen, her sentence reassured me that everything would go better if I slept well.

The track told me to take deep, slow breaths and took me through a process of tensing each muscle group independently and feeling the relaxation as I released it. The sequence methodically worked from my feet up, through my entire body to my neck, jaw, eyes and finishing at my forehead. I assumed that, as an elite cyclist, I was going to find tension and pain in my legs from training. Conversely, I found tension in my upper back, shoulders and forehead, my physical symptoms of stress.

At the end of the 10-minute PMR activity, my body was completely relaxed, and I made a note of areas of tension or pain that I'd found. Phil had told me that he'd had students fall asleep at this moment during his lectures. "Yeah right, it was because of the exercise?!" I'd sarcastically mocked him, but the technique genuinely relaxed me to the point of falling asleep within minutes. On the road, we would have this process honed to take just a few seconds.

———————————————

I knew that winning the battle in my mind was going to be important in breaking the record but until my self-awareness was heightened through these new techniques, I didn't understand the extent. For the first time, I'd been given a physical and a mental exercise that ran simultaneously; PMR had been easy, centring was a disaster. My body was mechanics; an engine with pistons and levers, as natural to me as the industrial world I grew up in. But psychology was still new territory and I began to wonder if I even knew my own mind. I'd been told repeatedly that getting to the finish line would come down to having a strong mind but, like so many lessons before, I hadn't truly believed it until I learned it for myself.

NINE

THE WHITE WALL

On Friday 13 April, I was back under the fluorescent lights of the laboratory at the University of Derby for an Endurance Threshold Test. The lab was emptier and more sterile than ever before. Excalibur sat in the middle of the room, facing a white wall. There were no visual distractions, no audio distractions and only Mark and a student in the lab, working in a far corner.

The test would last 4 hours. Every hour, the pedalling resistance would increase. A heart rate monitor was strapped around my chest and power was monitored through the pedals. Blood samples were taken from my finger every 30 minutes to measure lactate, as we had done in the incremental tests. Mark ensured that I was set up with everything I needed, understood what we were doing and was happy to begin. I clipped my shoes into the pedals and got settled on the hard saddle. The test began at a relatively low intensity, which I spun out comfortably for the first hour.

On the road, a bike moves beneath a cyclist continuously, over bumps, around corners, under braking and acceleration.

It's the romance of the bicycle; to move in harmony with the landscapes, to ride the undulations like a rollercoaster and to experience "flow" in the moment. But like the sword in the stone, Excalibur didn't budge. The heavy static bike might as well be bolted to the ground. Although the first hour was easy to pedal, the constant pressure on my wrists, feet and sit bones made them increasingly sore. *It's only for a few hours, just pedal through it,* I told myself as I continued to spin.

The resistance was ramped up at the beginning of hour two and I began to wrestle with the monotony of pedalling continually at the same cadence. On a static bike there's no respite offered by freewheeling on a descent or cruising with a tailwind, just the tedious left, right, left, right… My eyes searched the lab for any distraction but there was nothing, just the white wall in front of me. I looked forward to the blood samples being taken every 30 minutes, to being stabbed and having blood squeezed out of my finger. Those few seconds of human interaction were clinical and painful but they gave me something else to focus on. Every time Mark went back to the corner of the lab to work with his student, he seemed further away, and their hushed conversations were more frustrating than silence.

In the third hour, my mind began wandering. *I wouldn't be in so much pain if I'd slept better last night. This would feel much easier if I'd put more effort into training. I'm not good enough. Those biscuits I ate have sacrificed this,*

I should have more self-control. I relived old arguments in my head: *Why couldn't Dad ever be proud of me? Why has he become an advocate of creating a better future for society when he doesn't even call me or Emma, his direct connection to a better future? If he'd have been there for me, I'd be better than this now...*

In hour four, the resistance approached my threshold. *It's the last hour now, you've done most of the hard work, just keep going* I told myself. After 3 hours of continual pedalling, on a bike that didn't move, with pain in every contact point, no distraction except plain white walls and arguing with demons in my mind, the high level of physical demand began pushing me to my limit. My heart rate crept up to uncomfortable levels, my heavy legs began to burn, I felt tension in every part of my body, I gasped for air and sweat dripped from my face. Alone. Seconds seemed like minutes. Minutes seemed like hours. Every instant was physically and mentally excruciating. The mantra in my mind of *Just keep going* was replaced with *Just wait until Mark has finished with his student, then he can stop this.* However, the student didn't go and my frustration built with every pedal stroke.

Why am I so weak? Their whispering is intolerable. I don't care what anyone else thinks any more, they don't understand what I'm going through. When he only saw his kids one day a week, why didn't he do anything with us? How could they just sit there chatting when I'm hurting so much? The pain of negative thoughts multiplied, like a lactic build-up in my mind. Fifteen minutes passed in a state of agony and I kept holding on, waiting for the student to leave. *It'll be over soon.* The clock hit 20 minutes. *Just hold on, Leigh, it can't be long now, just hold on…* Mark and the student continued working.

"Arrrrrgggghhhhhhh!!!" I screamed as I stopped pedalling and slammed my hand on the handlebar over and over. Blood from my finger splattered over Excalibur and the white wall. "What the hell are you doing over there?" I shouted at Mark. "My heart is pumping out of my chest. My lactate levels must be through the roof. Can't you see how difficult this is for me? What the hell are you doing? Why aren't you helping me?"

After 3 hours and 25 minutes I snapped.

Mark walked slowly and calmly across the room to me, turned the power down on the static bike, and walked back to his student without saying a word.

I sat on the saddle, spinning the lactate out of my legs. Within seconds the burning ceased and my mind calmed. I felt embarrassment. Shame. *What have I just done? Who have I become? Where did that come from?* The student left the room, I got off the bike and apologized to Mark. He said nothing. The session ended.

Surrounded only by white walls, I had to look myself in the eye and be accountable for my own behaviour. I hated who I'd become in that moment and it was difficult to accept that I was that person. After all the work I had done, was doing, to change myself, I was gutted that this negative, angry part of me still existed. There was nobody else to blame and nothing happened that was out of my control. There was only me. For almost three and a half hours, Mark had watched me riding a bike without concern, and then "BOOM!" I lost my head.

Days later, when we debriefed, Phil disclosed that there was no such thing as an Endurance Threshold Test. Mark and he had cooked the idea up to see if my mental strength matched my physical strength. As I sat on Excalibur in psychological turmoil that day, my physical data suggested that I would have been comfortable to continue cycling at that capacity for hours longer. When everything was stripped back, it highlighted that physically I was in a great place but mentally there was a lot of work still to do.

I began to see a parallel narrative in the world record project and my experience of depression years ago. In both cases I had reached breaking point. On the depression timeline, I'd shouted at an audience of 100 schoolchildren, which had cost me my job. If I reacted in the same way on the road as I had in the lab, it could cost me the world record.

Starting the project, I hadn't been fully on board with psychology and I'd pushed against Phil's suggestions, much more committed to sponsorship and physical training. I'd believed that I was who I was born to be and there was one way, *my way*, of dealing with things. I'd argued with Phil that my mindset was so good it had got me around the world and questioned why I would need to change it. He'd said that my way of thinking was a "fixed mindset' and that I wasn't cycling around the world any more – I needed to adapt.

When I'd laughed at Phil about emotional regulation and falling in love on the road, this is what he'd really meant. It was a tough blow to take. It was personal. Until this point, my approach had been the same that I'd had for my whole life; hoping that Phil would have a one liner, the quick fix or the escape that would transform me. My old belief that I'd get through on legs and lungs, pistons and engines wouldn't work any longer, I needed to evolve. Emotional regulation was strength.

Performance psychology wasn't about making me a better cyclist, it was about allowing me to deal with any situation in a positive way, which would generate a better performance on the bike. Phil's analogy that we weren't reinventing the wheel, that I was the wheel, was perfect. He needed to ensure I was true and wouldn't buckle, that I could take the hits and keep on rolling, and that I had grip and control in all conditions. He needed to make a strong wheel before we could put power through it.

"You can't let that happen again, pal," Phil told me as we spoke about what I came to call the White Wall Test.

"Nobody can control if or when a crisis will occur, but you must learn to control your reaction to it. You've got to let those feelings out before they boil over." In my mind, I didn't feel as if I could ask for help as soon as I faced a setback; I had to push myself to my absolute limit first. That was my old mindset.

"Okay, I know," I conceded, "but you've been teaching me about tidying my room and sleeping and breathing. *How* do I let them out? When are you going to teach me the secrets of being a world record breaker?"

"Buddy, do you think I care how tidy your room is?" Phil asked. "Do you think I care when you go to bed? I haven't been teaching you to clean up, sleep or breathe, I've been teaching you control. Once you rein in your reactive thoughts, you have all the tools you need to make the most of your talent and your opportunities."

Phil told me to shout, count to ten, pinch myself or snap my fingers when I began seeing red. Once I'd escaped the emotional reaction, I should use the centring technique to become aware of my thoughts. I had to park inappropriate concerns that I had no influence over, like the notes in my phone, and come back to them later. Then control the controllables to create a solution-based plan.

"What if my plan doesn't work?" I asked.

"If there's a genuine reason the plan might fail, change it," Phil answered, "but if it's just doubt, you have to trust in your idea and commit to it. Like I told you before, you can't lose, only win or learn. Reflect on the outcome in a safe place, at the end of the day or after the event. If your plan didn't work, learn from it. If it did work you add it to your resource of proven solutions. Imagine you're creating your own utility belt, like Batman."

"You love a Batman reference, don't you?!" I joked at Phil before a flash of clarity. Through the previous months, Phil *had* been building up my Bat-belt. Tidying my desktop, organizing my bedroom, sleeping well and self-awareness exercises were all great skills on their own but mastering them *was* like doing reps in a psychological gym. In putting me through the White Wall Test, Mark and Phil had addressed all my concerns about confidence, uncertainty and coping on the road. I couldn't change what lay ahead, but I had to control my reaction to it.

Change was essential but, like my *why*, that change couldn't be external, it had to be intrinsic. Where I'd previously changed my surroundings or taken on new challenges, I now had to change my mindset. Throughout psychological training, Phil was arming me with the weapons I needed for my battle. Now I'd seen that my greatest enemy was within.

TEN

FAIL FAST

On 20 April, a week after the White Wall Test, Mark, Phil and I met in the foyer of the Human Performance Unit. In the three and a half months since training began, the team of sport science experts had created a world-class athlete. With six weeks until the start date of the world record attempt, all that was needed was a proof of concept – evidence that our scientific model worked in the real world.

The BBC World Service, who were interested in Phil's psychology training programme, had sent a reporter to record a radio article for their Health Watch programme. In a small office, we briefly explained our plan: a series of test rides over three days based out of the University of Derby, each designed to simulate a section of the world record course. Our strategy was to ride 4-hour blocks at defined power outputs with breaks in between. When things got tough, I was to rely on the psychological processes that Phil had taught me and draw upon the strength of my *why*.

The four of us rushed out to the car park and organized a track pump, toolbox, spare tyres, and a couple of thermal layers in the boot of Phil's Ford Fiesta. To keep me fuelled, we threw in a tub of energy drink powder and a large, clear plastic box of measured ingredients prescribed by the nutritionist. We did a quick radio check of some borrowed walkie-talkies between the bike and the car and Phil tucked a tenner into one of my jersey pockets for contingencies. The scientists and the reporter jumped into the car and prepared to follow me, while I clipped new carbon-soled shoes into the pedals of my "spaceship" bike. I was looking more like an elite cyclist, even if I still wore the same old clothes. Campus security lifted the gates to the university car park and my wheels began to blast along Derby's empty roads.

We left the city before rush hour to begin the flattest route I could plan from Derby; the long ride to Skegness. Spirits were high with jokes of eating fish and chips on the beach and visiting the donkey sanctuary while we were there, but the banter soon calmed to quiet as I cranked the pedals on the monotonous flat roads across Lincolnshire.

When I'd imagined being followed by a team, the support vehicle had been right behind me the whole time but in reality, traffic and road conditions meant it was rarely possible to stay together. I was only close enough to the car for radio contact every 20–30 minutes or so. As I vibrated across rough road surfaces through hours of uninspiring landscapes, I thought back to the first time I cycled to Skegness and back in a day.

Six months earlier, I'd ridden a borrowed bike without any technology; I didn't own a GPS or a heart rate monitor or even know about measuring power. A basic bike computer had recorded my speed and I had averaged 28 kph (17 mph). Now, on the test ride, I was cycling with my arms stretched out in front of me on aerodynamic bar extensions, on a customized, top-of-the-range, carbon-fibre road bike with a GPS unit that directed every turn and sensors that measured all my geographical and physiological metrics. I could translate those numbers to quantify my physical state and understand whether to push harder or ease off. My body and mind had been finely tuned into a performance machine that was cruising along at an incredible 35 kph (22 mph).

Just before 1 p.m. I pulled over at the side of a dusty, minor road and sheltered in the shade of a neglected farmhouse that stood alone between fields of short, dark green plants. My power had dropped and my heart rate increased. For an hour I'd been struggling, with my emotions getting the better of me. I was doing everything I was supposed to and I couldn't figure out what was wrong. Part of me wanted to blame Mark and Phil; there was nothing more I could do, so it must be something they weren't doing but I couldn't let this become another White Wall outburst. In all honesty, I didn't want to do centring exercises on the bike – I had enough to do – but I was aware of my bubbling anger beneath the surface and suppressed it. The car parked up behind me and Phil ran over.

"How you doin' there, buddy?"

"Honestly mate, I'm so angry right now," I replied, as calm as possible.

"Tell me what's going on, so."

"Something's not right. I can push harder than this but it's like I can't access my power. And I know it's not your fault but I'm *so* angry at you, just you. You should have been behind me," I said, more calmly than I felt. I'd been over it in my head, I knew I couldn't lose my cool again, especially with the BBC watching.

"Ah, sorry pal, your route went down a road we couldn't drive along, so we took a detour. Got back with you as soon as possible, like."

He was right, I had cursed the terrible country track I'd just ridden.

"Have a sip on this while I have a look at the data, brother," Phil said, as he passed me a litre bottle of water. I drank it all.

The winter of 2018 had been long and severe but, when it passed, it was as though the seasons suddenly snapped into summer. A heatwave sat over the UK and, in an unseasonal 26°C, I was dehydrating fast. Phil told me hydration is directly related to performance and I clearly needed to drink more, which explained my reduced power and increased heart rate. The nutritionist hadn't run hydration tests through training and climate was a real-world variable that I hadn't needed to consider in the controlled conditions of the HPU. Mark made notes to check my sodium electrolyte balance and a reminder that hydration awareness needed to be improved before the attempt. Weighing in at the end of the day would show a 1.5 kg loss due to dehydration. I kept a close eye on how much I was drinking as we hit the Skegness sea front, 185 km (115 miles) and 5 hours and 15 minutes of cycling time from home.

Shortly after we left the candyfloss-scented air in the bright landscape of fairground rides and "kiss-me-quick" hats, we stopped for a break and an interview. The BBC journalist had been speaking to Mark and Phil while they followed me and was interested to know how I dealt with the difficulty of operating at high performance for the whole day. I talked her through centring and the psychological interventions Phil had taught me in training but, in reality, they were still too new in my mind to be automatic reactions. When frustration had built through dehydration, I'd known that I couldn't vent my emotions on others and I'd done whatever I could to control it. When things were going well, I was enjoying the opportunity to use the legs that I'd spent 14 weeks training. It was the first time I'd unleashed them and I saw what I was capable of. I just loved being on the bike – it was freedom.

At the end of the day, a total of 362 km (225 miles) in 11 hours and 10 minutes gave us our first taste of ultra-endurance distance at world record speed. In the first 7 hours, we covered 241 km (150 miles) at an average speed of 34.7 kph (21.6 mph). We completed the remaining 121 km (75 miles) after lunch and interviews, at 30.2 kph (18.8 mph). We knew there was a lot of time to gain by reducing stoppage time and we could work that into the strategy. For the first time, we saw the fruition of our hard work playing out in the real world and started to understand what could be possible on the attempt.

———————————————

On the second day, we set off from the university at 8.30 a.m., into a mist that hung over the road in the fresh springtime air between the campus and Markeaton Park opposite. I headed out of town along familiar rural lanes I'd cycled with the club, before turning north to test my capacity in the hills. Roads in this part of the world don't follow the contours of the land – they plough straight over whatever stands in their way. As a cyclist, you hold on for your life as you fly downhill on loose gravel before clicking through the cassette to your lowest gears and stamping on the pedals to clamber back up the knee-crunching climbs. My consistent pace of the day before would become a distant memory on the route I plotted that criss-crossed Derbyshire's hills. Skirting the south-west border of the Peaks on exposed roads, I gazed out over the landscape that opened up to my left, with sweeping views for miles across Leek and ripples of land disappearing into the distance below me. Forty miles into the day, my route switched 90 degrees to take in the quintessential patchwork of green hills sewn together with drystone walls that kept flocks of sheep penned in. I traversed villages I recognized and passed small cafés whose steamed-up windows I'd sheltered behind on cold, rainy days in my youth. In Bakewell, I was absorbed in the sound of tourists' foreign accents and the sweet smell of delicious Bakewell puddings. Then I turned almost back on myself again, heading through the deep valley cut by the River Wye, and over the hilltops between limestone quarries on my way to Buxton. The steep roads would have been a hellish test if it wasn't for the ever-changing views and landscapes to occupy my mind.

With constant distraction, the morning passed quickly and before I knew it, I was halfway through the day, sitting in a layby overlooking the rugged National Park with Mark and Phil, shovelling the same food into my mouth as I had done the day before. I'd requested a meal plan from the nutritionist weeks ahead of the event but hadn't received one. A couple of days before we set off, he emailed me a plan with a familiar beige theme. There were no recipes – just a list of ingredients and the instructions, "Spread the potato/rice and cranberry wraps over the day and mix and match the ingredients to your liking. Anything not fitting in the wrap please eat it on its own – just make sure it is consumed."

The ingredients were tortillas, a mountain of white rice and boiled potatoes, two red peppers, a handful of cranberries, a malt loaf and a small amount of salsa. It wasn't long before I'd eaten the few tasty ingredients and I sat in the back of Phil's car spooning plain rice and cold potatoes into my drying mouth. The uninspiring diet which had caused me misery throughout training was following me on the road. Mark and Phil could see my frustration and passed what was left of their family pack of Kit Kats back to me. "You didn't get them from us, okay?" whispered Phil, I smiled and devoured them all.

Even with the previous long day in my legs, I was still performing well, so we decided to reduce the distance slightly, returning to the university sooner to prioritize a good, long sleep before an early start the following day. We traversed the National Park one last time, under the gritstone crags of Froggatt Edge and descended through the Chatsworth House Estate on our return to suburbia. My wheels rolled into the university car park at 5.30 p.m., having climbed over 2,800 m and covered 206 km (128 miles), happy to get a good sleep and hit the final day fresh.

Five-thirty on Sunday morning felt very early when I met Phil and Mark for the final test day. Half asleep, I closed the boot of my car on the cycling glasses I'd borrowed. One arm fell on the car park and the other into the car. It was going to be that kind of day. We loaded the bike spares and cycling gear into Phil's car and the same huge box of food – this time with three extra malt loaves and a multipack of Kit Kats – into the back seat and at 6 a.m. we left the university.

I pedalled into a 354-km (220-mile) day of mixed terrains around Derbyshire and the neighbouring counties. After averaging over 10 hours each day in old cycling shorts, the ill-fitting fabric had repeatedly rubbed the same area until it had become painful to sit down. I'd never experienced saddle sores before, even cycling around the world. The pain made everything worse, magnifying every small frustration. Chamois cream was added to a list of essentials for the attempt across Europe.

It was yet another hot day and keeping on top of hydration required catching up with the team regularly to refill my water bottles. In the early afternoon, the route went through the congested town of Loughborough, where roadworks and contraflow created a knotted mess of traffic. I tried to radio back to redirect the car but the walkie-talkies were out of range, so I carried on alone. I overtook the line of cars and trucks, dashed through the traffic lights and was miles down the road by the time I started to run low on water. Certain that the car would be through the town, I radioed back but there was only static on the line. *I'll just carry on until they catch me, it won't be long now*. Flat roads turned into undulations and every climb made me thirstier. I tried the radio again but there was still no signal. I kept riding, my mouth got drier, I got slower and frustration began to build.

I was convinced that Mark and Phil were testing me, that they'd stopped to relax with a drink while I was pushing flat out on the bike. *They should be with me by now, what are they playing at? It's fine for them, sitting in their air-conditioned car, they have no idea what it's like for me pedalling under the sun all day, eating rice and damn potatoes, hurting because of these shorts.* Miles passed without water. I was furious. I stopped, pulled my sweaty mobile phone from a jersey pocket and called Phil. Mark answered.

"Hello mate, how's it going, everything all right?" he asked.

"Mark, it's like the frickin' desert out here, where the hell are you both? I've been out here with no water for ages, what are you doing? I'm the one on a bike. All you've got to do is drive a car – can't you even do that?" I shouted down the phone.

"Sorry, Leigh, we got stuck in traffic back there, we'll be back with you again soon. Can you cycle slowly until we catch up?" Mark asked.

"No, I've been dehydrated for too long, I'll be standing right here until you find me," I snapped.

The car pulled up beside me 5 minutes later and Phil got out to fill my bottles. I could see in his eyes that he was angry, but he spoke to me calmly. He pointed out that

I'd just passed through a small town where I could have stopped to buy water with the contingency money in my pocket. If it wasn't possible to buy water, I could have slowed down to reduce dehydration and allow him to catch up. I'd let frustration override my thought process, just like in the White Wall Test. At least this time I'd gone three days rather than the 3 hours in the lab, and there wasn't blood everywhere. We were making progress.

Having collected all the data that Mark and Phil needed, we headed back towards the city. As the sky turned amber between wisps of cloud, I passed under the barrier and into the floodlit carpark of the University of Derby. I'd cycled 922 km (573 miles) in three days. Mark and Phil welcomed me with cheers and open arms.

"How's that feel, lad?" asked Phil.

"Strong as an ox," I replied.

We were all elated with how far we'd come. Overall, the test rides had been a great success and scientifically we were in an outstanding position for the attempt. We'd learned about environmental variables that needed to be accounted for on the road and areas of my psychology that could be improved. It also confirmed that, physically, my performance was exactly where it needed to be. Our scientific approach to the challenge was proven and we'd collected enough data to form the strategy for the attempt. As Phil had taught me, "You win or you learn," and it felt as though we'd done both.

A year to the day since I returned from cycling around the world, I had transformed my life and was in shape for a world record attempt.

"In six weeks' time we'll be on the road to success across Europe," laughed Mark. "Go home and order yourself a pizza – you deserve it."

———————————

Ten days after the test rides and just over a month until the start line, Mark, Phil and I met in Blends for a debrief. Despite taking time out individually since the test days, excitement was still high. We fist-bumped and hugged, impressed by our results. Now we understood what we were capable of on the actual attempt. It was agreed that, given the data, 250 miles would be a good and achievable daily objective. That set a target of 16 days. We could not only beat the existing record of 29 days; we could virtually halve it.

"Sixteen days is our best-case target, but we don't tell the media that," said Mark.

"That's right. Even though it would still smash the record, we don't want to over-promise and under-deliver," replied Phil.

"Exactly. Okay, twenty days. That gives us plenty of contingency," replied Mark.

Mark and Phil's animated conversation continued as the smile and enthusiasm slowly drained from my face and I sat quietly. There was something I had to tell them. I had expected sponsorship to come to me in the same way as the kindness of strangers that had got me around the world, but it hadn't. A number of local businesses had committed small amounts of money to the project but, with only five weeks until the start date, I was 30 per cent short of funds. I'd spent the previous week concluding discussions with companies I believed would become the headline sponsors. One by one they'd come back to me with rejections.

I thought about all the people I would let down: the team, the charity, my friends and family. I couldn't imagine myself standing on the start line anymore. No matter how much potential we had, I didn't know how I would be able to take a team to Portugal.

Mark and Phil remained incredibly supportive. They explored every alternative option with the same level of detail as they had the original strategy, using our test data to model different scenarios. We could use the final few weeks to train for an unsupported attempt or I could take a driver, who could meet me at strategic points to offer support.

Since the beginning, our project had been about mitigating risk and finding my peak performance, to discover what I was truly capable of. As much as I wanted to just get out there and bring the record home, as Steve had told me, I should never compromise.

It looked like we might have to call the whole attempt off.

ELEVEN

TICKET TO RIDE

I sank into the car, closed myself off to the outside world and slumped over the steering wheel. Deflated, I called Steve. "I told the team I wasn't willing to compromise, I couldn't go for their alternative options," I told him. "I just don't know what I'm supposed to do now."

Steve and I spent the weekend cycling together and developing a way to move forwards. Utilizing the long daylight hours and warm weather of June was no longer an option – still, there was potentially another window of opportunity in September. I'd ruled it out previously because it overlapped with Mark's wedding day and the scientists would be occupied with the new academic year but if I could form a new road team, the attempt could still go ahead. The summer would be enough time to secure extra funding, build that team and make the necessary changes to the strategy. The University of Derby confirmed they would remain supportive and I told the press we'd be heading to the start line on 10 September 2018. We would come back from this adversity stronger than before.

The attempt was back on but, behind the scenes, it was as though I was starting over. Mark explained that physical performance couldn't continue improving indefinitely, my training was set on a trajectory to peak in June and it would need to be reset for September. Physically, I had to go "off the boil" and ramp up my strength again later in the summer. With the third phase of training complete, my cycling was reduced to social rides. In mid-June, there were moments when I felt superhuman as my physical performance peaked, then I watched my fitness decline with science on hold.

Physiology, psychology, nutrition and physiotherapy were all paused, and I used this interlude in training as an opportunity to shake up the project. The first thing Steve and I did was ensure nothing was holding me back. We emailed the nutritionist, suggesting that he seemed too busy developing his own business to dedicate the time and energy required to the record attempt and that we'd continue without him.

I then turned my full attention to funding and the business aspect of the project began to develop with unexpected pace. Since first putting the project outline together, I'd believed it would appear amateur to pursue less "professional" funding strategies while approaching global businesses for investment. When high-level sponsorship failed to materialize, I opened a crowdfunding page. After an article in the Derby press about the change of start date, sponsorship came in from friends, family and the local community, raising £2,500 in a matter of days. The generosity and support from people who wanted nothing more than to see me succeed was overwhelming. The kindness of strangers still existed – I'd just needed to open an opportunity for others to support me.

I'd teased Phil relentlessly about his "bullshit bingo" phrases, but "the kindness of strangers" was one of my own. I used this so many times when explaining how I had survived on my round-the-world travels that new friends soon repeated it back to me parrot-fashion. We laughed, but it was true. The help of people I met at the roadside enhanced my travels enormously when living out of panniers. The same was now true on the record attempt.

It's difficult to say with certainty what changed when the start date was put back but, in a short space of time, funding from corporate sources started falling into place, too. The dozens of generic emails I'd sent out remained unanswered. Conversely, businesses I'd chatted with over a cup of tea, who had seen me at speaking events or who had connected with my blogs, began to commit to the project. I was in back-to-back meetings through the beginning of the summer and rapport seemed to be my key to success. Whether I was on a doorstep in a distant country sharing my dream of cycling around the world, or in a boardroom explaining how I would break a record, my enthusiasm infected those around me. A month after all that uncertainty, I had enough money in the bank to make the project happen.

Though sponsorship had grown quickly, with corporate investment came additional responsibilities and obligations that had to be fitted into an already hectic diary. I still had no equipment, no transport, no schedule, no thorough strategy and no road team. *And* there were only two months remaining until a trial run. *And* I needed to find a replacement nutritionist.

The upmarket café of an expensive racket club on the outskirts of the city was bustling with the smell of coconut shower gel and freshly ground coffee when I met Nicky Gilbert. About 5-foot tall, with a big smile, she had the lean build of a marathon runner. I went in for a hug as she simultaneously gestured to shake hands. We laughed as we walked to the bar, ordered coffees and chatted about Mark and Phil, the nutritional background of the project, and some of the problems. Nicky talked about her work as a registered sport and exercise nutritionist and her successes with Olympians, premier league football teams and World-Cup-winning cricketers. Enthusiastic as she was, she seemed more passionate about making scientific theory accessible to all. She discussed her work as an assistant professor at

Nottingham University and her novel projects supporting health and wellbeing in the workplace.

Nicky asked what test procedures I'd gone through to set my dietary targets in training. I told her they were based on the previous nutritionist's preferred body fat percentage for athletes. She assured me that there wasn't a generic number that worked for everybody and that I shouldn't continue reducing my weight without reason. She was shocked at the lack of variety in the foods I'd been eating, exclaiming that I was potentially deficient in essential micronutrients. She asked what kinds of supplement and hydration tests had been run in preparation for the attempt.

"None," I told her.

It was late in the game and we were short on time to get the nutrition aspect of the project correct. Nicky asked for as much data as I could deliver, as soon as possible. I described the incremental tests that had been conducted since our first day of training and that the next one was scheduled in two days' time. I invited her to join us – it would be the perfect opportunity for her to analyze fresh data and speak to the team directly.

"I'll be there," she said.

Mark and Phil stood beside Nicky, studying the monitors in the HPU, and together they examined the data that echoed my exertions on Excalibur. She requested detailed breakdowns of my energy expenditure data and recorded every measurement necessary to put together a comprehensive nutrition strategy. Mark had always been sceptical of Jonathan's working practice but when I asked his thoughts on Nicky, his eyes lit up.

"The difference is massive, mate," he told me. "Jonathan wasn't willing to collaborate on our innovative approach, he was stuck in tradition. But Nicky, she's on the same page." Nicky joined us and, for the first time, the preparation team felt solid. We were connected by a mutual respect, driven towards the same targets and our personalities gelled.

Nicky and I regularly met in the racket club to check in and map out fuelling plans for the attempt. She calculated how many calories I needed to ride 400 km (250 miles) a day and, comparing the result with the energy stored in my body fat, the numbers concerned her. If I could only consume two-thirds of the required daily intake on the road, which alone would be a huge demand on my system, I would burn through all my body fat by the second week of the attempt. It wouldn't only be catastrophic to the project, it would be life-threatening. The old ethos of "ride the wave of the crave" was reversed and I was told to listen to my hunger and eat.

Our approach to nutrition took a dramatic turn and, to my relief, Nicky prescribed a diet based around foods I wanted to eat. Flavour returned to my life. On the new diet, crusty rolls with tuna and pitta with houmous were introduced. Nuts, yoghurt and chocolate were allowed, and we even discussed using cake. For me, the most positive change was my introduction to an app that tracked my calorie intake and expenditure. I was given back the autonomy to make my own decisions.

While training, we tested and recorded every nutritional variable to create a handbook for the road. I received regular calls and emails from Nicky, outlining what she had implemented and what needed input from me and the team. When outdoor training rides resumed, we used the hot, dry summer to run hydration tests.

Nicky ensured that I was hitting all my dietary targets in an approach that was personalized and her attention to detail transcended nutrition. When she asked me to get blood checks from the doctor for iron, magnesium and vitamin D, she also reminded me to check whether I needed any vaccinations or inoculations for the countries I was travelling through. As she was unable to join me on the road herself, Nicky also began to draw up a list of contacts to potentially join the team.

Every scientific aspect of training resumed and when long training rides began eating into my schedule, the days seemed to get shorter. There was still a lot of work to do before we were fully prepared for the attempt; to simply get the wheels turning we had to finalize the strategy, test the equipment and bring the new team together. It required another three-day trial run to ensure these elements worked and flag up anything we needed to develop. Like the test rides I'd done with Mark and Phil earlier in the year, this trial would be an ultra-endurance ride and needed to be timed so the physical exertion would benefit my training schedule. Only one month remained until that window of opportunity.

―――――――――――

Earlier in the summer of 2018, Sean Conway had covered the media headlines once again. On his second attempt, he'd cycled across Europe, from Cabo da Roca to Ufa in 24 days and 19 hours. It could take months for Sean to submit all his evidence and for Guinness to verify his attempt, however, hypothetically the record I was going to attempt had become more difficult. The upshot was that he was raising the profile of the record and referencing my upcoming attempt as the reason he'd started so early in the year. I was happy about the coverage but bigger things concerned me. As the clock counted down to my own start date that couldn't be changed again, I was losing confidence that I could pull this project off. With more people and money invested, I was consumed by a growing concern that I'd bitten off more than I could chew.

Steve and I drew up a comprehensive to-do list. It was seven pages long and included finding a driver, a mechanic, a physiotherapist and a nutritionist for the road. Hiring a motorhome, planning the route and researching facilities along it. I had to contact embassies, organize media presence, fixers, permits and border issues. I needed to research, design and order clothing and equipment, allowing for production lead times and delivery timescales. Strategies needed to be planned for first aid, communication and electrical charging. The list also quantified visa application deadlines and the increasing expense of flights. Some tasks relied on the completion of others, and many depended on the names of team members I didn't even have. The attempt that had started as a simple idea in response to a magazine article now had £50,000 behind it from businesses who I'd convinced to support me and I worried about what would happen if I let them down. I knew what Phil would say – *control the controllables* – but all I saw was a knot of responsibilities. With no experience, I was learning how to do every job from scratch and each one I completed seemed to create two new ones. Life in the small spare room at my mum's house was frantic. With too many parallels to life in the third floor attic room in my 20s, themes that were all too similar to my struggle with mental health were creeping back into my life.

It seemed as though every task I took on filled my "stress bucket". I'd read this metaphor in a mental health article years before. It described some people who seemed to be able to take the weight of the world as having a large stress bucket, while other people had a small bucket that filled up quickly with everyday responsibilities and pressures. At times, I thought mine must have been the size of a thimble. The article described the consequence of the bucket overflowing as a fight, flight or freeze response – that irrational kneejerk reaction that always seemed vented at the wrong person – and the instant regret afterwards. To avoid this overflow, it was important to have a "tap" on the stress bucket that released the build-up. This could be exercise, the arts or mindfulness.

Over time, I realized that cycling was my stress tap and as pressure built through the course of the world record project, I needed to turn to it again. But cycling had become work. Every training ride had specific targets to hit – date, duration and power output – and I repeated the same flat routes on every ride to maintain continuity. My stress tap had been taken away and became an additional stressor. It was one of life's confusing contradictions that I was increasingly aware of. Lost somewhere between the adages, *do what you love, and you'll never work a day in your life* and *never turn your passion into a job*, I was beginning to side with the latter.

As project deadlines loomed and the pressure built, social rides with Cycle Mickleover kept me sane. It was a small piece of cycling that I kept just for me. Sitting on the back of a group at 20 kph (13 mph), there was no need to prove myself. Like most others who waited in the car park to ride with their friends, club rides weren't really about the cycling. I was there to chat, share my worries and listen to others share theirs. It was a time to remember that, outside of the robotic nature of training and putting together the attempt, I was still human.

Chatting in a psychology session about the overwhelming demands I was experiencing, Phil described a man walking towards a goal. Without any forces acting against him, it was easy. He then asked me to imagine that same man trying to walk but with ropes tied around him, pulling him back. Depending on the force of those ropes, he might never get to his goal. I was that man and each of those ropes was a demand or expectation pulling me away from breaking the world record. To reduce the forces against me I needed to look through my to-do list, evaluate what was pulling each rope, how strong it was, and what we could do to cut it.

Phil reminded me of the time we met in the student bar at the beginning of the year, when my disorganized lifestyle had spewed over the table. I needed to use the same tools that he'd taught me then: to maximize efficiency and control the controllables. Success wasn't down to me proving that I could do everything myself. My role on the team was to be the best cyclist and we could all pull together on the other tasks. I had to delegate.

During Mental Health Awareness Week, I ran workshops in local schools and blogged about my own experiences of depression to raise awareness of the cause that was close to my heart. It was personally important for me to show that even those who take on challenges like cycling around the world continue to battle their own demons. I never considered that those actions would have a positive impact on the record attempt.

Out of the blue, I got an email from entrepreneur Rob Hallam. He wanted to discuss financing my project. I was dubious. Steve was convinced it was a scam; nobody ever approached anybody with the unconditional offer of money. Rob and I met in a glass-fronted café that looked out on to the market square of a small town just outside Derby. He was joined by a friend, Martin. The two of them sat in red faux-leather armchairs, covered in tattoos with short hair and chiselled jaw lines. Ex-military.

Rob spoke openly about sensitive issues. Upon retiring from "The Mob", which I came to learn referred to the military, a lot of his friends had struggled with PTSD. Rob's businesses and investments were doing well, and he was passionate about raising awareness of mental health. He had read my blog and saw that we shared the same values. He genuinely wanted to support me for all the right reasons and was willing to contribute a generous amount of money towards the project. Martin was softer spoken. He shared Rob's sentiment and explained that his new company could also offer help, specifically where I needed it.

Martin was developing an indoor training facility for cyclists in the basement of a new apartment building around the corner from the café. The relief of walking downstairs from the heat of the summer into the cool of this underground gym lent it a foreign air. Under industrial ceilings, the fluorescent-lit space was full of static training bikes and analysis equipment that a cycling nerd like me could geek out on all day. When Martin became a sponsor of the attempt, I moved my project headquarters from the dressing table in Mum's spare room to one of his offices.

We repurposed a widescreen TV from a training area, so we could watch the Tour de France while drinking strong coffee from his espresso machine as we worked. Martin became "Marty" and, spending every day together, we brought companionship to each other's demanding projects. We created a cyclist's dream in his underground gym and it was just what I needed; an antidote to the nightmares I was having alone at home.

A year before, Marty had been on the support team for an ultra-cycling record attempt through the Americas. He had first-hand experience of overcoming the logistical challenges that stood between me and success. He explained things that had worked and things that could have been done better, equipment that was necessary, and workarounds for problems. Although the scientists were innovating a new approach to training, I didn't need to reinvent logistics. Where every task had previously taken days of research for me to learn from scratch, Marty helped me to make informed decisions in minutes. One of the ropes that were pulling me was cut.

I had no idea at the time, but my relationship with ACE Sameday Couriers began in January, when two members of their sales team had been in the audience for a keynote speech I'd delivered at a major business event. The presentation about stepping out of my comfort zone, taking a chance and finding my place in the world struck a nerve with the local community. ACE were looking to raise their profile and become more visible in the Derby business network. They also had a marketing budget. I was in the right place at the right time.

In the summer, ACE signed up as the headline sponsor of my record attempt. In an office beneath the flight path of East Midlands Airport, their team of logistics experts scheduled and tracked urgent deliveries across the nation. In transporting goods from A to B as quickly as possible, my attempt was in their area of specialization and the skills and knowledge they brought were invaluable. They quickly became an integral part of the project, not only financially but dedicating time and manpower to delivering the world record on the ground.

With preparation time quickly running out, building a road support team was my top priority and a close second was resolving how to transport them across Europe. I needed a plan in place with everything booked and schedules arranged that I could plug the team into as soon as it was formed. Over Jaffa Cakes and instant coffee, I asked how ACE could help and within days they came back to me with the solution. Considering border crossing restrictions and limited resources, our only option was to hire a motorhome from Moscow and drive it to Portugal before using it as the support vehicle on its return to Russia. Even with the best price they found, their proposal would put me almost £7,000 over budget. It was impossible. I didn't have another area of the project to divert funds from and my own research into British and European rental companies reached a dead end.

I felt foolish for believing that, with sponsorship secured, the business side of the project would be straightforward all the way to the start line. I continued to struggle balancing the equation between money, time and effort. It seemed all three were running out and I was going to need to raise extra funds to buy my way out of the problem, *again*.

———————————

Throughout 2018, I asked everybody if they knew anyone who could help me with the project. One of those conversations led me to Jerry, a friend of a friend, a cyclist, and a successful businessman. I parked outside his large, glass-fronted house on the edge of the Peak District, walked down the long drive, past a sports car and a large, covered vehicle and shouted through the open door. Jerry greeted me with a smile, a firm handshake, and a frenetic energy.

We sat on leather stools around the central island in his modern kitchen, chatting about my cycle around the world and his races around Mallorca, realizing that we fundraised for the same charity. Our conversation about the record attempt was interrupted by a business call and as he spoke on the phone, I wandered out of the wide patio doors into his manicured garden and gazed out over the rolling Derbyshire countryside.

"So, how can I help?" he asked as I walked back in.

"I was just wondering, what have you got under that cover on your drive?"

"That's my motorhome, I take the kids to Europe in it every summer. It's like our bond, you know, it keeps us together since me and their mum separated."

"No way, you're into motorhomes?! I don't suppose you know anybody who'd be able to help me with a problem I've got, would you?"

After a short discussion, I secured the transport that would get the as yet unknown team across the continent. Jerry's motorhome was perfect – it slept six, had masses of storage space and was left-hand drive, ready for European roads. I told the team at ACE and they came back with a logistical plan that worked with my budget.

To save money, I originally planned to drive the motorhome to Portugal myself, complete the record attempt and drive home from Russia. Thankfully, Jon, the owner of the courier company, invested himself in the project personally to ensure we had the best chance of success. He suggested that one of his employees could deliver Jerry's motorhome to Lisbon airport, where we could pick it up and drive it as the support vehicle to the Russian border. While we were crossing Western Europe, Jon would fly to Moscow and collect a hired motorhome. He would drive the rented vehicle into Latvia, swap it with us and drive Jerry's motorhome back to England. The team and I could cross the Russian border quickly with native licence plates and continue to the finish line in Ufa, where we could leave the hired vehicle and fly home. With this logistics strategy, we would arrive in Portugal fresh to begin the attempt and not be faced with a week-long drive back from the middle of Russia after cycling 4,000 miles.

The uncompromising strategy gave us every chance of success. It was planned to run like clockwork and ACE were meticulous with every detail. Every risk was minimized, and I put my complete trust in them to deliver. In return, they put their trust in me to make it across Europe with their name on my back, but they were reluctant to say the same about the vehicle.

The motorhome was 16 years old and the chance of a breakdown was a risk they didn't like. When Jerry returned from his family holiday, his motorhome had its own vacation in the workshop at ACE headquarters for rigorous servicing and maintenance. They ordered replacement parts and spares, stripped it down and rebuilt it to a standard they believed could cross a continent.

All I needed was to find a team to join me on the road.

TWELVE
THE ROAD TEAM

My greatest challenge and biggest regret in changing the start date was that Mark and Phil could no longer join me on the road. They knew every psychological reaction to expect from me, the "physical gears" I had, and the buttons to press to get the best from me. I was still learning about myself, but they understood me. What's more, we had grown to be like brothers and the attempt that had always been ours was taken away.

A new road team had big shoes to fill. The individuals I selected had to glue together all the elements that delivered a world record. They had to take the scientific knowledge of a lab-developed product and deploy it on the road, hitting strategic targets while dealing with unknown variables. Team members would be living together 24 hours a day, seven days a week, in the back of a small motorhome, deprived of sleep, under pressure, and every second could be a crisis moment. It sounded like the trailer for a nightmare reality TV show and I didn't want it to become one.

Replacing Mark and Phil with similarly trained doctors who were available was impossible so, with Steve's advice, I stripped my requirements back to basics. The strategy could function with the skills of a sports therapist, a cook, a mechanic, a film-maker and a driver. Those abilities had to be fulfilled by as few people as possible to create one tight, mobile unit.

I needed people I could trust and who could meet the demands of the challenge. Steve suggested that I select the team members based on three characteristics: personality, mindset and ability, in that order of priority. Considering personality before ability to produce a world-class performance sounded backwards. Steve explained that specialist ability was important, but no more than a capacity to adapt, think on their feet and deal with a crisis. These qualities couldn't be judged in an email or CV, I had to feel a connection with each person before I included them in the team.

Having the right people with me on the road was critical.

My conversations with Nicky sent me to London, where she sat on the board for the nutrition degree courses at St Mary's University. She'd advertised the role of road team nutritionist to their masters students. Of the CVs received, we shortlisted three and one immediately stood out. There was a student who was about to graduate with a masters in nutrition, who already had a degree in physiotherapy.

Jahna Drunis walked into the café, wearing brightly-coloured sportswear, smiling as she introduced herself. Australian and in her late 20s, she'd not long come back from a ski season in France and still had that carefree air about her. We took our coffees out into the street where it seemed everybody was commuting by bike in the warm weather. Jahna told me about the trip she was planning to Italy in a couple of weeks, cycling around Lake Como.

We walked along the River Thames, past crowds of tourists and between the runners who jogged along the wide path beneath famous bridges. People-watching from the grass in a small park, we chatted about her work with the NHS and the Diabetic GB Futsall Team, who she'd recently supported on a European tour. As the conversation turned to my record attempt, she explained solutions she'd developed for ailments I hadn't even considered, while volunteering as a physiotherapist for the cycling equivalent of a marathon. She was excited to join the team and it felt as though I'd known her much longer than a couple of hours.

While Jahna had all the right characteristics and skills to carry out the nutrition programme on the road, her commitments leading up to the start date meant she had little time for preparation. A gap was still left on the team for an expert who could quickly develop a menu of recipes that covered my nutritional demands. Nicky brought Phil

Woodbridge on board, a professional nutrition consultant and author of *Plant-Based 4 Running*. Phil worked tirelessly behind the scenes, number-crunching and creating recipes that not only hit the nutritional targets set by Nicky, but that would also be quick and easy for Jahna to prepare on the road. With Nicky, Jahna and Phil on board, nutrition was no longer neglected, it was micromanaged with care and enthusiasm.

With the first member of the road team confirmed, I returned to Derby to face a decision I'd been putting off. For months I'd been looking for the right mechanic to join the road team. They had to be someone who knew their way around a bike and who was confident to drive the support vehicle across Europe. I was struggling to find the right person. The best mechanics in Derby weren't available, others I rejected for their questionable "upgrade" suggestions, and friends had warned me against the ones that remained. Marty recommended Anthony "Jem" Jemmett, the operations manager from the world record attempt he'd worked on through the Americas, but to meet his fee I would be left with no contingency in the budget. When every other avenue had revealed a dead-end, and with options and time both running out, I made the call.

When Jem answered the phone in his Geordie accent, I was immediately taken back to memories of joining the mountain bike club at university in Newcastle. He used the same military slang Rob and Marty had, describing his appearance as "rebelling against the Mob". With long grey hair and a beard, built like a brick wall in a black T-shirt, I could imagine him riding into the sunset on a Harley Davidson. However, like those friends from university, Jem's passion was for push bikes.

After retiring as a military helicopter mechanic in his mid-40s, Jem started a company called Epic Performance – a specialist outfit that project-managed endurance bike events. He was a mountain biker living in Edinburgh and as I described my student trips to the nearby haven of Glentress Forest, he told me how much the trails had expanded since then. Although it was the first time we'd spoken, it felt like I was chatting to an old friend. Jem and I spoke the same language – mountain biking. I could outline specific components and strategic problems I was having trouble with and he understood immediately without needing an explanation. As he discussed his background, Jem talked of helicopters that didn't fall out of the sky because of a "right first time mentality" and a culture of "no excuses". He shared Steve's *no compromise* approach and he had bullshit bingo to rival Phil.

Jem's skillset was perfect: he was a bike maintenance instructor, a vehicle mechanic by trade and already had experience of managing the road operations of an endurance cycling record attempt. His mindset was proactive and focused from his military training and he seemed to have solutions to problems I hadn't even come across yet. I knew Jem would get along with Jahna, too. Unfortunately, he seemed indifferent about being on the team. I was honest about the financial restrictions of the project and that the rest of the team were in it for the opportunity to pioneer techniques and push the limits of endurance cycling. It seemed that, for all the credibility the project would bring, it would just be another job to Jem and he remained unwilling to budge on his fee. The best he could offer was a list of suppliers from whom he could pass on cost price goods and that was it. "Take it or leave it."

It was a tough call. Jem was the right, if not the only, person for the team. I'd learned from the first nutritionist that employing the wrong person could cost more than money. Also, with the multiple roles that Jem could fill, he and Jahna could effectively run the performance team on the road between the two of them. I crossed my fingers in the hope that his discounts on equipment would justify his fee and committed. Jem was in. It would be one of the best decisions I made.

I emailed him my seven-page to-do list and he immediately replied with solutions. His experience was invaluable from the moment he joined. A problem that had stumped me and the science team for a while was how the bike and support vehicle could track each other's live location when separated on the road. We'd considered beacons, websites and cycling apps but while it was easy to get intermittent locations of the bike and logs at the end of the day, none provided a solution for real-time tracking both ways.

"Do you use WhatsApp?" Jem asked.

"Of course," I replied.

"Then use the 'share live location' feature."

Obvious. It was the same with other aspects of managing the road project. In the way that Marty and ACE shared their years of experience in logistics and preparation, Jem brought vital understanding of road operations. Modelling, theory and innovation were key to preparation, but experience was essential to make the project work in practice.

An obstacle that stood in the way of building a road team that gelled was that the three roles demanded different types of people. A scientific mind for nutrition and physiotherapy, a logical mind for project management and mechanics, and a creative mind for film production. The specific dilemma with finding a media producer who fitted in with the team was finding one who understood sports and the outdoors.

Back in 2017, while visiting the Kendal Mountain Film Festival, I'd caught up with a producer who had lectured on my university course. He'd introduced me to a 20-year-old film-maker called Kerr McNicoll who was producing his own fell-running documentaries. Kerr and I bonded there and then over our shared experiences of mountain biking, and studying film under the same lecturer. I hadn't asked Kerr about joining road team earlier because I'd envisioned having an extreme sports cinematographer on board – a happy-go-lucky, energetic, fun-loving character. Kerr was different to that; he was headstrong and liked to provoke reactions, he dug deep into his subjects and pushed their buttons to create interesting footage. Nevertheless, his experience of mountain sports could be the connection that made the team work. I hadn't spoken to Kerr in over six months and when I called him seven weeks before the attempt, it was late notice. He was already committed to another project on the weekend of the trial run but he had availability to film the attempt across Europe.

The road team was assembled.

THIRTEEN

THE PEOPLE'S REPUBLIC OF DERBADOS

Derby Arena, an imposing gold, silver and bronze structure, stands tall over Pride Park on the outskirts of the city. It's the cycling hub of Derby and in 2018, another cycling team was evolving on its velodrome; the Huub Wattbike Test Team. These four relatively unknown cyclists took science to the next level, challenging traditional strategies and using data to significantly improve their performance. They won medals and championship titles on the track, beating national teams in ways that no one expected. They brought recognition to Derby as the independent team who regularly topped scoreboards populated with international squads. In a nod to this, the team began calling our home town a nation, even designing their own flag, and in the world of cycling our city became known as "The People's Republic of Derbados".

The engineering mind behind Team Huub Wattbike was ex-Formula One aerodynamicist, Dan Bigham, and his sound advice also brought significant gains to my record attempt. Dan shared Mark and Phil's philosophy that there was no "one size fits all" solution to making a cyclist go faster. He recommended controlled testing of various bikes, equipment and body positions, and using that data to make informed decisions on what, and how, I rode. Ten days before the trial run, I visited Dan at the velodrome and put myself through his test procedure.

A young female cyclist wearing a Team GB skinsuit cruised around the track at a low cadence, seemingly effortless at a million miles an hour. For a second, the whoosh of tyres on wood enveloped everything, before echoing shouts across the enormous empty hall returned and she vanished to the opposite side of the oval. Then zoomed past again. Then vanished. Metronomic. I paused in the centre of the oval track where Olympic champions had stood, looking up at the gym where I'd first sat on a Wattbike with Cycle Mickleover less than a year before. On Tuesday evenings, we'd laughed and joked in group sessions every week, staying active through winter with club friends. I'd come a long way since then.

Dan completed my initial setup on the flat, blue "infield" beside the track. Anxious to begin the test, I waited leaning on the chrome handrail built onto a glass wall. On the other side, he finished configuring and calibrating his databases and timers.

"I'm sure I don't need to tell you how to ride on the track, so feel free to warm up when you're ready," Dan shouted.

"Erm, hold on," I replied.

I had never stood on a velodrome track, let alone ridden on one. The intimidating banked corner loomed high above, like an ocean wave only a few metres away, about to crash over me.

"Okay," Dan reassured me, "it's easy. Just ride along the flat blue bit until you're doing more than twenty-five kilometres an hour, then you can move up the banking. Go too slow and you'll clip a pedal, which will be sore and embarrassing. Try to stay between the black and red lines."

Echoing sounds. Blue paint. Glass and chrome. It was childhood swimming lessons and having to let go of the edge of the pool. I loosened my grip on the handrail, cycled timidly towards the bank of wood and followed the flat around the first curve. I accelerated and committed my wheels to the boards on the back straight, moving up and flying around the banking. Incredible. I zoomed around the "wall of death" with a grin on my face, pushing hard on the pedals. Cycling indoors was fast – really fast.

Dan ran the session with military precision. Each cyclist's body, technique and aerodynamic footprint is unique and to calculate what would work for me, everything had to be tested. He analyzed various handlebar positions, bottle styles and helmets. I sat upright, then tucked, hands on the brake hoods, the drops and the aero extensions. As each test was completed, he brought me off the track, changed the setup and sent me back out again before my legs had a chance to cool down. From the saddle, each change was too subtle to notice, with the exception of a time trial helmet. In an upright position, air buffering around inside was noisy as hell, but in a shrugged position, it faded to calm. I would never compare myself to legends of the track, but in this unique experience I felt somehow connected to the greats I'd watched on TV. Within that thundering silence, I understood the thrill of the iconic hour record.

Off the bike, Dan went through the numbers with me and systematically explained where I could make gains. Data took the guesswork out of cycling; everything could be quantified. At 40 kph (25 mph), I could save almost 50 watts by shifting from an upright position to tucking my head down with shrugged shoulders and my arms out front on the extensions.

"Fifty watts? How did you find that?!" the young GB cyclist shouted across to Dan and me, as he explained his results. Years into honing her position and technique, she was testing in the hope of finding an extra 5 W, which would still be impressive. Although my lower speeds on the road would reduce aerodynamic benefit and the perfect position was unsustainable for long durations, the gains we made on the track were huge. It would be difficult to gain 50 W of power over five years of training in the gym.

Changing back into casual clothing and packing away my bike, I asked Dan for any last-minute advice that would help me go faster across Europe. He started naming friends who could digitally model the course and analyze the road surfaces and gradients to optimize my strategy and setup, before he stopped and looked up from his monitor.

"Actually, mate. Don't brake, it slows you down."

That was it. I had done all that I could in a year to improve my performance and I realized how naive my expectations of preparing for a world record had been.

In the early 2000s, I watched a television series called *The Long Way Round*, which documented Ewan McGregor and Charlie Boorman riding motorbikes around the world. It had inspired me to do the same myself on a bike. The first episode covered their preparation; getting a motorbike sponsor, planning a route, packing their bags and a few comedic falls on an off-road training course. My preparation for cycling around the world had been similar; I took three months to buy the equipment, build a website and plan a rough route.

That was the difference between an adventure and achieving my best. To cycle the world, I put minimum time into preparation. Instead, I lurched into situations and worked out how to deal with them en route. For the world record, there was no time to learn on the road, we had to know what we were up against and have a ready-made solution. It took the best part of a year to prepare for two weeks on the road.

Abraham Lincoln said, "Give me six hours to chop down a tree, and I will spend the first four sharpening the axe." My old mindset used to just pick up the axe and start hacking away. Now I understood his sentiment. After a gruelling 11 months of business plans, sponsorship pitches, rejections, setbacks, mistakes, lessons learned, delays, agreements, disagreements, interviews, stress, distress and the hardest year's work of my life, the axe was sharpened and excitement finally arrived.

Mum's house started to resemble an Amazon distribution centre. Parcels were delivered by the hour, my room filled with stacked boxes, and the garage filled with tools and hardware. The motorhome was parked on the driveway, the bike was set up, and custom-made clothing arrived with a new helmet and expensive eyewear. I had been transformed into an elite athlete, I had the best equipment I could buy and I was surrounded by a professional team.

It felt incredible. Everything had come together, as it should be, at the right time. I felt ready.

One month before the start date of the world record attempt, the scientists and I met the road team to hand over the project. We sat around a long desk above the HPU at the University of Derby, in a boardroom decorated with macro photography of red athletics tracks. Mark, Phil Clarke,

Nicky, Jem, Jahna, Phil Woodbridge and me; it was the first time we'd all been in the same place and an air of excitement filled the room, knowing that we were embarking on an amazing journey together. The team enjoyed each other's company. *Relief.* The following day, we would begin a full dress rehearsal; the trial run. Mark walked us through the strategy for the road and the range of "physical gears" he planned to use, splitting the day into hours and cycling at a defined power output for each one.

Jem spoke up. "Not in the real world, mate."

"We've tested and calculated it, Jem. Don't worry, it sounds tough, but we know Leigh can do it," replied Mark.

"I'm sure he can pedal that in a lab, like, but what about junctions, traffic lights, roundabouts, rain, punctures, y'know? We haven't got those ideal conditions in the real world."

Jem had experienced situations that Mark hadn't accommodated for and that none of us on the preparation team had considered. It was an important meeting, each expert sharing their experience, knowledge and solutions. For the handful of potential issues that were raised, many more solutions were found. I was touched that they had put so much effort into the project – everybody wanted to be part of the same incredible result. I saw each team member's hard work come to fruition and was pleased with how every aspect fitted together. Physiology, psychology, nutrition and road operations overlapped to ensure scientific procedures would work in the "real world".

Again, as with the first session in the lab, the experts spoke about me as though I wasn't there. Phil walked Jem through a psychological analysis he would perform on me at the end of every 4-hour block of cycling through the trial. It listed 25 emotions across a broad spectrum from *happy* to *depressed*, *alert* to *mixed-up*, *calm* to *panicky*. At each break, I would have to rate how much I was feeling each emotion from one, "not at all" to five, "extremely". The team put together templates to record my physical data. Lines of communication were created between the road and the lab and WhatsApp groups were set up. I was left out of it all. At that point, I became the cyclist and *only* the cyclist. I relinquished all other responsibility to the team.

It's strange how much I wanted help when I was stressed and working alone, but how hard I found it to accept when support came. Letting go of the project management was one of the hardest things to do and something I don't believe I fully did. I was too attached to the project. I'd created, developed and trained for it. I'd fought for it and funded it. I personally knew everybody who had been involved at every stage. I knew every piece of equipment and the way every hour had been spent building up to this moment. As much as I respected the team, I didn't believe that anyone else would put as much effort into continuing it as I would. Maybe it was a symptom of my first time leading this type of endeavour, that I was too precious of it. This was more than a project to me; it had become my life.

Jem, Jahna and I pulled up at Mum's house and she rushed out to meet us, offering cups of tea and coffee. "I'll just stay out of the way," she'd said before I left but, as much as the preparation must have been uprooting her whole life, Mum was excited to meet the team and be a part of what was unfolding. I could see that she was proud of how far I'd managed to develop this attempt but I knew that, in her heart, the default emotional response was maternal concern. As we stood chatting around the motorhome with mugs in our hands, the supermarket delivery arrived. Full carrier bags covered the driveway. The amount of food needed for the team, for only three days, was staggering. It was physical evidence of how my budget was disappearing fast; simply keeping us alive and moving was expensive, even before considering a record attempt. We spent the afternoon removing all Jerry's personal effects from the vehicle and set it up as a mobile performance unit. Jem had everything squared away, ready to be found instantly.

As we drove to the campsite, Jem and I discussed our approach to the trial run. He asked whether I'd done this earlier in the project. "Yeah, I did a trial with Phil and Mark a few months ago, when we were scheduled to start in June. We met up at the university each morning for three days and they followed me around Derbyshire," I told him.

"So, you didn't camp or cook or run an operations strategy?" Jem asked.

"No, why?"

"That wasn't a trial run, mate, you went on a bike ride. *This* is a trial run."

The long weekend gave us an opportunity to test every aspect of the project, from strategy, to equipment, to teamwork, as it would be across Europe, on a small scale and a small budget. It would allow us to understand what worked and what didn't in order to knock the bugs out before the attempt. I plotted a three-day route that took us around England, hitting the target distance the science team were confident we could achieve of 270 miles a day and minimizing elevation gain, as I aimed to do across the continent. A Derby to Derby round-trip via the New Forest and Great Yarmouth. The project had stepped up. Only four months earlier, Mark, Phil and I had covered 922 km (573 miles) close to home, with a box of food and a Ford Fiesta. Now I would cycle 1,314 km (817 miles), fully supported and overnighting on the road. Suddenly it felt very real.

We arrived at a campsite on the southern outskirts of Derby early that Friday evening. There were families who had set up collective camping "villages" with music, barbecues and lights. Children ran around the site in shorts and T-shirts, screaming and playing games in the warmth. We found a corner out of the way and set up camp. Jem serviced the bike, Jahna cooked dinner and I put up a tent to sleep in. A separate tent was intended to provide a quiet space where I could rest while the team worked in the motorhome, but I found it difficult. I wanted to be with the team, to share in the camaraderie, to know what they were preparing and help, but my job was to rest. I was still holding on to the project. I found it hard to focus on my job alone.

After a couple of hours, as the sun began to set, a pale-looking film-maker with black hair and dark clothes was dropped off by his girlfriend. The media company that Kerr worked with had sent Damien to stand in for him. This was the first time we'd met and it appeared he was there begrudgingly. He grunted as the team and I introduced ourselves and it seemed his only interest was how quickly he could get out of there. I went through our intentions; I wanted him to collect as much information as possible about media requirements – charging, filming logistics on the road and the kind of shots that would be possible. Jem explained the team dynamic and that, although it was understood he would need to focus on media, he was also a part of the team as a whole and would need to chip in with other responsibilities.

I left the team to finish their tasks and by 10 p.m., as it went dark in the tent, I turned off the head torch and closed my eyes.

FOURTEEN

TRIAL RUN

11 AUGUST 2018: TRIAL RUN, DAY ONE
Distance: 431 km (268 miles)
Start: Derby, Derbyshire
Finish: The New Forest, Hampshire
Weather: 27°C, sunny

As set out in the strategy, I woke at 6 a.m. on Saturday to the sound of activity in the motorhome. I hadn't slept as long as planned; it was the first time I'd been in the tent since cycling around the world. The familiar yet forgotten smell of camping equipment distracted my mind and, instead of falling asleep, I'd reminisced on the adventures of a past life. However, rather than feeling fatigued, I woke excited about the day ahead – my first day of a proper trial run with a professional setup.

As part of the road operations schedule, Jem had me create a kit bag containing everything I needed for the evening, overnight and next morning. I rummaged through the bag and put on a crisp, new jersey and bib shorts, emblazoned with sponsors' logos. I shook the damp from the tent as I stepped into the fresh air and wandered around to the motorhome. Jahna had an enormous plastic bowl of oats waiting for me and Jem was already drinking his second cup of coffee, brewed in a cafetière that he brought from home. The two of them had bonded over their love for quality coffee.

The first day was supposed to be relaxed, or so we had planned. Over the three days we would increasingly build in more strategy. The routine already felt military to me. I was out of bed, fed and ready to go in 30 minutes. Jem carried my bike along the gravel path, stood with me at the roadside and took the phone from his pocket to create a short video for our *Guinness World Records* documentation. As the adjudicators from Guinness weren't attending my record attempt, I had to provide an evidence pack that had strict requirements including witness statements, GPS tracks, logbooks, media articles, photographic evidence and 10 minutes of video from each day.

Due to his experience from previous successful world record attempts, Jem already had it all planned out. Even though this was only a trial run, he hit record on his phone, "Zero six thirty. We're in Beechwood Park, Elvaston. Beginning of block one, day one. Kilometre zero. Ready to roll out." Jem repeated his ritual at the beginning and end of every 4-hour block of cycling. I spun up the wheels and set off alone from the cool, damp valley, leaving the team to pack the support vehicle. Thumbs up, head down, I pedalled hard into the first day.

Fast legs made for a happy mind. Hedgerows blurred into green backdrops as smooth road surfaces buzzed under my wheels. When my body warmed it felt safe, tucked into a thermal cocoon, protected from the morning air that crept in through zips and down my neck. Alone, forging my way across counties, I felt strong and the sensation was confirmed by data screens on the GPS.

The morning warmed into perfect cycling conditions. By 8 a.m., it was already 20°C under blue skies. With the team right behind, I pulled into a service station to remove a layer of clothing. Sitting on the cool concrete in the shade of the forecourt, Jem pulled my leg warmers over my shoes and Jahna put fresh bottles on the bike. I ate a banana, went to the toilet and was back on the road within 5 minutes.

Progress was better than expected – my average speed for the morning was a rapid 34 kph (21 mph). Then, only 3 hours 20 minutes into trial day one, the unimaginable stopped me. On the Fosseway, 110 km (68 miles) from Derby, I crested the brow of a climb, shuffled down through the gears and tucked into the aerodynamic position for a fast descent. Looking up, I saw a white transit van a few hundred metres ahead, facing me on my side of the road. Something was wrong. I sat up and freewheeled. As I approached, the small group of people in the road waved their arms to slow me down. I stopped 50 m before the van and the thrill of the morning drained from my body and mind. In front of the smashed windscreen and dented bonnet of the van, lay a motionless body. I was one of the first on the scene of a motorbike fatality. My concerns of beating a record paled into insignificance.

I pinched myself and snapped out of it, back to the moment. I hated myself for such blatant lack of sympathy, for such selfishness, but what could I do? Nothing. Drivers and passengers rushed over from their cars, stopping on both sides of the road. I would be in the way if I stayed, besides I had a job to get on with. I pulled the phone out of my back pocket to call the team but there was no signal. I sent a message on WhatsApp with the location, explaining that the road was blocked and traffic would be delayed for hours, they should find an alternative route. I slowly pedalled around the sobering scene and past an extending traffic jam on the opposite side of the road.

After 4 hours it was time for our first scheduled break but there was no sign of the motorhome. I still hadn't had a reply to my message. It was the same situation that had me shouting at Mark and Phil in April. I stopped and called Jem.

"Where are you, brother?" he asked. "We've been driving up and down the route and haven't seen you."

"I sent you my location at that accident, did you get my message?" I replied.

"That was nowhere near the route, man, thought it was a mistake. Tell ya what, do us a favour, turn on your live location and keep riding. We'll find you."

When we met 30 minutes later, we realized the bike GPS had gone off track at a junction and an autoroute function had taken me on the most direct route to my destination. I was way off course. Jem put the team GPS on the bike and we switched back to the planned route.

By the time we stopped for the second break, 8 hours 30 minutes into the day, we'd circumnavigated the north of the Cotswolds, around Cheltenham and Gloucester, and stopped on the border of Wiltshire and Somerset. I sat at the dining table in the motorhome, dripping with sweat. With 275 km (171 miles) on the clock, it was mid-afternoon and almost 30°C; the still air inside was suffocating. Jahna had prepared a pasta and bean salad, containing every calorie and nutrient I needed to power through the rest of the day but I felt overwhelmed just looking at the enormous plate of food.

In comparison to the test days that we ran in April, the new nutrition strategy was heavenly; food was tasty and varied. I wasn't shovelling cold rice and potatoes into my mouth in the back of the car, I was served delicious meals that had been prepared for my needs. Jahna delivered the programme that Nicky and Phil Woodbridge had developed for the specific demands of the attempt. Their nutrition plan maximized the opportunity to eat these tasty real foods, containing about 2,000 calories per meal, at break times. However, to replace my 11,000–12,000 calorie daily energy expenditure, I needed to top that up with supplements on the bike. I was to drink a bottle of energy drink every hour and take a gel every 15 minutes, a total of 56 gels per day. Although we'd made great progress with nutrition, at 174 cm and 67 kg, I found it difficult to stomach such huge quantities.

"I'm sorry Jahna, I can't eat this," I said, returning half the portion of pasta and bean salad to the table.

"Okay. Well, what can you eat?" she replied.

"I'm sorry, I dunno." I stepped out, made the evidence video with Jem and cycled away.

What do I want to eat? How am I supposed to know? She's the nutritionist. I need to ride this bike fast, I need to... Pinch. *Is that thought useful?* I remembered Phil's centring technique and focused on what I could stomach. I knew what I liked the idea of, although it sounded stupid, childish. *Screw it, I looked childish going around the world, pointing at my mouth to suggest hunger and then at what I wanted to eat, and that had always worked. Maybe it'll work.* The next time I caught the motorhome in a traffic jam, I shouted through the window, "I know what I want!"

"Go on," replied Jahna, reaching for her notepad and pen.

"Spaghetti hoops! Oh, and Liquorice Allsorts, but without the liquorice!"

"I'll see what I can do!"

Training had put me in a great place physically and psychologically. From the saddle of the bike, in moments of flow, the first day of the trial run felt like a dream.

We took our final break to the south of the Dorset Area of Outstanding Natural Beauty and as I cycled alone for the final 30 minutes of the day, I made a detour to check off a personal milestone. I'd cycled from the furthest place from the sea to the south coast of England and, by bike light, I caught a glimpse of the English Channel before turning to meet the team. When I reached them, the dark silence of nature was broken by the rattle of the diesel engine and the yellow shafts of light that leaked from the motorhome, like a giant refrigerator in a car park of the New Forest. I showered before eating and debriefing with the others at the vehicle's kitchen table. We'd covered the 431 km (268 miles) in 14 hours, an epic achievement we were all ecstatic about. But we agreed that problems and delays we'd experienced in the near-textbook conditions would grow exponentially over the duration of the actual attempt. With all the delays, the day had gone on longer than expected and it was almost 11 p.m. when I arrived at the location Jem had found to sleep for the night.

On top of the motorbike accident, the GPS going off route and the nutritional problems, Jem explained the difficulty he'd had starting the motorhome, and how the awning we'd used as shelter for a physio session wouldn't retract and needed repairing. Our dress rehearsal was revealing the flaws that had to be resolved before the curtain went up on the attempt.

As the team got on with their chores, I went to my tent. After seven years of wild camping around the world, I knew exactly what I looked for in a campsite; a place hidden from passers-by, positioned to catch the sunrise in a place of natural beauty. Jem had put the tent on a patch of grass at the side of the road. It made me uncomfortable, certain that someone was going to move us on.

I lay in my sleeping bag, checking my phone for messages. Friends and family back in Derby were amazed, congratulating me on cycling so far, but they appeared more concerned about the trauma of seeing the motorcycle accident. It brought back to the forefront of my mind the scene I'd witnessed that morning. Watching headlights catch damp canvas, I thought about the family of the man lying there. Today somebody had lost their father, brother or son. It struck me that life can take years of conscious effort to change. It can also change completely in a split second.

---

12 AUGUST 2018: TRIAL RUN, DAY TWO
Distance: 439 km (273 miles)
Start: New Forest, Hampshire
Finish: Winterton-On-Sea, Norfolk
Weather: 29°C, sunny

It was light when I woke but I hadn't slept well. It was already late when I got into bed and I was kept awake with a busy mind and the sound of cars passing close by. After 6 hours' sleep, at 6 a.m., I wearily attempted to keep to the strict morning timings and unzipped the tent to reveal the landscape that had gone unseen last night. A river ran through picturesque rolling fields, where wild horses grazed in the shadows of trees. If it was a round-the-world morning, I would have sat and enjoyed the view. Instead, I busied myself in preparation for the road, which took forever, then struggled to eat a family-sized portion of oats with raisins and honey and threw back a freshly brewed coffee. Jem held the bike ready for me on the road and read the location, time and distance into his phone for evidencing. I was 15 minutes late – wheels rolled at 6.45 a.m.

With the prevailing wind behind me, the second day flew by with an even faster average speed than the first. At lunch, after hours on the road, cycling close to Oxford then Cambridge, destinations that tourists travel across the world to visit, all I had to talk about was road conditions. No landscapes or points of interest to speak of, just the potholes and tarmac surfaces of endless major roads. After consulting the science team in Derby, Jahna had picked up a tin of spaghetti hoops and some mini malt loaves as alternatives to half of the gels, ensuring I was motivated to replenish the energy I was using. I thanked her, demolishing a plate of spaghetti hoops on toast and cramming the malt loaves into my pockets.

The physical freshness of day one was gone and fatigue

began to set in. At the end of each 4-hour block of cycling, as well as physio treatment, Jahna had me stretching to compensate for the crunched position I held on the bike. As I wondered what motorists thought of a Lycra-clad man doing yoga at the side of a major road, Jahna asked if I was experiencing the back and neck related problems she'd treated on the charity cycling marathon she'd chatted to me about on the day we met in London. After a quick body scan that I'd done so many times through Phil's PMR routine, it was reassuring to report that, with the exception of the niggle that I'd had in my left hamstring throughout training, everything felt good. Psychologically too, things were going well. Considering the lack of sleep, the vast distances I was covering and my constant view of little more than tarmac, I was in surprisingly good spirits.

The only problem we encountered that day was one I'd worked hard to avoid. By mid-afternoon, Damien, the film-maker, decided he'd had enough and needed to get back to Derby. He asked to be dropped at the nearest train station, which required an hour's diversion for the support team. Jahna made sure I had enough food and drink, Jem put essential spares in my pockets, and they left me to make their unplanned journey. When we debriefed in the evening, Jem was annoyed.

"The guy was an absolute oxygen thief, man! Acting like he was out here on a jolly." Damien had filmed a few shots until his camera battery ran out, then did nothing to help out. He'd slept while there were jobs that needed to be done, watched as Jem coordinated the logistics and resources, and ate Jahna's food. He'd put added strain on the rest of the team and it took away from the positive energy that we needed to maintain. The problem with Damien hadn't bothered me at the time – the team had kept going and I'd been able to achieve the distance I expected – however, I was concerned about the impact on team morale. With so much to do on the road, team motivation and enjoyment was a priority. Under the high pressure situations we were going to encounter across Europe, tempers could flare easily and I knew how these could turn out from my own emotional outbursts. I just hoped I'd made the right call with Kerr.

At the end of another long day on the bike, I found the motorhome and tent tucked into a large, gravel layby on the east coast, beside a pile of rubbish and a locked barrier. It was a dump. But it was a dump in the right place. On this relatively low budget record attempt, I couldn't afford hotels every night – we had to make the most of what we had. Between the two options of sleeping earlier in the tent or being kept awake by the team working around a motorhome bed, the former would deliver better performance on the bike. Again, Jem had positioned us in a location exactly at the end of the route, where I could eat, sleep and we could stick to the strategy. Exhausted, I fell asleep instantly.

---

13 AUGUST 2018: TRIAL RUN, DAY THREE
Distance: 444 km (276 miles)
Start: Winterton-on-Sea, Norfolk
Finish: Derby, Derbyshire
Weather: 26°C, sunny with isolated showers

Something was wrong from the moment I stepped out of the tent. There was a sharp pain in my left knee. I knew it wasn't fatigue. I complained and procrastinated with Jem and Jahna over breakfast. Multiple alarms went off in the motorhome, signalling the time for me to start cycling. Jem leaned against the counter, staring back and forth between his watch and me. "Come on, Lofty, you're into your own time now, get out there," he demanded. To be honest, I had no idea what or who Lofty was – it was a nickname Jem gave to a lot of people – so I guessed it was another one of his military terms. I got on the bike 10 minutes late.

Jem made his evidencing video and I turned the pedals. It was agony, as though metal nails tore at nerves deep inside the joint with each rotation. I rode slowly, hoping it would ease off, hoping it was in my mind and that I would be able to cycle my way through the pain. *Jesus, I'm 270 miles from home, what the hell am I going to do, I'm never going to make it.* Two hours later I phoned the team. The pain was too much – we needed to do something about it.

The physio couch was already prepared in a driveway off a country road when I pulled alongside the motorhome. Jahna treated my left leg and taped up the knee. She noticed swelling that looked like an insect sting and gave me an antihistamine and Ibuprofen. I swallowed the pills and put extras in my pocket for the road. The discomfort subsided and I increased my power.

The day was flat and underwhelming in a part of the world I'd become familiar with over the previous year. I cycled around East Anglia and The Wash, passing Skegness *again*; all test rides seemed to lead there and the town had seen me getting faster with every visit. I watched the squalls of micro-storms beneath black clouds that ran across the wide-open landscape, hoping not to get caught under one.

When we stopped for a break at 8 p.m., having just left the Lincolnshire Wolds, there was only half an hour until sunset and I still had over 100 km (60 miles) to cycle. I was concerned about my condition and my ability to make it home, and I was concerned about the team – we would be late arriving in Derby. *Did they want to pack up and drive home? Would their accommodation be all right? Did they have work tomorrow?*

The sun set and I cycled onward into the small patch of road illuminated by my bike light. Cycling feels faster in the dark. The wind feels colder. It feels like cars overtake closer. Every sense is heightened. With doubts in my mind and increased fear of my surroundings, we turned onto a dual carriageway. I pulled straight over to the hard shoulder.

"Are you sure I can cycle down here, mate?" I shouted to Jem through the window of the motorhome.

"'Course you can, it's not a motorway," he shouted back.

"But it's horrible," I moaned.

"You better get used to it, mucka, off you go."

I pulled on some warmer layers and shivered back to the edge of the tarmac. The motorhome stayed behind me with hazard warning lights flashing but as the queue of trucks and cars built up behind us, Jem overtook me and moved up the road. In the vehicles that passed, every driver and passenger seemed annoyed at me, beeping their horns, swearing and shouting at me.

"Get off the road!"

"Stupid cyclist!"

"It's illegal to ride on this road, dumb-ass!"

I was over it. Under my breath I cursed the road and every stupid driver on it. I didn't want this but there was only one way home and it involved pedalling. I kept going. With 40 km (25 miles) to go, I joined the A52 – another busy dual carriageway – a familiar road that I'd driven hundreds of times before but I'd never once thought of cycling. The silver lining was that being on it meant I was less than 2 hours from home.

At midnight, in the orange light of Nottingham's empty suburban streets, the motorhome pulled alongside me and the smell of coffee wafted out of the window. Jahna pointed her mobile phone camera at me and called out, "Where have you been?"

"Everywhere!" I shouted.

"Where are you going?" shouted Jem.

"I'm going home!" I replied with an emptiness in my legs and fatigue in my eyes. Delirious, we all laughed.

As I turned onto Mum's street I was 14 again, returning home after riding as far as I could with my friends. I rode onto our driveway just before 1 a.m., absolutely shattered. The motorhome shuddered behind me as the diesel engine was switched off and Jem and Jahna jumped out. We had covered 1,314 km (817 miles) in three days. We'd endured accidents, mechanicals, disagreements, injury and exhaustion. The trial run had taught us a lot of lessons but we'd come out stronger on the other side.

Our tired, sweaty, group hug was like no other.

FIFTEEN
A PEP TALK

I woke up the next morning and my left knee and ankle had swollen into unrecognizable spheres of flesh. I couldn't feel my toes. I could no longer walk, let alone ride a bike.

The swelling Jahna had seen on the trial run wasn't a sting.

"It's an inflammation of the proximal tibiofibular joint, increased tone of the peroneal muscles, with associated peroneal nerve pain," Ruth told me in an emergency physio session. The prognosis wasn't good. My lower left leg was solid and the tensed muscle had caused nerve damage, leading to the loss of sensation in my foot. It would take six months for the nerve to recover. The good news was that the muscle wasn't injured and, with treatment, the problem could be resolved before the attempt.

The inability to cycle was torture. There were still four weeks until we flew to Portugal, four weeks when I could potentially squeeze out any last drops of performance. My mind raced, thinking of the fitness I'd built up over the year wasting away. More than once I took the bike out believing that it was all in my mind, that of course I could ride, but the familiar pain shot through my leg immediately. I confessed to Ruth and Jahna, who reassured me that I couldn't change anything now, I wouldn't improve anyway and my fitness wouldn't disappear. I just had to rest and ensure I got to the start line in the best condition for the attempt.

Training stopped. I was in physio twice a week and I returned to Andy Brooke, the bike-fitter, to make adjustments to the bike. He assured me that the rest of the team would get me to the start line in peak condition and he would ensure I had a bike I could ride to the finish. Still, in the back of my mind, I was concerned about what would happen if we didn't resolve the problems. I was troubled by the thought of not being physically able to start the attempt and, even worse, that I started and failed halfway through for the same reasons as others before me. My attempt was all about mitigating risk and not compromising on performance; this could jeopardize everything.

A week after the trial run, I made the 5-hour drive from Derby to Edinburgh, to process express visa applications at the Russian embassy. Jem invited me to stay with him and his wife for the weekend, in the brand new house they'd recently moved into. It gave us the opportunity to get to know each other outside of the team environment. As I looked through the boxes of suspension forks and drivetrains for his clients' bespoke bike builds, we chatted about cycling and the record attempt. Discussing the previous projects he'd worked on, I began to understand his unenthusiastic acceptance when joining my team.

"Marty told ya we worked on another record attempt a few months back, right?" Jem asked.

"Yeah, I mean, knowing some of the inner workings of that attempt really helped me prepare for this but, to be honest, he didn't tell me much about what happened," I replied.

"Not surprised he didn't tell you much – it was absolute shite."

I looked at Jem, who didn't seem like the type to get emotional. He filled his mug from the cafetière and put it down gently on the new marble worktop between us.

"That project was meant to be all about raising awareness about mental health, y'know? Rob probably told ya, a lot who served struggled after leaving the Mob. Anyway, I put loads of my own time, money and gear into that project, thinking we were really going to make a difference."

"Good on ya, man, that's awesome."

"Yeah, well the guy we were supporting didn't see it the same way. Turned out, it was all about him. Never gave us credit in his socials – we just wanted a mention, a bit of recognition, but nah. All about how amazing he was. Expected us to sleep in the vans while he booked fancy hotels, like. Marty's missus, Clare, she was out there with us, sleeping in the wagon, too. And, get this, right – as well as spannering and navigating for that absolute Cheggers, his film crew expected us to feed *them* too. Would *they* help us? Would they bollocks. We were threaders, man, worked to the bone for nothing. Did me in. Had a worse effect on my well-being than it helped others. Clare, man, she's still struggling."

"Ah, sorry about that, mate."

"It's not the only time. The project before that, I was taken on as mechanic but turned out the rest of the team had no experience – ended up doing all their road ops just to get them to the finish line."

Jem had been stung before. I understood why he was wary of the same thing happening with me, how the film-maker on our trial run had affected him and how he would be feeling about working with a team of theoretical experts who had no experience with the variables of the road. In that moment it became very clear to me that every one of us was influenced by what we had experienced before. Jem was actually incredibly passionate about endurance cycling projects. When he spoke about the good times, the sunrises, the camaraderie and the successes, he became animated and excited. He lived and breathed for this – he'd just had too many bad experiences.

We climbed into Jem's VW camper early Monday morning and drove through the grand roads of Scotland's capital, into the side streets behind Hibernian football ground. Jahna was cycling in Italy but Kerr stood waiting for us, holding his camera and tripod, when we arrived shortly before 8.30 a.m. I was happy to see Kerr already there and hoped this would make a good impression on Jem but I think his opinion of film-makers was already soured by his previous experiences. Jem seemed to have his guard up when I introduced them. We walked among imposing Georgian architecture, before waiting in front of a characterless concrete building with no windows, the Russian Visa Application Centre.

Inside, we sat on hard plastic seats in an undecorated room that smelt of second-hand smoke. The walls were plastered with immigration warnings and dog-eared 1980s holiday posters. A handful of chairs were occupied by Russian nationals and truck drivers who appeared to be regulars there. With no tickets or queuing system, we had to remember who was ahead of us and assert our place if anyone approached the desk before us when the clerk shouted, "Next!"

In our interrogations, Jem and I completed the application forms, answered the questions and paid without fuss. Things were different for Kerr. The strict guidelines that we all had stated the exact size and quality of passport photo required but Kerr had brought a photocopy. We knew it was trouble as we overheard the Russian clerk telling him, "Come back with correct photo. Office close in one hour."

"What's occurring, Lofty?" Jem asked Kerr as he walked back towards us.

"I thought this photo would be all right, like, but..." Kerr replied.

"But what, man? Did you even read the guidelines?"

Jem rolled his eyes as his expectations played out in front of us. You never get a second chance to make a first impression. We piled back into Jem's camper and rushed to a supermarket where Kerr could have an appropriate passport photo taken and returned to submit his application just before the office closed. We were told to collect our visas at 4 p.m. In the time it would take for them to be processed, I'd arranged to visit Mark Beaumont, the world record holder for the fastest cycle around the world, as we were in his hometown.

In many ways, Mark had long been a marker of success for me. Ten years previously, when he had just completed his first record-breaking circumnavigation of the globe, I watched him speak to a packed hall at the Assembly Rooms in Derby. Afterwards, I lined up to speak to him about my own upcoming round-the-world adventure but, when I got in front of him, an assistant asked what I'd like Mark to sign and I was ushered along with the crowds.

When I returned from my own circumnavigation, he reached out to congratulate me. Over the course of the following year, he'd given me tickets to the Kendal Mountain Film Festival and arranged for me to attend a corporate dinner he was speaking at. Now, here we were, chatting in his home. An international cycling icon wanted to spend time with me. *I must be doing something right.*

Mark was working on an attempt at the penny-farthing hour record. We took a miniature version of one of the bikes into his garden, where he set up a short course around cones and under trees, and raced around the lawn in the sun. After he won, we sat outside and made a short video for social media, joking about training on the penny-farthing and that I'd come back and win next time. When we were finished, we joined Jem and Kerr indoors at the dining table and the four of us discussed my project.

Mark was kind and honest and offered advice but, with his knowledge and experience, he pointed out what he believed were weaknesses in my plan. He contested the scientists' strategy of focussing on sleep and riding faster for a shorter time, telling me that the power range I was aiming for was too high and that I should sacrifice 2 hours' sleep for extra time on the road. Mark also pointed out what he considered to be my weakest link: my reliance on Jem. Jem's role's included road management, navigation, mechanics, evidencing and driving, and Mark didn't believe that one person could fill all those roles. Jem was adamant that he could, arguing that he'd just returned from an ultra-endurance project where he did exactly that, daily, for three months.

After a year of being certain that we were innovating a new "better" approach, I was struck by doubt. When I returned to Derby, I told Steve what Mark had said.

"Well, he's right, isn't he?" confirmed Steve. Like Mark and Phil, Steve wasn't just there to cheer me on – he challenged and pushed me and didn't sugar-coat the truth. Given more time and budget, it would have been something we would have worked on but now it was too late in the game to change anything. Visas, flights, hotels, roles on the team… everything was booked and names were allocated.

I just had to trust in Jem. *Was I doing the right thing?*

"There are people that dwell on a situation and focus on what's happened – you've been that person," Phil told me from the other side of the table. "But you've changed – you know what to do now. This is it, pal, you're stepping up to the starting block and there's no looking back. You have to tear out those pages and write the next chapter. No regrets."

After four weeks of doubt in my physical and mental ability, I returned to the University of Derby, where Phil and I sat in the corner of an empty seating area outside his office. Sunlight caught the white text of motivational quotes stencilled on the light blue walls behind us. Maya Angelou's words – "People will forget what you said. They will forget what you did. But they will never forget how you made them feel", – beside a quote of Vince Lombardi, "Perfection is not attainable, but if we chase perfection, we can catch excellence." I drank an Americano with an extra shot and Phil sipped his dishwater tea. My leg had healed, the bike fit was adapted and the crowds may as well have been chanting in the stadium in the last minute before we stepped out into the game as he gave me his dressing room pre-match pep talk.

"Let's go through your thought processes," Phil started. "Give me an example of when you overcame a difficult situation in training."

About three months into this project, shortly after we introduced training outside on the road, there was a day when I got out of bed already feeling tired. I followed my morning routine and was on the bike less than 60 minutes later, for 2 hours of training at high power. Still yawning and cycling into a headwind, my legs ached and I fought to keep the numbers up. I recognized the repeated phrases of my inner critic: *the power's too high, I can't hold it that long, this is too difficult*. At that point, there was nothing I could do to change the session, I had to complete it. So I asked myself if I could ride like that for 10 minutes. It seemed much more manageable. I stopped thinking about time, scrolled to a page on the GPS that only showed my power output and concentrated on that.

"Did you get through the session?" Phil asked.

"Yeah. Once I got into it, everything was fine."

Phil explained that the reason I had those reactive thoughts was because I'd just woken up and that I did the right thing. I snapped out of it and committed to a controllable, solution-based plan. I'd always known how to do this; I broke down the challenge into manageable chunks and adjusted my mindset. It was just a matter of self-awareness, of recognizing the pattern.

Nevertheless, it was only going to be harder in Europe. "On the attempt, you're going to get to a point where you'll be thinking, 'I don't know if I can get through another fourteen hours of this,' and it'll be like there are two wolves battling in your mind." Phil imparted another of his analogies. "One wolf is the positive thoughts that will keep you going and the other is the negative thoughts that will stop you. The wolf that wins is gonna be the one you feed."

To support his point, Phil reflected on the third day of the test ride in April, when I'd shouted at Mark because the support car wasn't with me when I needed water. On that day, as I stood at the roadside having a tantrum, my reaction had directly affected what I achieved. The clock kept ticking but I wasn't moving.

At the train station in Ufa, the end point of the world record, the only person I was going to have to justify my finishing time to was myself. "If you stopped on the record attempt, how would you justify losing that time *to yourself?*" Phil asked.

"I couldn't. After all I've gone through this year, I'd be gutted. I'd be so angry at myself," I replied.

Phil used this to create an intervention. He took the version of me from the finish line and put him on a metaphorical balcony that I could look up to at any difficult time and ask my future self for advice.

"What would *future you* shout when you stopped because you were angry at the team?" Phil asked.

"Just keep pedalling!" I shouted, like a sports enthusiast shouting at his favourite team on TV.

"Exactly. Just remember that view from the balcony."

Phil wouldn't be there to help acknowledge my thoughts on the road – that would always be my responsibility. Hopefully centring and PMR had trained me for that. However, he could create a shortcut to positive thoughts that would help me feed the right wolf. His plan was to tape positive messages onto my handlebars. Phil and I wrote a list of concise statements and quotes that we had used through our sessions over the year, condensing nine months of psychology into a page of individual sentences. We wanted to remember ten; we remembered 31. It was the ultimate round of bullshit bingo.

Breathe. Left – Right, Repeat. Control the Ropes. Relax Your Shoulders. Be Your Best. New Beginning. Test Yourself. Define Yourself. No Excuses. The list went on.

We also printed large quotes to stick on the walls of the motorhome, to act as encouragement to get back on the bike at the end of each break. *Be the best at skills that require no talent. Control the controllables. What advice would future Leigh give you? Be where your feet are. Not many people in the world, when they have given everything, can put their left foot in front of their right foot and continue on.* And finally, of course: *What's your why?*

"That's it, buddy," Phil said, returning from the printer and handing over the laminated motivational quotes in a cardboard folder. We had proven I had the physical ability. Now breaking the world record was going to depend on my discipline. It was a mental game of chess and only I could control the outcome. I had given 100 per cent to training, the team had left no stone unturned, and we had the best possible strategy based on science, experimentation and practice. Preparation was complete.

Every lesson I'd learned over the last year had been taught to me before as I cycled around the world. I'd overcome great hardship, I understood what was important to me and I knew how to achieve more than anybody had expected of me. In spite of this, I'd always struggled to make the solutions work outside the dream world of cycle adventure. Preparing for the record attempt had taught me how to apply these lessons in "real life" and use them to achieve my full potential.

Phil and I walked out of the air-conditioned university and into the warm air outside. After everything we had gone through, I was sad that he wouldn't be with me on the road. We hugged.

"I'll be there for ya pal, make sure you call me," he said. "Now go get 'em, and write that next chapter like it's your last." It was the end of a very special time. I walked away and didn't look back.

The moment had come to break a world record.

It was just me against myself.

PART TWO:
RACE ACROSS EUROPE

SIXTEEN

MISSION CONTROL

7 SEPTEMBER 2018: THREE DAYS TO GO
Sintra, Portugal

In the early 1990s, when they first met, Al took Mum on her first holiday abroad and not long after, he did the same for Emma and me. As Elton John's "Rocketman" played through the plane, Emma and I sat excitedly on the runway ready to take flight to Tenerife. While we mocked the safety briefing actions and clicked through the in-flight entertainment, Al secretly asked the flight crew if we could visit the cockpit. Mid-air, a flight attendant came over to the seats where Emma and I were staring out the window at the world 30,000 feet below, crouched beside us and asked if we wanted to meet the pilot. Stunned, we looked back at Mum and Al, with big smiles on their faces. They nodded, "Off you go." We walked into the cockpit in wonderment at the wall of switches and gauges and the panoramic window. It was dusk and the pilot told us to look outside; the sun was setting in the west and the moon sat on the horizon in the east, separated by a gradient sky. It was magical.

That same memory came to mind on every plane I took since. I pushed my headphones into my ears and pressed play. "Rocketman" filled my ears, as it had on that memorable flight. Jem, Jahna and Kerr sat in a row together, with the aisle between them and me. Wheels thundered along the runway and we were pressed into our seats as the plane rose into the stillness of flight. Everything we needed was in the motorhome somewhere 7 miles below us, finishing its five-day journey from Derby. I was locked in; no matter what happened now, the world record attempt was underway.

The automatic doors to the arrivals hall of Lisbon Airport slid open and as Jem, Jahna and I walked through, Kerr pulled a skateboard out of nowhere and skated between the holidaymakers and suitcases.

"The hell zat," exclaimed Jem, "a frickin' skateboard? He's got a skateboard? What does he think this is? He's not at school! Hey! Lofty! It's not playtime!"

As we pushed our luggage towards the glass entrance of the airport, the motorhome came into view in glorious Portuguese sunshine; Jem and ACE already had logistics on point. We ran over and threw our luggage on the back bed. Chris, the ACE driver got out and told us he was so worried about losing the bike that he hadn't let it out of his sight for the whole journey. As I went to thank him, the airport police whistled and shouted with unmistakeable physical gestures, ushering us to leave. I leaned out the window shouting, "Thank youuuuuu," as the motorhome rattled out of the drop-off bays and onto the motorway.

In the front passenger seat, I finished a bag of fresh Portuguese custard tarts that we'd picked up en route, as Latin music played on the radio and we drove west towards Sintra, the closest town to Cabo da Roca. Jem connected his phone to Jahna's wireless speaker and loud R&B pop beats filled the warm air.

"I chose us this song, a theme for the world record, like," Jem laughed.

"Are you kidding?" I rolled my eyes. "This song? Really?!"

But Jem had spoken and that was that. With his hand in a horns gesture, he nodded his head to the beat as "No Brainer" by Justin Bieber played on. I looked behind to see Kerr and Jahna nodding along too – the project had its anthem. *No Brainer* – after months of psychology preparation, the irony wasn't wasted on me.

As the music played and we continued to drive, I logged into my *Guinness World Records* account and was met by a surprise. The 4,000-mile cross-Europe cycle record I was on my way to attempt, which had stood at 29 days for over two years, had been broken. It wasn't delayed confirmation of Jonas Deichmann's or Sean Conway's attempts. It was by a man who we hadn't heard of called Paul Spencer. The only thing Jem and I assumed had differentiated Paul from the others was evidencing. The team at *Guinness*

World Records are notorious sticklers for detail; attempts don't get acknowledged without fulfilling their specific requirements. We speculated that maybe Sean and Jonas hadn't documented theirs thoroughly.

Only a few hours separated the completion times of the three most recent attempts – it seemed as though the threshold of what was possible had been reached. The new official record stood at 25 days and 4 hours.

We arrived at the beautiful location that would become mission control for the next couple of days: a two-storey white house with a terracotta roof, on the outskirts of a village overlooking the edge of the Sintra-Cascais National Park. Within minutes, the homely, welcoming interior was turned upside down, transformed into a bike workshop and editing studio. Every socket was connected to charge equipment, Wi-Fi passwords were shouted around the house and boxes of bike components were stacked for examination.

Kerr edited the day's video for a social media post as Jem did an inventory check on everything in the motorhome and Jahna cooked lemon chicken. In the evening we sat around the kitchen table for dinner like a family; the food was delicious, the company was great and warm dry air blew gently through the open back door. For a few minutes we weren't a world record cycling team – we were a group of friends on holiday in a foreign country, enjoying each other's company.

After we tidied the kitchen together, we all went out the back and stood on the steps that led down to the yard behind the house. A hot air balloon drifted across the evening sky, which had turned a deep purple over the terracotta roofs and dusty trees. It would have been a perfect holiday, if we weren't launching an epic cycling challenge to Russia in 48 hours' time.

---

8 SEPTEMBER 2018: TWO DAYS TO GO
Sintra, Portugal

Twelve months to the day since I'd submitted my application to attempt the record. Twelve months of hard work, lessons and sacrifice. It had been a hell of a journey just getting to the start line.

Mission control was alive with activity in the morning; Jem had the bike on a work stand in the shade out the front of the house and Kerr was in the lounge, rummaging through bags, with media equipment spread everywhere. The air filled with the aromas of oatcakes and endless fresh coffee as Jahna prepared the nutrition for the road. Jem walked into the lounge and stopped dead in his tracks to avoid standing on a skateboard.

"What the?" he shouted.

"All right?" Kerr asked as he looked up.

"Get all of your shit in one sock, man!"

"But I've already had a shit this morning."

"No. Look. Your shit…" Jem gestured towards the equipment haphazardly cast around the room "… In one sock," he concluded as he brought his hands together and grasped them tightly. The room was an accident waiting to happen and Jem needed the space to be tidy. He was obsessive about organization and tidiness for good reason – it was efficient. Jem had the most equipment to manage but it took up the least amount of space.

In the kitchen, he and I looked through the project management paperwork. I'd brought a folder of documents collected through preparation, which passed all my knowledge on to the team. Jem had also created two folders of his own – one full of spreadsheets for evidence gathering and the other for physiological and psychological data collection, which he would photograph and send to the science team for real-time updates. My confidence grew – the devil is in the detail.

Jem and I went through Mark's daily plan, calculated using specific data the science team had collected through training. Our strategy prioritized 7 hours of sleep per day. On an average day I was on the bike for 14 hours, starting at 5 a.m. and finishing at 8.30 p.m. This time was broken down into blocks of cycling; three 4-hour blocks, and one 2-hour block. The remaining 3 hours of the day when I wasn't sleeping or cycling, were designated for breakfast, dinner and break times. Precision was key.

In our review of the trial run around England, we had analyzed every area that had cost time, the main concerns being my timekeeping and procrastination. On the second and third day of the trial, I had been at least 10 minutes late setting off. I'd wasted 5 minutes on every block changing clothes and stopping for the toilet and, when I was uncomfortable, I pulled the team over to question plans and expend further time. We quantified the impact that this would have on the record; if I wasted 5 minutes at the beginning and end of every block, it added up to 40 minutes a day. Multiplying that by the 20-day target we had given to the media equated to almost 14 hours. I could gain a day on the world record through the core principle of an elite athlete's lifestyle; be the best at skills that require no talent.

That afternoon we drove out to the lighthouse at Cabo da Roca. The doors of the motorhome slammed shut with the force of the wind blowing in off the Atlantic. It was surreal. The place I'd visualized 100 times or more in research and centring exercises was a tangible building in front of me. The team and I stood beneath the tall, rock monument with a white crucifix on top that honoured the western extent of Europe and marked the start point of the world record. Tourists from around the globe disembarked by the busload to walk the sandy paths and lean against the wall to take selfies in front of the ocean. The next land beyond the clifftop wall was the east coast of the United States, some 3,000 miles away, a distance that seemed impossibly huge.

Then I remembered I was cycling 1,000 miles further than that in the opposite direction.

In the commotion of a tourist photo shoot, it was difficult to prepare for the record. We climbed back into the motorhome and set off on Jem's recommendation to recce the first 30 km (19 miles) of the route. The road climbed inland, up a steep gradient towards a small village at the top. Before we even reached the village, Jem stopped the vehicle.

"What's up?" I asked.

"That's your route there, mate," Jem pointed down a steep gravel trail that disappeared towards a farm and into scrubland of the national park.

"Haha! Yeah right, mate, pull the other one!"

"I'm not kidding, check it for yourself."

I scrolled to the map on the bike GPS and held it up. It pointed straight down the trail. I zoomed in, double- and triple-checking it, but couldn't escape the fact that Jem was right, it was my worst-case scenario. We continued driving and as far as we went, the route I'd plotted was riddled with tracks and paths unsuitable for a highly tuned road bike and unnavigable in a motorhome. I couldn't believe this disastrous oversight. In route planning I'd thought I had been uncompromising in every detail.

Marty and I had spent weeks plotting routes across countries. Starting with the most direct path, we removed motorways, and rerouted around unnecessary climbs to create the shortest and most efficient route. It had been a challenge from the outset of the project but rather than geography, it was politics that posed the biggest obstacle. The most direct route went straight through Belarus, an option I'd had to dismiss from the beginning because only Russians or Belarusians could cross the border between their countries. The best alternative seemed to be through Ukraine and so I plotted that route and committed to it through months of preparation.

In researching vehicle hire with ACE, I'd been faced with a new problem. For insurance purposes, European hire companies wouldn't allow their vehicles into Ukraine and Ukrainian companies wouldn't let their vehicles into Russia. The route I'd committed to demanded two vehicle swaps, which would create a logistical nightmare and potentially create long delays. As an alternative, I'd begun researching the route to the north of Belarus, through Lithuania and Latvia. On a flat map of the continent, it appeared much longer than the southern options but it was an optical illusion. Due to the curvature of the Earth, it was remarkably similar in distance. There was the additional bonus that going north avoided the foothills of Southern Europe's mountain ranges, creating a route with much less elevation.

Theoretically, when modelled on a computer, the whole route – west to east – was perfect but I'd overlooked a significant real world factor: road surface. With one day until the start, the whole itinerary needed to be reviewed with a fine-tooth comb. Jem and I went through the first day's route that evening and contacted Marty, one of our sponsors in Derby, who made the time around opening his new underground cycling gym to review GPS files and send them out to us day by day. Jem's 30 km recce saved us from disaster.

---

9 SEPTEMBER 2018: ONE DAY TO GO
Sintra, Portugal

I woke at 4.30 a.m., put on my cycling clothes, crept downstairs and wheeled my bike out into the dark morning. Mark had prescribed a 1-hour leg spinner, which I used to get into the routine of a 5 a.m. start. Calm and in control, knowing that the team had prepared everything meticulously and with the empty Sunday roads to myself, cycling in darkness was heavenly. Under streetlights every sense was heightened but, unlike the dark dual carriageways on the trial run, it was serene. The cool morning air felt fresher, the lingering smells of cafés and bakeries were sweeter and electric gear changes zipped and chunked louder. Riding on the right-hand side of the road reminded me of cycling around the world, and I gently pedalled from village to village and memory to memory. For that hour, the morning was mine alone and I loved it. The bike was everything it had been to me throughout my life – a love, an escape, a dream. I returned to mission control and crept back into bed.

After a few extra hours of sleep, I showered, shaved and went downstairs. All three of the team turned and laughed at me.

"What? What have I done?" I asked.

"Are you, like, some kind of Wolverine?" asked Kerr.

"Haha, are you hopin' that'll make you go faster, more aerodynamic, like?" laughed Jem.

I looked in the mirror. I'd missed big chunks of beard in the same place on both sides of my face. I did look like Wolverine. I turned around and imitated metal claws coming out from my knuckles, laughing at myself with them.

With only a few hours until we had to check out, our focus was on finishing anything that needed the internet, charging every piece of electrical equipment and organizing the motorhome as a support vehicle. Food supplies were stocked, fuel was topped up, water tank filled, physio and mechanic areas prepped. I found Jem giving the bike its final checks and stuck my motivational quotes on the aerodynamic handlebar extensions. *Breathe*, *smile*, *positive* and *new beginning* were written on masking tape and positioned so I could see them whenever I looked down at the GPS.

Throughout the months of psychology work with Phil, he'd asked me to compile three music playlists to help manage my state of mind on the bike. One to pick me up, one to help cope with boredom, and one to calm me down. Among all the other demands, I'd neglected making them and now, at the last minute, I realized I was about to cycle into weeks of silence. I spent the last couple of hours at mission control trying to remember my favourite songs from the previous 35 years and added them to the anti-boredom playlist. At that moment, Kerr was unoccupied so I asked him to compile the playlist to give me a boost when needed.

"Okay. What kinda music do you like?" he asked.

"It's gotta be uplifting stuff. Phil mentioned an Eminem song, 'Till I Collapse'," I pretended to know what I was talking about, "and I was thinking of that Black Eyed Peas one, 'Pump It', you know?"

"Right. What about Kanye?"

"Erm. Sure. Why not."

"DJ Khaled?"

"Who?"

"DMX?"

"I've got no idea what you're talking about, mate. If it's uplifting, add it to the list," I conceded. With minutes to spare, I downloaded the audiobook of Geraint Thomas's *The World of Cycling According To G*, decided that a chilled-out playlist of only six songs would be enough and disregarded the podcasts that Phil had suggested. Mission control was returned to its previous state as a comfortable townhouse and we left without a trace.

The wind howled as we parked up on the roadside close to the lighthouse. Just as we had done on the trial run, we planned for me to sleep in the tent and for the team to sleep in the van. However, there was nowhere to pitch the tent in the visitor centre car park and, even if there was, the wind would have blown it away, so I opted to sleep in the motorhome with the team. We would all get an early night if we prepared for tomorrow in advance. Considering its large appearance and how cumbersome it was to manoeuvre through small roads, living conditions in the back of the motorhome were surprisingly cramped. Each movement was like one of those sliding puzzle games; one person had to step out of the vehicle, the others individually took their turn to move, then the final person got back in. Each job became a royal pain in the arse.

I put myself firmly in everyone's way, sticking the laminated quotes that Phil had created for me around the walls of the communal area, explaining them to the team. I also taped a reminder of my positive thought process beside the exit door, and the front page from my diary that I'd written when crossing the Himalayas. It read:

Leigh, you are only going to be here once and at times it will be soul-destroyingly difficult. Don't wish for anything else – face it and embrace it. Live in the now – this moment is all there is. Look around you. Breathe. Smile. Pedal.

It was a reminder that I had been in this position before. I had pedalled and pushed and struggled to get myself and my bike up the mountains and onto the Tibetan Plateau, only to realize that the climb was only the beginning. The real difficulty was the daily grind of simply existing in the harsh environment I'd put myself in. Here, now, everything was in place; we had climbed the mountain, and we were ready to start.

SEVENTEEN

DAY ONE – DON'T BE SHIT

---

10 SEPTEMBER 2018
Distance: 411.2 km (255.5 miles)
Start: Cabo da Roca, Portugal
Finish: Vilar Formoso, Portugal
Weather: 30°C, sunny

It felt like the middle of the night when I woke to the sound of clanking pots and the click, hiss of the gas stove. I checked the clock: 4.30 a.m. I dressed under the stark LED light that burned streaks on my retinas after the blackness of sleep. The inelegance of squeezing into Lycra was amplified in the tight confines of the motorhome and, as I dressed, I cast disturbing shadow puppetry onto the curtains for the world outside. I pulled back the fabric door and stepped through to the kitchen area, where fresh coffee and a trough of oats waited for me. My filled bottles and the GPS, loaded with the route, sat on the table ready to go.

"Hey, don't forget to open today's envelope!" Jahna chirped as I finished my breakfast. A couple of weeks before the attempt, Marty's girlfriend, Clare, had visited the team and me at Mum's house. She brought homemade banana bread and gave me a card. Inside were 20 envelopes; one for every day on the road. Each contained a chocolate and a handwritten quote to motivate me. I chose one at random, opened it and read it aloud.

"Don't be shit!" I exclaimed.

"Classic Clare, man! Classic!" Jem laughed. "Now come on Lofty, it's time."

Walking out of the motorhome and towards the start line replays in my memory like an out-of-body experience. A view I could never have seen, cast in low contrast night vision. A wide-angle shot from above, over the roof of the motorhome, the lighthouse to the right, the crucifix down a cobbled path ahead of us, the dark turbulent waves crashing at the base of the cliffs beneath us. We left the comfort of the vehicle and walked into the cold, towards the westernmost point of Europe. The team went two steps ahead of me, Jem carrying my bike. The moment plays out in cinematic slow motion, hair blowing in the wind, the scene growing darker as we walk away from the lights, the white noise of the ocean behind.

We stood at the monument at 4.55 a.m. Fully prepared. I'd been visualizing this moment through preparation, expecting to be pumped on adrenaline, but I wasn't. The end of training had been emotional. The flight had been emotional. The ride on Sunday morning had been emotional. However, the 5 minutes leading up to the start of the world record attempt was unremarkable. I knew the road that lay ahead and I knew what I had to do. All that remained was to turn the pedals.

Jem checked the bike and patted each pocket on the back of my jersey to ensure I had the equipment I needed and that it was switched on. A phone, a Spot GPS tracker, the Garmin bike GPS and the Fenix GPS watch, full bottles, snacks and lights. He repeated the words I would become very familiar with, "Phone. Spotty. Garmin. Fenix. Nutrition. Bottles. Lights. Good to go. Rolling out." At 5 a.m. I hit start on the GPS and clipped into the pedals as the bike bumped over the uneven paved footpath beneath me. I followed the beam of my front light into the hills. The clock was ticking.

In darkness, I cycled perfect black tarmac that wound its way upwards through the leafy streets of sleepy terracotta towns and around the outskirts of Lisbon. After 2 hours, the sky began to brighten and, with the support vehicle behind me, I reached the top of a long climb surrounded by rolling green hills. We traversed a ridge and, as I peered into the deep valley to our right, I saw that we'd already climbed above the clouds. It was breathtaking. Windmills spun slowly on hilltops all around, poking through the top of a cotton wool landscape that churned in slow wisps, trapped between the deep folds of the earth. The sun sat low on the horizon, casting a pink hue over the panorama and, for a few moments, reality was transformed. It was freedom, it was movement and it was total sensory immersion. I knew this feeling – it was practising tricks in the woods after school, it was mountain biking trips to the Peak District as a teenager, it was travelling the world by bike. It was everything I loved about cycling.

The route followed unmarked single-track roads through rural Portugal, around the contours of rolling hills, between the pinstripe green vineyards that accentuated the shallow gradients of the land. Acres of agriculture punctuated by the flaking white paint and bowed tile roofs of crumbling abandoned farmhouses. I cycled through the serenity of being awake before the world, the sun warming my skin. Birds sang in the small villages I passed through, the bakeries began filling the sleepy streets with aromas of freshly baked crusty rolls and the cafés awoke with the hissing of milk frothers and the clinking rattle of cups and plates being arranged. Locals shouted to each other across the street, Portuguese was a mysterious song in my ears. This was the natural habitat of around-the-world cyclists; empty roads through peaceful towns and, in scrubland away from populated areas, I spotted perfect places for wild camping.

Crossing Europe, I once again got to appreciate the multisensory detail and variety of the world from the saddle of the bike every day, from sunrise to sunset. But this time I wasn't cycling at a speed that suited my mood, I was attempting to break a world record. There was no time to stop and savour foreign delights – instead I passed them at pace. We had a scientific strategy, hypothesized and proven to a limited degree, and hanging about to smell the flowers wasn't a part of it.

By 9.47 a.m. I'd cycled 129 km (80 miles) and had run slightly over time for the first break. We'd left the windy and lumpy coastal landscape to follow fast, flat floodplains where the motorhome was parked in a dusty driveway at the side of a long, straight, flat road. Break times became a well-oiled routine with the team. Jem always managed to find a safe place to park as the clock hit the end of a cycling block and the equipment would be ready to use. I got off the bike and left it for him to check over, while I "jumped" onto the physio table and Jahna put a massive box of food in my hands that I had to eat as quickly as possible. As I filled my face, she ran through a quick sports therapy session on my legs. While Jahna organized my nutrition and physio, Jem took the GPS and uploaded all the data from the previous block for the science team in Derby, downloaded the route I needed for the next 4 hours and put it back on the bike. He then ran through Phil's brief psychological analysis with me. Meanwhile, Kerr filled the small bag on the top tube of my bike with supplements and snacks and recorded interviews and cutaways. Jem held my gloves out so all I had to do was push my hands into them, he put my helmet on my head and put the bike at the side of the road. I got on it, Jem made a quick evidence video and, "Ready to roll out," I hit the road.

I pressed play on the long playlist that I'd planned to get me through monotonous days of pedalling. The second block of cycling undulated through the countryside as close to the course of the River Tagus as possible; long distance cycle touring had taught me that following the course of rivers provided the flattest, fastest routes. The road unfolded beneath tall, silver-barked trees and the bike cruised effortlessly over the smooth, grey road. Dipping in and out of villages and towns, I caught glimpses of myself in convex mirrors on driveway exits; a pale Englishman speeding through the country on his rocket ship bike. A smile spread across my face; I was doing it, I was attempting a world record, another dream on the way to becoming true.

Through the middle of the first day, the temperature settled around 35°C. The team must have been feeling it in the motorhome and, as I cycled under the cloudless sky with my unzipped jersey flapping, I saw them pulled over on the opposite side of a quiet road. I hadn't even noticed I was burning until I was stood like a scarecrow with Jem lathering sunblock all over my arms, legs and neck.

Stopping at 1.21 p.m. for the second break, the team waited for me behind the metal Armco barriers, on a patch of gravel beside a turnoff to an industrial storage depot. Our two-stroke generator screamed in the background, filling the air with sweet fumes, the solution I'd developed to keep Kerr's laptop charged for film editing on the road. I sat on the physio table, already prepared with a selection of foods and drinks to consume and our Formula One pitstop routine was executed for the second time in the day.

The team constantly adapted their plans and, instead of taking time to apply sunscreen separately, Jahna switched from using massage oil to sunblock for sports therapy. We multitasked every job when it was safe to do so.

Back on the road at 2.01 p.m., over a dam and around a reservoir that invited me into its deep blue waters to cool down after 9 hours on the road. Not today. Head down, I joined the service road following the *autoestrada* up to Castelo Branco, where smooth horizons became more textured. Riding at around 500 m in altitude, on empty roads with the motorhome behind me, I dipped down into the aerodynamic position, reaching my arms out front on the extensions. On a day with so much climbing, it was rare that I got the opportunity but when I did, it was as close as I could get to flying.

I pulled into the paved car park of a petrol station, just outside the hilltop town of Penamacor, at 6.05 p.m. With almost 2 hours until sunset, the team had set the physio table up in the shade of the motorhome. Even there, it was still 33°C. When I'd discussed the strategy with Mark, Phil and Nicky, we agreed that getting the hardest part of the route out of the way on the first day would be physically testing but would put me in a strong psychological position going forward. The road through Portugal was 411 km (255 miles) in distance, with 5,000 m of climbing – half the height of Everest. Completing it on Day One would utilize my freshness and adrenaline, I would already have ticked a country off the list and I'd get the biggest day of climbing out of the way. It required extending the final block of the day from 2 hours to 4. The pit stop routine was completed for the final time of the day and at 6.41 p.m., I set off on the final stint towards Spain.

The warm afternoon with views over dry valleys below faded to the dark of night as I cranked the pedals over the toughest climb of the day, lifting myself onto the hilltops at 900 m altitude. As the sun dipped beneath the horizon behind me, the mountain air quickly dropped from 30 to 15 degrees. Jahna passed me a gilet and arm warmers to put on before the team went ahead to recce the border, find a place to sleep and prepare dinner. In the pitch black country roads, the narrow beam of the bike light caught something in the road ahead. As I approached, it spread its bright, wide wings and the owl took flight directly over my head. *Woah! Amazing!* What a day this was. The world around me was incredible and I was sailing through the attempt quicker than we ever thought possible. *The team and I must have overprepared or underestimated my ability, we're setting ourselves up to beat even our own expectations.* I pedalled towards the Spanish border with a smile on my face and energy remaining in my legs.

At 10.11 p.m., half an hour ahead of schedule, I arrived in the border town of Vilar Formoso, where I heard Jem and Kerr shouting, "Yeahhh! That's it!" even before I saw them. I coasted the bike to a standstill and they greeted me with a pat on the back and a high five. It was a great moment. The day had been perfect – we'd made it perfect. We took a photo under the streetlights outside the border control office and recorded the final evidence video of the day before heading round the corner to the motorhome. My legs were heavy, my hands and legs were filthy, and I was sticky with sweat and sun cream but I couldn't have been happier with how the attempt was going as I climbed off for my first night's sleep. This was a day that dreams were made of.

EIGHTEEN

DAY TWO – CHANGES

---

11 SEPTEMBER 2018
Distance: 359 km (223 miles)
Start: Vilar Formoso, Portugal
Finish: Santa Maria Del Campo, Spain
Weather: 34°C, sunny

One of the qualities that differentiated our attempt from those that had gone before was the primary focus: sleep. Previous attempts gained time by sacrificing sleep and cycling longer hours at a slower pace. We cycled smarter, ensuring thorough recovery for maximum daily performance. Our strategy prioritized 7 hours of sleep every 24 hours. Having added 2 hours of cycling to Day One, we maintained sleep duration by reducing my cycling time on Day Two, starting 2 hours later than normal.

Although science proved that more sleep led to greater performance, it still seemed counter-intuitive. I felt irked that it cost 2 hours on the bike – even at a slow pace that would be a loss of about 50 km (31 miles). However, I woke refreshed and was on the bike in daylight, on time at

7 a.m. Crossing the border into Spain we changed time zone and, although we continued to work to British Summer Time, local time jumped an hour ahead. The change in country also radically transformed the landscape. From the close, green hills of Portugal, the vista opened into infinite yellow plains. The sun-baked tarmac of Spanish service roads cut straight lines through endless fields of dust as they followed the Autovía de Castilla on a beeline through the country.

On the first break, after a solid 109 km (68 miles), I looked around my surroundings from the comfort of the physio couch. On the highest point before the descent to Salamanca, with expansive views, I was just a tiny speck in this vast emptiness.

"Is there a reason why the breaks are twenty, then forty, then thirty minutes long?" Jem asked.

"I don't think so, mate. As far as I know, it's what the science team figured would work best. I like that it gives me a longer lunch time, ha!" I replied.

"Totally get that. Thing is, we can't get everything set up and broken down again in twenty minutes, it's a mad rush for us to do everything. Can we change to three thirty-minute breaks?"

"Yeah, man, that works for me."

It was another solution to a strategy that had seemed fine in the lab-based models but needed adjustment to work in practice.

The first 4-hour block had gone to schedule – I'd sat and cycled through the miles on autopilot. However, in the second block, challenges seemed to be thrown at me from every angle and I couldn't get into a rhythm. In the city of Salamanca, my route led onto a gravel trail. I found another option on the GPS, let the team know where I was going and turned on my WhatsApp live location. The alternative road I joined was closed for roadworks and I had to follow a diversion. After the diversion, the original route deteriorated into more impassable conditions that I had to map around again. When I finally made it onto a smooth main road, I got a puncture. In the first hour and a half, I only covered 25 km (15 miles). I swallowed my disappointment as I watched the daily target slipping away and, with the spare wheel on the bike, pushed on harder, determined to make up distance before the next break.

That day, you could fry an egg on the metal barriers at the road's edge. They creaked and pinged, expanding in the sun and radiating heat onto the road. It was a scorching 34°C on the Spanish plains without respite from the direct sun and my frustration at the delay was compounded by the nutrition strategy, which became difficult to tolerate in the high temperatures.

During training through the summer, Nicky and I had monitored my hydration levels in relation to weather. In these extreme conditions, we knew I had to drink a litre and a half every hour to avoid dehydration – an enormous

6 litres every 4 hours, 21 litres a day. Consuming 11,000 to 12,000 calories on top of that was bordering on painful. The large meals I ate on every break left me with that post-Sunday dinner feeling of unavoidably falling asleep in front of the fire. Except I couldn't nap, I had to ride 120 km (75 miles) in the next 4 hours before eating it over again. I became so bloated that I couldn't tuck into an aerodynamic position and it felt as though my body was so busy digesting that I had little power to push through the pedals. In comparison to what I could achieve in training, on an empty stomach and in perfect conditions, it felt like cycling through treacle.

My mind switched to frame everything negatively. *I can't believe this route is still so bad. The research never showed this kind of temperature. I can do better than this, I shouldn't be eating so much. I could cut it down and ride faster. Jahna is playing it too safe.* When it came to the next break and another huge bowl of food, the frustration came to a head. The team counted out the empty gel wrappers to track my calorie intake; in the heat, I hadn't even eaten half of them. When they reminded me to take a gel or bar every 15 minutes, I snapped, "Are you serious? Look at the amount of food in this bowl, I'm trying my best and you want more? Come on!"

They said nothing and let me get back on the bike.

My own angry voice replayed in my head as I cycled. I realized what I'd done, recognizing the pattern in my behaviour. It was infuriating that, when calm, I knew how to react and could keep a cool head but in moments of weakness, heated words flew out of my mouth uncontrolled. That wasn't who I wanted to be. When I caught up with the team for fresh bottles, I opened up about how I felt.

"I'm sorry, guys. There are sides of me that even I don't like and I'm trying to deal with them. I'm sorry I snapped at you like that."

"Don't worry, you have every right to snap, you're constantly pushing your limits, it's to be expected," Jahna replied.

Still, it wasn't fine to me. I'd spent months working on psychological interventions with Phil to stop this happening but that knee-jerk reaction was still there. He'd told me there was no quick fix to change psychological reactions but I was disappointed that I hadn't adopted that perfect, positive mindset. I was in the wrong and put my hand up to admit it. At least clearing the air helped us work on what lay ahead rather than dwelling on the consequences of past actions.

At the end of the day I went back to Jahna with an idea. Instead of the 2,000 calorie meals that I was eating on each break, supplemented with a drip feed of 80-calorie snacks every 15 minutes on the bike, I asked if we could find a middle ground that involved smaller meals and higher energy snacks. Jahna agreed it was a good solution and began work on a strategy.

We were out of the honeymoon period but the reality of the task ahead was still far from kicking in. After the fantastic first day of a fast, uphill 411 km (255 miles), Day Two had been a testing 359 km (223 miles) and not even half the elevation to climb. I was disappointed. I'd proved to myself that I could do better than this and was certain I had a lot of potential in my legs – I could feel it. Yet I told myself it was okay – I was sure I could make up for lost time tomorrow with a full 14 hours on the bike. Things were looking good.

NINETEEN

DAY THREE – THE DESCENT

---

12 SEPTEMBER 2018
Distance: 377.4 km (234.5 miles)
Start: Santa María del Campo, Spain
Finish: Magescq, France
Weather: 30°C, sunny

I'd been looking forward to this day since plotting the route with Marty. After crossing the high-altitude plateaux of central Spain, I was to descend 1,000 vertical metres through the Pyrenees to the French coast. It was sure to be a record-breaking fast day.

For the first 8 hours, I cycled comfortably across flat terrain at just below 32 kph (20 mph), through plains of wheat fields, soft blankets of yellow that covered the landscape. We circumnavigated the city centre of Burgos, hugging the outskirts on the broad, two-laned boulevards between shops and business districts. From Burgos, we tracked the path of the *autovía* heading north. I followed this for most of the day, fast and steady, through to Vitoria-Gastiez, where peaks of mountains began to appear over the horizon. From here, the road was swallowed by the landscape. From featureless vistas, the surrounding geography was turned on its head, becoming rugged vertical rock faces and tunnels. The Pyrenees. This was where I planned to make up time. From the topography of the map it looked as though I would exchange a 200 m ascent to gain a huge 700 m downhill. That whole day of climbing I'd put in through Portugal was saved up like a coiled spring and was about to be released. The road began to drop away and my speed increased. My legs spun out in the biggest gear. I tucked into an aerodynamic position and flew down the mountains.

The descent was wild but I'd overlooked that it was only 20 km (12 miles) long. Even a dramatic increase in velocity would make little impact on the average over a 400-km (250-mile) day. As it happened, moving speed was the least of my concerns. The only route I could cycle passed through busy market towns with narrow cobbled streets and steep gradients that Jem struggled to negotiate in the motorhome. Built-up areas were a logistical nightmare of one-way systems, restricted roads and a congested infrastructure. To add to our problems, we reached them at rush hour.

The team minimized my loss on the road. They drove ahead to each junction, GPS and Google Maps at the ready to guide me turn-by-turn through a solution. Yet, only 40 minutes into the block, a bollard blocked the route. Jem pulled onto the pavement and switched on the hazard lights.

"I can't drive through this, mate. I'm gonna have to join

that motorway and bypass the towns," he pointed to an overpass ahead. "We'll meet you at the French border."

Jahna put full bottles on the bike and I spun back in the opposite direction to the motorhome. I continued to follow the GPS, bunny-hopping up and down kerbs, swinging between parked cars and sprinting through gaps in the traffic. My moving speed only dropped 2 kph but everything other than gravity seemed to be working against me. After fighting my way through the bustling towns higher up in the mountains, I hit the Basque Country tourist hotspot of San Sebastian and the historic town of Irun. Every light changed from green to red and I lost 40 minutes, not from cycling slowly but due to standing still.

My expectations for descending the Pyrenees had been so great yet it had been a disaster. Three hours after the team left me to join the motorway, I saw them waving to me from the motorhome in a car park before the international bridge across the Bidasoa River. I chatted to them briefly about the nightmare I'd had while Jahna put fresh bottles on the bike and food in my pockets. Even though another country had been ticked off the list, I was dispirited. I'd lost yet more time. It was extremely frustrating to feel the strength in my legs but not be able to unleash it. *I just need a bit more time* I told myself, like the panicked request for an extension on an impending deadline.

I pushed on into France and my surroundings became different again. In a short space of time I'd gone from a dusty high-altitude plateau to rugged mountains, to bustling towns, to busy cities and now, although still heavily populated, I was surrounded by woodland. It felt closer to Britain – the ground was grassy, the trees dense, the air cool and damp. I arrived at the motorhome on cue, as the clock ticked over to 4 hours. I conferred with the team in the small town of Bidart about extending the 4-hour block to 5 in an attempt to make up time. I still had energy and could cycle faster in the daylight and without a full stomach. They agreed and I pushed on, but even through the following hour, progress was restricted as the road passed through busy towns around Biarritz.

On the final break at 7 p.m., Jem ran through my psychological analysis. Feelings of *happy* and *calm* were down from scores of five to three, while *angry*, *anxious*, *worried* and *downhearted* all increased.

With only 1 hour left on the bike for the day, I passed through Bayonne and the population density reduced almost instantly. Major roads became dual carriageways and the red and white lights of Renaults, Peugeots and Citroëns sped past me in a blur. I put my head down and punched through the air as fast as possible under an increasingly dark sky. I tucked my head down and watched the back of my hands, averaging speeds of 35–40 kph (22–25 mph). After a frustrating day in the saddle, I was flying. Still, no matter how hard I pushed, I couldn't make up for stoppages and totalling 377 km (235 miles) for the day, I was a long way from covering the distance I'd expected.

TWENTY

DAY FOUR – WHERE IS MY MIND?

13 SEPTEMBER 2018
Distance: 413.8 km (260 miles)
Start: Magescq, France
Finish: Chauvigny, France
Weather: 20°C, cloudy

I was now officially on the longest elite sports ride of my life.

It was a relief to leave the oppressive heat and nagging delays of Spain behind. Now came fast cycling on the smooth roads of France, a country I was already fond of. As far as cycling went, it had been my favourite country of the 51 I'd visited around the globe. It was where I'd watched the Tour de France, the most iconic bike race in the world, and local cycling fanatics had conversed with me through their car windows as they drove past me on my touring bike.

The day started in the tranquillity of Landes de Gascogne National Park, south of Bordeaux. In comparison to Spain, France was lush and leafy. I cycled between wildflower meadows and dense woodland. Spiderwebs in the long grass caught droplets of dew that twinkled, reflecting the bright colours of sunrise. The buzz from the freewheel and the click of gear changes startled roadside deer that ran beside me before darting into the undergrowth.

Cycling across a plain of low ferns between tall bare trees, the sound of a stampede thundered through the air to my left. It seemed so close that if I were stood still, I'd feel the ground shake. *Glasses of water must be trembling somewhere as a T-Rex approaches.* Suddenly, two muscular silhouettes burst out of the bushes, millimetres from a collision with my front wheel. I swerved and slammed on the brakes as the tusked wild boar obliviously chased each other across the road, becoming a dance of moving shrubs as they disappeared on the other side. *Woh!* Adrenaline dilated my pupils before diluting in my bloodstream as I returned to calm. *Am I riding through a scene from* The Lion King? *A part of this migration of wild animals, all running towards a precipice where a baboon is about to hold a lion cub aloft as the sun bursts through the cloud?* "The Circle of Life" from the Disney soundtrack got stuck in my head for hours.

My mind conjured up such odd stories in the saddle. That morning, I also developed a narrative about an angry hippopotamus who lived with a fun-loving mouse who was into ceramics; a happy potter mouse. The hippo sat in an armchair next to the phone in the shoe that they lived in and, whenever it rang, he made a point of picking it up before the mouse. There was always great confusion between calls for the hippopotamus and the happy potter mouse, and the hippo got increasingly irate as he began conversations with animals who didn't want to speak to him. One day he snapped and shouted loud expletives at his little friend.

My mind drifting to imaginary worlds or creating stories from the scenes I passed through was a sign that things were going well. I didn't need to focus my thoughts – my legs were on autopilot and my mind passed the time in its own bizarre, dreamlike state. However, my thought process on the bike was far from consistent.

For 14 hours a day on the bike, my internal clock distorted as the continual ribbon of tarmac disappeared beneath my wheels. Usually, my mind was 20 metres ahead of me, watching traffic and road conditions, keeping me safe and avoiding obstacles. On the right roads, it could become the perfect moment of "flow". Hours could disappear as I became one with the world, cycling the racing line, feeling the wheels grip on corners and hearing deep section carbon rims thundering over the road at speed. Sometimes, I was completely focused on the GPS to monitor my speed, power and heart rate, making sure that I was hitting targets and pushing my speed up, forcing tired legs to drive the pedals.

At times I slipped out of experiencing the world around me, unconsciously immersing myself in the process, the strategy that had sounded so exciting when the scientists and

I planned it. By Day Four I lived in the automated scientific spreadsheet, a lifestyle governed by alarms, organization and statistics. Everything was under strict control in this life experiment and it led to repetition. On long, featureless roads, the bike could have been Excalibur – to sit on it was the same as staring at the white wall. The view ahead appeared as a series of mirrors that cast a repeating world into infinity and to my side a pantomime backdrop rotated to reveal the same landscape, over and over. There were times when my mind was not just 20 metres ahead, but miles away, lost in strategic concerns. *How much money are the team spending? Will the budget run out? Is that squeaky wheel on the motorhome going to be all right? Are the team in contact with the scientists?* I still had trouble letting go of project management and being where my feet were. I flicked through playlists to break the boredom and wake my mind or rummaged through the bag on the top tube to find interesting snacks to stimulate my taste buds – Phil's interventions for motivational variety.

The first break of Day Four was carried out with usual Formula One efficiency. Bike check, eat, drink, physiotherapy, psychological analysis, GPS update, gloves, helmet. The world spun around me while I ate and recovered on the physio table. Breaks were the few times that Kerr had an opportunity to interview me about my feelings and how the ride was going. As the action unfolded, he pointed his camera at me and asked a jarring question.

"So Leigh, can you tell me, where do you draw the line with the team?"

I didn't quite know what he meant and struggled to respond. After a moment's contemplation, I replied with the kind of business answer that Steve would expect of me.

"Everybody has their role on the team, it was organized before the attempt began and—" Kerr stopped me before I could finish my sentence.

"Yeah, but, look around you. Jahna did her job *and then* put sunblock on you, Jem has done his mechanic and logistics work *and then* put your gloves and helmet on you. Everyone is doing more than their role, so where do you draw the line?"

At that moment, as though on cue, Jem emerged from behind the motorhome with the bike. "Alreet. Time. On your bike, Jack." He evidenced where we were, checked I had the correct equipment in my pockets and I cycled away with Kerr's question in my mind.

In the 4-hour blocks alone on the bike, whatever thought I was left with from the previous conversation stuck with me. That morning, I mulled over Kerr's question. *What does he mean? Why would he ask that? Do I expect too much? Am I a bad person?* I analyzed the situations and tried to assess how the actions that Kerr had asked me about even started to happen. *Why are other people dressing and putting sunblock on me? Have I asked them to do this? Am I going crazy? Am I unreasonably demanding?*

After hours of reflection, I settled on an explanation that added up in my mind. The team wanted to drive me to the finish line with such conviction that they were willing to even take on my responsibilities if it helped us perform better as a whole. At lunchtime, I walked into the motorhome and tapped Kerr on the shoulder, poised with my response.

"All right, mate, I've been thinking about your question from this morning and I've got an answer."

"What question?" he asked.

"You know, where do I draw the line with the team?"

"Oh yeah, don't worry about it. I've got pages of questions I've prepared to ask you – that was just one of them," Kerr told me.

I'd spent 4 hours deliberating over something that meant nothing to him.

All I needed to do on the bike was focus on the demands of each moment, however, my mind overcomplicated it. Reflecting on what happened, it was easy to draw parallels between my thought processes through this ultra-endurance event and through my experiences of depression. The feelings of being alone, that *nobody understands what I'm going through* and *everyone else is enjoying their life except me*, were certainly there. It didn't take much of a push to tip me over the edge into dwelling on a situation and focussing on why it happened; the traits that Phil had urged me away from. I should have been where my feet were, controlling the controllables, but I struggled.

Eat. Sleep. Ride. Repeat. Regardless of the ebbs and flows of my psychological state, it felt as though life on the road found its rhythm. Our pace increased and we began covering the daily distance that I had seen I was capable of through training. The days started to feel like routine and my lifestyle adopted the scientific strategy. When I'd initially looked at breaking an endurance cycling record, I'd assumed that the hardship would be in riding the bike fast but it was not. Endurance was a battle of attrition and each piece of the puzzle – sleep, nutrition, psychology, mechanics, logistics and physio – had equal importance in keeping everything on target.

TWENTY-ONE

DAY FIVE – THE COMPETITION

14 SEPTEMBER 2018
Distance: 391.3 km (243.1 miles)
Start: Chauvigny, France
Finish: Saint-Soupplets, France
Weather: 22°C, sunny

On my website was a map of Europe, upon which spun the legs of a tiny, animated Leigh Timmis and a tiny, animated Sean Conway, pedalling from Cabo da Roca to Ufa in a race across the continent. Although Sean didn't hold the record, his was the most recent and the most publicized comparison and he kindly agreed to let me use his data. The graphic updated every 5 minutes and had "dot watchers" in the UK glued to it.

On Day Five, the route turned east into the heart of France, skimming Tours and Orléans before it skirted the south of Paris. Rural roads crossed quaint bridges and wound through rustic towns of crumbling, sandy brickwork. Shopfronts sported the words of my school language textbooks, "Pharmacie", "Supermarché" and my favourite, the delicious "Boulangerie". Old ladies shuffled along the pavement, tiptoeing between the shadows of trees and buildings to avoid the hot sunshine in floral streets, where hanging baskets adorned lampposts and homes.

After 56 hours in the saddle in four days, my skin was now brown. Not the toned, manicured and bronzed beach body I'd have preferred but the colour and texture of an old leather handbag. I'd cultivated sharp tan lines at shorts and sleeve length and down the sides of my face where the helmet strap sat. I once again deserved the nickname that I'd been given in Australia, "Top Deck", a milk chocolate bar with a layer of white chocolate on top.

Within the first 2 hours of the day, the total distance ticked over the 1,000-mile mark, not that I noticed. On the bike I don't work in miles; speeds read too small and distances take too long to pass, I get a better exchange rate in kilometres. A quarter of the challenge already completed proved that Mark's training programme had worked. Physiology, the area of training that I'd initially believed to be the most important factor for success, had ticked away healthily in the background. As always, my legs were powering through the challenge, regardless of obstacles I had to overcome. Mark had taken a good cycling body and tuned it up; I was pedalling incredible distances quickly. Where previous challengers of this record averaged a moving speed of 25 kph (15 mph), I was averaging over 30 kph (19 mph). The scientists' innovative approach was delivering a world-class performance.

On the first break, Jahna put a cup of coffee in my hand, dropped my trainers in front of me and told me to walk around the supermarket car park to give my digestive system a nudge. Holding the aerodynamic position – my torso in an almost horizontal position over the bike – meant food was struggling to move through me and I was getting bloated again. Kerr thrust his camera in my face and as we walked he asked me about the competition against Sean.

I spoke of my respect for Sean – what he'd achieved was impressive. To ride across Europe unsupported, he had to do his own shopping, mechanics and evidencing, as well as finding places to eat, sleep and cycle. Kerr's opinion was that I had done the same for seven years cycling around the world. His comment disturbed me somehow; it was correct, I had done the same but not in a race. In my opinion, this record attempt was very different to touring around the world with Dolly and on reflection Sean's approach was a compromise – somewhere in between.

There were times when my approach had been framed negatively in comparison to Sean's attempt and previous attempts before that. I was hurt by critics pointing their finger and accusing me of having an unfair advantage by taking a support team, when creating that team and the strategy we used had demanded a year of enormous sacrifice. Others suggested that there should be separate supported and unsupported records, to which Kerr had an entertaining answer.

"In that case, would you say it's unfair that Usain Bolt would beat my window cleaner in a sprint, because he had the help of experts? Should there be a separate hundred-metre world record for ma buddy?" he would ask. For viewers who only saw the attempt itself, it was impossible to have an informed opinion on what was unfolding. Nobody knew what I was battling with beneath the glossy achievement that was presented.

The "animated" Leigh was now half the width of France ahead of Sean. Hundreds of miles stood between us. In my opinion, comparing our attempts demonstrated the difference between an adventure and the pursuit of an elite sporting performance. Adventure was spontaneous – dealing with challenges as they arise, taking risks. Elite sports were calculated – everything was considered and planned for in great detail. That comparison also made me realize the scale of personal change I'd gone through. Without the guidance of Steve, I would have done exactly what Sean did. I would have flown to Portugal and taken my chances, just as I had going solo round the world. Assuming I didn't get ill, or lost, or injured, I would possibly have knocked a couple of hours off the record.

"You're so far ahead of Sean now, why do you keep pushing?" Kerr continued.

Again thinking of my first impetuous plans, simply breaking the world record had been my aim when I first applied to Guinness but that had changed too. Phil had shifted my motivation. If breaking the record was my only aim, I could now ease off the gas, but I hadn't been comparing my result to the previous record for a long time. Once the team and I had drawn up the target of 16–20 days, comparison to others had disappeared. I wasn't looking at the time. I wasn't looking at Ufa. I wasn't even looking to the end of the day. I was just looking at what I could do in that moment on the bike. I kept pushing because I was pursuing my own best. I was defining myself.

TWENTY-TWO

DAY SIX – HUMAN AFTER ALL

15 SEPTEMBER 2018
Distance: 418 km (259.7 miles)
Start: Saint-Soupplets, France
Finish: Kessel, Netherlands
Weather: 18°C, sunny

I cycled in leg warmers and a thermal layer as the sky brightened behind electricity pylons that stood like giant robots holding skipping ropes from horizon to horizon. The day took me through agricultural landscapes of hay bales, vineyards and leafy green crops above which sprinklers caught the sun and painted rainbows in the air. It was familiar; the world record course crossed the round-the-world route that I'd begun in the same country eight years before.

Roads passed through small villages where I'd camped in farmers' fields and been welcomed in for traditional French breakfasts. I remembered dipping baguettes into bowls of hot chocolate made with milk, fresh from the cow, and drinking endless cafetière coffee in the smoke of

Gauloises cigarettes. I was racing through the same region where I'd stumbled across a bonfire where local people were celebrating the Feux de la Saint-Jean. That night I'd been swept into the celebration, never spending a minute without a cup of champagne in my hand, the villagers riding Dolly around the town. I wondered how far I was from the people I'd visited back then. Those years had taught me that cycling around the world wasn't about the bike; rather, it was the key that opened the door to experiences with the people that I met. Those experiences had expanded my understanding of the world, I missed those spontaneous, uncertain adventures. It was a sacrifice I made in dedicating myself to this project because I was looking for something different this time. Rather than understanding more about the world, I was learning more about myself. This time it wasn't chance encounters with strangers that enriched my journey but the professional stoicism of my support team, at home and on the road, that unlocked the experiences and lessons I was learning.

I'm certain that each member of the team would tell a unique story about the record and each would be radically different to mine. When possible, they drove behind me to offer protection from overtaking traffic and support for nutrition, navigation or mechanical problems. However, most of their days were spent rushing around, shopping, refuelling, recharging equipment, finding a place to fill the vehicle with water, planning the day, adapting the strategy, evidencing, communicating with the team in Derby, film-making and running a social media presence. As Jem navigated and drove the motorhome, Jahna chopped vegetables on her lap in the front seat and Kerr edited footage in the back. The support vehicle was a mobile kitchen, physio studio, bike workshop, office and hotel, with staff on call 24/7.

Each member of the team had their own priority and wanted to achieve the best within their discipline. Jem told me that when driving through beautiful landscapes, Kerr would ask to stop the vehicle so he could climb onto a bridge for the perfect opening shot of me cycling into frame. Jahna would push him to catch up with me because we were 2 hours into the block and I'd dehydrate if she didn't get water to me quickly. Jem himself had to reel in their expectations and prioritize essential tasks, asserting that if he didn't fill up with diesel within the next 20 miles, nobody would be doing anything.

The team were always positive around me but I got the sense that the dynamic between them was frayed at times. My impression was only based on the breaks I shared with them and every day they spent 14 hours without me. I didn't see Jem and Kerr together often and, when I did, Jem was usually dictating a list of important tasks he wanted help with. Jahna put her heart into everything, making scientific expertise from Derby work with the facilities on the road across Europe. She looked after everyone's needs and was selfless with her time, combining science and compassion. Jahna became good friends with Jem but I felt that she was sometimes stuck in the middle of him and Kerr.

There were times when the team worked perfectly together and I could mistake the record attempt for a road trip. It was like that when we came together for the first break of Day Six. The two-stroke generator screamed in the background, filling the air with sweet fumes as it charged electrical equipment and the nutrition buffet was set out. Kerr followed me down the road on his skateboard, recording my arrival, and Jahna welcomed me with a smile. "Sublime" was blaring out of the motorhome's speakers; the team were playing my playlist. I lay face down on the physio couch, in a layby just outside a small rural town and Jahna covered me with Kerr's black down jacket to keep me warm. Lying motionless, with the hood over my head, I looked like a dead body. Jahna tucked it all around me, Kerr filmed it and every Geordie slur that came out of Jem's mouth had us in stitches. We laughed together; we were more than a team and it was these light-hearted moments that made a difference. I missed that fun when I got on the bike for another 4 hours alone.

I flew along the smooth roads of France that transitioned to perfect bike paths beside the main roads of Belgium. We finished the day in the Netherlands, having successfully traversed three countries and covered the longest distance of any day so far – 418 km (260 miles). Jem met me at the side of the road, we videoed our end of day evidence, shut down the bike lights and GPS, and he ushered me into a campsite they had booked. He chatted to his wife on a video call as we walked over the gravel driveway, turning the phone to me so I could say hello. She sat on the sofa, drinking wine with her girlfriends. I'd been so immersed in the all-consuming challenge that I hadn't even considered it was Saturday night for everybody else. I smiled and chatted, two things I hadn't really done much on the road. The variety of talking to different people about something other than cycling or analyzing my physical and psychological status was liberating. I remembered Jem wasn't only a mechanic, he was a husband and a father, Jahna was a sister and a daughter, Kerr had a new girlfriend at home, and I was a human being too.

The campsite was an unexpected luxury. We were never slumming it on the road; we had all that we needed but it was far from the expensive restaurants and personalized mattresses delivered to hotels that the Tour de France cyclists were used to. My tent was set up on flat ground in the space beside the vehicle. We connected to mains electricity and had the opportunity to fully charge everything. The hot water of the power shower was divine; I turned to wash my body and bare skin didn't touch cold plastic walls like it did every day in the motorhome. I connected to the Wi-Fi and received messages of support from friends and family at home. I missed them and wanted to reply but there wasn't enough time. I'm sure the whole team felt the same. We were all human, trying to do the best we could in difficult circumstances. The lights of the motorhome that illuminated the tent went off as the team fell asleep.

TWENTY-THREE

DAY SEVEN – OVER AND OVER

16 SEPTEMBER 2018
Distance: 382.1 km (237.4 miles)
Start: Kessel, Netherlands
Finish: Peine, Germany
Weather: 20°C, sunny

"Hey, buddy. Sorry, man." Kerr's voice woke me up.

The night at the campsite had been a welcome luxury – the shower, the flat ground and the peaceful environment made for a good night's sleep – but still, its duration was limited. I recorded 6 hours' sleep, from a total time of 6 hours 30 minutes in my sleeping bag. We were up and away with the usual efficiency; oats, coffee, equipment check, video evidence and Jem's "Ready to roll?"

Wheels turned out of Kessel and 45 minutes later, after 20 km (12 miles), I crossed the border into Germany. The cycling infrastructure through the Netherlands had been fantastic, with segregated bike paths away from the roads. However, they were potholed and broken where tree roots grew beneath them. When I used them, I had to stop at every junction to let cars through and when I joined the main roads, I was shouted at by drivers who were frustrated by me cycling in their space. I was happy to be back on the fast roads of Germany as I cycled through the built-up towns that surrounded the major western cities of Düsseldorf, Essen and München.

This was the sixth country I would cycle through in seven days. Cycling around the world, I'd realized how wonderfully varied Europe is as a continent; 45 countries with different landscapes, cultures, languages and foods, all within easy reach of each other. For all the diversity and the sensory immersion cycling across a continent offered, on this challenge I had become more immersed in the daily routine that, conversely, never changed.

I'd now spent a full week on the bike. Having racked up almost 100 hours in the saddle, I was overcome by tiredness. Instead of a physio session on the first break, I climbed straight into the back of the motorhome and took a nap. When I woke up to eat, Kerr was unusually calm and reassuring, almost dragging the positives from me as he recorded our interview.

"How much did you do in that last block?" he asked.

"A hundred and twenty-something kilometres," I replied through a mouthful of banana.

"That's good, mate. Like we've said, you've got to have the lows to appreciate the highs."

"Getting in bed will be a good high," I laughed.

Statistically, I was cycling well and averaging a high speed, but my senses were dull. Mornings were a mental and physical struggle, as though I became desensitized to my surroundings, riding numb. Confused, I lacked concentration. Like the drifting drowsiness of a long drive at night, my eyes wished to be closed and I fought to bring my mind to the game. After five days of headwind and a day of still air, I was finally starting to pick up the prevailing tailwind that I'd planned to profit from and I wanted to make the most of it. In the saddle, I focused everything on getting the power down and it left me drained.

Kerr asked how difficult I was finding the attempt on a scale of one to ten. I gave him an eight, telling him it wasn't just the cycling, it was everything. I'd always thought that pushing my physical limits on the bike would be the difficult part but, in reality, there was no respite from the continuing routine for 24 hours every day. Break times were ill-named – rather than a time for relaxing, they were a busy 30 minutes of teamwork while competing in an eating competition. Every basic daily need was monitored; even sleeping had start and stop times with required outcomes.

Nutrition was repetitive, too. Even with the team's amazing work, the great demand for calories unavoidably translated into a lot of the same foods. After a week of continuous eating, I was uninspired by the same ham and mayonnaise wraps and peanut butter, banana and honey-filled brioche buns. I was tired of cramming gels and malt loaves into my mouth while cycling. I asked Jahna if she could mix it up for me and she did what she could. The team began passing me new shaped treats wrapped in foil with promises of slices of cake and hamburgers. When I opened them, I found the same old wraps and buns, shaped to fool me. I loved their humour, and I knew it wasn't the nutrition team's fault we couldn't change; we had a plan that mitigated risk and we had to stick to it. It would have been unsafe to start trying new things that might not agree with my stomach. I knew this but it didn't make the repetitive routine any easier.

Phil had described the attempt as a "mental game of chess" in our pep talk and he was right, there were so many intricate pieces to play and every move had a consequence.

Jahna passed me the plastic wallet full of small envelopes from Clare. I had been opening them since Day One, and it seemed that every day, the note I picked directly connected to what I was going through. The one I opened today read, "Left leg... Right leg... Repeat!"

Back on the road, it was clearly Sunday. The empty streets of sleeping towns were organized into tidy rows of parked cars in designated bays, outside large, white houses with gable roofs. House. Car. House. Car. Left. Right. Left. Right. In the second 4 hours on the road, we left suburbia and entered fields of agriculture. I picked up the pace significantly and, head down, forcing the pedals along the flat, made good distance. To either side, perfectly aligned meadows of green crops, ploughed dirt and geometrically organized polytunnels flashed by. Germany was engineered, precise and consistent and our strategy continued, like clockwork, in the same way.

One of Jem's military posts had been in the region of Germany we were passing through. Two of his "mates from the Mob" came to meet us in a car park in Bielefeld, where we were eating lunch. By Day Seven, I was wearing arm warmers throughout the day and the morning and evening temperatures were dropping colder than I had expected. Maybe I'd mentioned it or maybe Jem just sensed that it was important but, without me knowing, he had asked his mates to bring a bag of extra base and thermal layers for me. It was a generous gesture and I thanked them, wishing there was something I could do for them in return. They stayed with us for the break and signed the witness book. As we chatted about the cycle from Portugal to Germany, a wild lady dressed in bright colours and floral patterns came over and preached the word of God. I didn't have the energy to deal with it, so I went inside the motorhome. I'm sure I heard her saying that Jem was the devil and the thought crossed my mind that maybe it could be true – the devil is in the detail after all. I was glad he was on my side.

The third block of cycling repeated the ones before with good speeds and good distance covered. The days began ticking away with precision – no diversity, no change, no choice. Identical timetabled duplication. One block ends and the next one begins. Copy. Paste. Left. Right. The monotony of the pursuit became tiresome. We'd always known that dealing with boredom was a prerequisite for success, that's why we had interventions in place. Still, I wished for variety – anything to break the repetition.

Our approach had factored in utilizing my different physical "gears" throughout the day, and the final 2 hours had always been dedicated to cooling down. Inevitably, delays I encountered every day meant that I'd still been pushing hard to make up time as I cycled into the night. As I set off for the evening block, under red and purple clouds, Jem went through the equipment checklist before telling me, "Remember, chill, tranquillo. Just 'av a nice steady one." It had been another productive day and achieving my best didn't mean I needed to hammer myself all the time, I could ease off. Like the "time out" that Phil had insisted on in preparation, I began to realize the importance of 2 recovery hours.

"I'll enjoy the sunset," I said and rode a steady pace, spinning my legs out for recovery and setting the next day up to be a strong one.

TWENTY-FOUR

DAY EIGHT – BE CAREFUL WHAT YOU WISH FOR

17 SEPTEMBER 2018
Distance: 354.2 km (220 miles)
Start: Peine, Germany
Finish: Diedersdorf, Germany
Weather: 26°C, sunny

The GPS beeped and I followed the instruction to turn onto a canal path. I didn't think to question it. I was in the routine, following the script and the route had been perfect for days. However, the narrow path quickly deteriorated into potholes and bricks coated in slimy mud, bottles and cans strewn all over. On one side of the trail was a large bank up to a housing estate and on the other, a drop into the canal. Suddenly I was on high alert. I manoeuvred the bike extra cautiously over the obstacles, taking care not to make any mistakes that would throw me into the water. Pssssssshhh. Suddenly every bump jolted through the bike. Only 35 minutes into the day, the rear tyre went flat in an instant. Though I'd been craving a deviation from the routine, this was not what I'd envisioned. *Be careful what you wish for.*

I pushed the bike to a bridge a few hundred metres up the trail and climbed up onto the road where I could assess the damage without getting covered in mud. The tyre looked like it had been sliced by a piece of glass. I was running tubeless tyres and couldn't fix it myself. I phoned Jem.

"Y'alreet, mucka G?" he asked.

"Nah mate, gotta puncture. Can you come and help me please?" I shared my live location on WhatsApp.

It couldn't have been worse timing. The team had made the decision to restock food supplies that morning and were in a supermarket half an hour away. If I was honest with myself, there was more than one option for me in this situation. I could have tried fitting the spare inner tube I was carrying. If that didn't work, I could have used the old mountain biking trick of filling the tyre with grass or I could have started walking. Yet, still suffering the fatigue that had led to napping yesterday, I discounted those options immediately. I waited at the roadside stretching and consuming as much as I could from my on-bike food store.

I'd sat at the roadside fixing punctures hundreds of times before while cycling around the world. It had been an excuse for a rest and a snack every time. It had also been a time to meet people; a sweaty foreigner with a bike in pieces was a magnet for attention. I'd been surrounded by laughing children playing in the sun and had been invited into family homes to escape the rain. No matter where it happened, people always appeared out of nowhere. I daydreamed about those previous adventures; now into the second week of ultra-endurance routines, I missed those carefree days.

Dust kicked up into the air as the motorhome pulled up on the roadside in front of me. Jem jumped out and fitted the spare wheel, while Jahna put fresh bottles on the bike and filled my pockets with snacks. Pit stop complete, I was good to go in seconds. That puncture was the only mechanical problem that cost us significant time during the attempt and, even at that, I was moving again 40 minutes after it happened.

An amended route delivered me back into industrial Germany at the Wolfsburg Volkswagen factory; an enormous square box with four tall, narrow chimneys and a big VW logo on the side. If a child was asked to draw a factory, it would look just like this. I imagined lumps of metal delivered into one end and cookie-cutter cars rolling out the other. If the scene was drawn in crayon, I would swear I was in a kids' cartoon. Maybe the roadside rest was what I needed – my brain was again painting abstract narratives with an upbeat spin. I was physically refreshed too. In the face of losing valuable time that morning, I picked up speed, rocketing through the urban sprawl surrounding the colossal manufacturing plant. In the first block of the day I'd still managed to cycle 90 km (56 miles), I couldn't be too disappointed with that.

At lunchtime, as I chatted to Kerr, I was in good spirits. From the physio table, I talked positively about the day. I was glad that we'd passed through the busy west German towns on Sunday – they would have been horrible with today's heavy traffic, and cycling through east Germany was a pleasure. We had left the industrial plants and riding through woodland reminded me of being at home in Derbyshire, my adventures with friends after school and my last wild camp of cycling the world. The sun was out and the roads were cast in dappled light through the canopy of trees. The tailwind that I'd struggled to catch yesterday was filling my sails.

The natural landscape continued through the afternoon. Heading towards Berlin, I expected Germany to become increasingly populated, but approaching the capital, I spent a lot of time in nature. Across the low-lying flatlands, I passed through wind farms, where turbines slowly spun above me as evidence of my gentle tailwind, before the rolling pastures were exchanged for densely wooded nature reserves. Minor roads were buckled and fractured under trees and my game of constantly dodging ruts and potholes reminded me of England. I resorted to cycling the smoothest patch I could find, down the middle of the road. Still in dense forest, I came within 10 km (6 miles) of

Berlin without even knowing, and continued cycling east towards the end of the day.

Checking my messages in the tent that night, I read a supportive text from Mark Beaumont: "Looking good out there. Keep it up." Through all the psychological struggles I'd experienced, one of the most difficult was the thought that *nobody knows what I'm going through, nobody knows what it's like for me.* Although this day had been easily broken down by the puncture and changes in landscape, 14 hours on a bike can be a very lonely place.

Mark's message reminded me that I was not alone – others had gone through this before. A short note from someone who understood became a big message of hope.

TWENTY-FIVE

DAY NINE – PERSPECTIVE

18 SEPTEMBER 2018
Distance: 395.1 km (245.5 miles)
Start: Diedersdorf, Germany
Finish: Gostynin, Poland
Weather: 26°C, sunny

Riding east, I had the privilege of cycling towards the sunrise every morning and the ninth one was beautiful. Wheels started rolling at 6.02 a.m. local time with only 25 km remaining on German roads before I crossed the border. When the sun rose over the horizon at 6.45 a.m., it painted a golden sky over the River Oder as I cycled across the bridge into Poland. The new country seemed much more agricultural than the Germany I had cycled through the day before; smoky farmyard landscapes encroached on the potholed roads that I shared with antiquated trucks, under dishevelled trees. Countries don't usually transform instantly at borders, they slowly transition in landscapes, peoples and customs but on this occasion it was as though the backdrop had been changed between scenes while the curtains were closed overnight.

Over the previous few days, in an effort to stay focused on the bike, I'd switched from the "easy listening" to the "pick me up" playlist. Pressing play, I'd hoped to hear house, electro or rock; music that connected me to times in my life, experiences and people. The soundtrack that Kerr had created for me filled my ears with heavy metal and rap. What uplifting meant to me, I realized, was different to what it meant to somebody else. From then on, whenever I had time, I connected to the internet to download tracks with personal resonance.

At 10 a.m., after 4 hours in the saddle, a brief radio interview was scheduled. I pulled into a filling station forecourt, where the team were already set up, and sat on the physio table for a phone call with the BBC. "So, how far have you cycled to date?" asked the presenter. I had no idea. I told him about the way I broke the challenge into small, more manageable chunks. I generally looked at the distance I covered each day and judged it against my target, but I hadn't measured the combined total distance. In the 4-hour block of cycling that had just passed, my total distance would have ticked over the 2,000-mile mark. I was over halfway, not that I had any knowledge of it.

Everyone saw a different view of what was unfolding on the road. Listeners of that interview would have heard a cyclist conversing at ease about a project that was going well. Friends and family saw my animated icon racing across the map of Europe at a blistering pace. The science team in Derby saw a project that was on target to hit their best-case scenario. Those watching our social media saw short montages of quotes and camera shots, carefully edited to represent the best of that 24 hours on the road.

Personally, I had to look at what I was doing, moment to moment. My focus couldn't be on the bigger picture – that was too big. One hundred miles is a long way to cycle, and knowing that you must do that 40 times to get to the end is too much. I could interpret information like being halfway positively or negatively depending on my state of mind at the time. On Day Nine, I could see it as a blessing – *great, only the same to go again* – or a curse – *I have to endure another nine days of this*. We had a lot of plans to keep me upbeat in the moment; I played my music playlists, tried to find the positives in each situation and tried to stay in the moment by enjoying what I was doing and where I was cycling.

I jumped off the physio couch and opened the day's envelope from Clare. The note read, "If you're going through hell, keep going – Winston Churchill." I spent the day on narrow, busy roads, flanked by trees spaced 10 or 20 m apart, occasionally punctuated with wonky advertisement boards for agricultural supplies. On a ride that headed due east for the whole day, the sun rose in front of me, hung overhead and sank down behind me, the fields and other cyclists I passed on the road. Throughout the day, I overtook old men in trousers and shirts, on their sit-up-

and-beg commuter bikes between the fields of dried mud. It wasn't long ago when I had ridden a touring bike, wearing second-hand clothes from the people I'd met on the road, meandering around the world in the pursuit of happiness. Now I wore expensive Lycra and pedalled an aerodynamic bike, racing to the finish line as quickly as possible. I looked at the old men, cycling as if they had all the time in the world, absorbing their surroundings. In return, they looked at me as if to ask, "Where on earth are you going in such a rush?" My own perspectives on what cycling could mean had changed. There was ample space for both worlds, and everything in between.

After the final break, the sun went down and the road became a poor concrete surface that tyres rumbled over with a jarring bump where sections didn't align correctly. Mounds of dusty earth were piled at the roadside with steel rods and construction equipment. The road led away from heavy traffic and it seemed only me and the team were heading out on a road leading nowhere. At that time, all that existed of the world was present in the beam of the headlights, cast in monochrome shades of black and white.

Suddenly, the patch of light disappeared to black. I swerved left, taking a bumpy, rutted path down a steep embankment, struggling to hold on to the bike. I skidded to a standstill in the bottom of a ditch and looked back. A bridge was missing. The road stopped and became a 3-metre drop into a dry riverbed. I looked up from my uncomfortable resting place. Jem cast long, sci-fi shadows in the motorhome lights that cut through the dust-filled air. He stood looking over the drop and the narrow, mud track diversion. The motorhome wouldn't make it – they would have to backtrack and find another way to meet me. I carried the bike across the riverbed and resumed pedalling, hoping another hole didn't appear and swallow me into darkness.

As I rode alone, a car approached from behind, slowed down and drove beside me. The driver wound down the window and shouted to me from his beaten-up Lada. I shouted back that I didn't understand, I was English. In broken English, he asked if I wanted to stay at his house. From his point of view, I was a cyclist in the countryside, on a broken road in the dark, and he was kind enough to offer support. He could never have known that I was attempting a world record and that there was a support team waiting for me ahead. As the chancer that cycled around the world, I would have said yes and another adventure would have unfolded. As it was, I tried to explain why I had to decline his offer. I doubt the driver understood my reason but upon my refusal, he drove away.

I carried on, cycling into the small circle of light that was all I could see ahead of me, oblivious to everything else blanketed in darkness.

TWENTY-SIX

DAY TEN – THE FALL

---

19 SEPTEMBER 2018
Distance: 411.3 km (255.6 miles)
Start: Gostynin, Poland
Finish: Gervenai, Lithuania
Weather: 26°C, sunny

Tiredness was getting the better of me. Running the entire project on British Summer Time, as we moved east the sun came up almost 15 minutes earlier every day. Over one or two days the small time difference was unnoticeable, but after ten days the sunrise was a full 2 hours earlier because of the vast distance we'd covered. In my fatigued state of mind, it confused me. I left the motorhome at 6.05 a.m. local time, certain I'd woken up too late because the sky was already light. In a perplexed daze, I lumbered into a road already busy with commuters. Still waking up, I rubbed my eyes and looked at my surroundings. Not a cloud in the sky. The scruffy Poland of the previous day seemed to have had a shave and a haircut.

It was a perfect day for cycling. There was a consistent tailwind and, on the flat roads of Poland, it was a great opportunity to bank some long distances. However, tiredness followed me through the morning. I struggled to concentrate, repeatedly dropped drinks bottles that Jahna passed me from the roadside and found it difficult to motivate myself. *I'm too tired for this*. Mornings had been physically and mentally difficult for a few days. I was perceiving a much higher exertion than I should for the power I was outputting and I was drowsy, my eyes wanting to close while riding. *I need to rest*. I motivated myself with the incentive that on the second break I would take a power nap – a strategy that had worked for me over the previous three days. After 4 hours of lacklustre cycling, the tailwind helped me cover an impressive 114 km (71 miles). I met the team at the side of the road and they rolled out the break time routine with precision, as always.

I knew I could do better in the second block, so I went out onto the road with the attitude to push on a bit harder. Still weary, it was hard to motivate myself. My speeds were still great and, with the tailwind still pushing me along, I could get away with doing so little. Feeling the fatigue in my legs whenever I pushed harder, my mind referred to the negative monologue that it was too easy to slip into. *I can't do it*. With a daily total of 8 hours on the road and another 118 km (73 miles) on the clock, I cycled towards the end of block two thinking of nothing but getting on the bed in the motorhome.

Speeding down a descent, I saw the team standing on the opposite side of the carriageway with the motorhome tucked around a corner, already set up and ready for me. I aimed towards them and leaned into the 90-degree bend without thinking. The front wheel twitched on a patch of gravel. *Take off.* Time. Slowed. Down.

From the saddle, the road had been a smooth black ribbon, seamlessly transporting me across the remorseless contours of nature. Always my friend, no matter where I was in the world, the highway was with me, guiding my future, leaving my past behind me. It was easy to forget that the road was unforgiving; solid rock, smashed into fragments and glued together to form the hardened surface that tyres hum over. Easy to forget, that is, until I was hurtling towards it.

My body slammed hard onto the asphalt. Stones ricocheted across dusty potholes as the bike clattered to a standstill. Ten days and 8 hours into the record attempt, I lay on the road, broken and defeated, with one thought repeating in my mind – *No more, just no more, I've got no more.*

I caught sight of Kerr running over to me, video camera in hand. *A bike crash is just the kind of jeopardy he'd love for his documentary, I have to get up before he makes it to me and starts asking questions.* But I was too slow. By the time I was sitting up, his hand was held out above me. I grabbed it and got to my feet, turning without considering thanking him. I just wanted to get in the motorhome for the rest I'd been looking forward to all morning. I was half in the door when Jahna shouted over to me, "What are you doing?"

"I just need to sleep," I replied.

"Not like that! Look at the state of you." I hadn't thought to examine myself until that point. I looked down to see the blood running down my leg, the bruising swelling up and my torn clothes. Downhearted, I realized that falling off had just exchanged the 30 minutes of sleep I wanted for 30 minutes of suffering on the physio table.

I pulled myself onto the table, set up like it was on every break with a selection of foods and drinks to consume while Jahna made sure I was in optimal physical condition. This time, she wasn't giving a sports massage. After putting a Tupperware box of pasta in my hands, she went to work cleaning the grit out of my cuts and disinfecting the grazes, while I ate in silence.

Why on earth have I put myself in this situation?

I was so disappointed with myself. I didn't know what I was doing or thinking at the time I fell. I'd seen the team waving me in from the road – or could they have been warning me to slow down? *I wasn't paying attention, what an idiot.*

I started to doubt myself, wondering who I thought I was to put myself out here. I was a "normal" person; had all those travels led me to believe I was someone special who could take on world records? *So stupid*. I was taking on established adventurers and athletes, I was out of my depth. As my internal thoughts spun out of control, every touch of antiseptic on my wounds stung and every mouthful of lunch was difficult to eat. I didn't speak to the team about anything while I ate – I just sat there deep in thought and self-pity.

Jahna fixed up my wounds and reassured me that the injuries were just superficial. I pushed myself from the physio couch and back to my feet. My body was good to go but, as Mark had told me the first time we'd met, "You could be the fastest cyclist in the world but it means nothing unless you've got a mind that's strong enough to get you to the finish line."

My 30-minute break was over and the relentless strategy continued. Jem patted the pockets on the back of my jersey to make sure I had everything I needed before saying his usual line, "Ready to roll out?" I wasn't ready to roll out, I was ready to roll into bed – but that wasn't an option until the end of the day now.

"Just get on that wind, mate, just tap it out and you'll be alreet," Jem encouraged. He must have been able to see how tired I was, he'd have known I'd be tempted to stop. As soon as I pushed the pedals, the pain of my clothing catching on the cuts startled me. Pressure pulsed through the swelling bruises as blood returned to my legs and I was frustrated by the discomfort of first-aid dressings.

"Smile, yeah?" Jem shouted as I slowly rolled away from the motorhome. "Smile…" I turned back and grimaced a fake smile at him. "Good lad!" he praised.

I cycled away from the team into the loneliness of repeating negative thoughts. *Look at the state of your riding – terrible. You are your own worst nightmare. You can't keep going like this, you're going to crash again and get yourself killed.* Thoughts of pushing on for a productive afternoon were gone. Uncomfortable on the bike, I pedalled gently, just hoping to not injure myself again. My average speed was 2 kph down on the morning.

After 25 minutes alone on the road, the team caught up with me. When they pulled alongside, I looked around, pre-empting a shout for me to "pick it up" or "get on with it", the kind of thoughts that my own monologue repeated. But when my eyes adjusted from the bright daylight to the dark of the cabin, I saw Jem. His words resonated deeply on a personal level.

"Eh mucka! What's the view like from the balcony?" he shouted.

"You bastard," I shouted back, nodding as a smile grew across my face.

Jem knew exactly what he'd said and why he'd said it – they were Phil's words. At the end of the record, when I looked back on what I achieved, the only person I would have to justify my finishing time to was myself. If I stopped, quit or slowed down – if I did anything other than my best – I was the only person who had to live with the consequences. All of my challenges would be over by then, my negative feelings would be a memory, and I wouldn't want to regret my actions.

I decided to empty the tank, go full gas – half motivated to define myself, half motivated to ruin everything and drive myself into the ground. *Screw it, let's go.* I ate a whole bag of Haribo. Plugged in my headphones. Turned the volume up to max. And I hit play on *my* pumped-up playlist. Da – da da da – da da da – da da daaaaaaaaaaa. Cymbals. Guitar. Piano. Bass. The opening riff from "Eye of the Tiger" punched my eardrums. I stamped on the pedals and sprinted past the support team with my finger up at Jem, laughing.

"Yeah, come on!" he shouted out of the window, banging his hand on the outside of his door.

I had needed to hit rock bottom, this time literally, to find out what I was capable of. I hadn't seen my heart rate above 120 bpm for days; suddenly it was 160. *Bring it on!* I had more in the tank than I'd been telling myself. Twenty minutes later, tucked down in the aero position, I was still pushing. *I've bloody well got this,* I roared as I bared my teeth. My legs burned, my lungs gasped and my brain told me *no more* but I didn't listen. The beautiful churches in the colourful small towns went unnoticed, blurring into the background of a man on a mission.

In the 3 hours and 36 minutes I had left of that block, I covered 120 km (75 miles). Eighty km (50 miles) of that, I cycled at an incredible 38 kph (23.6 mph). On Day Ten of the attempt, when I was exhausted, when I hurt, and when I wanted to give up, I put in the fastest block of the whole world record.

We rushed through the last break of the day, still on a high. I was back in the game. "Remember, do not switch off until the border, go go go! Get on iiiiit!" Jem shouted as I got on the bike and rode into the night. I rocketed through a world that became streaks of white and red lights on black backgrounds. An hour later I pedalled up to the motorhome, parked at the side of the road, hazard lights flashing. In front of it was a blue road sign with a circle of yellow stars on it.

"Oh yeah we did!" I shouted over the rattle of the diesel engine.

"Go on son!" laughed Jem.

The sign read "Lietuvos Respublika". We'd picked up the pace at the right time and we were on track in Lithuania.

TWENTY-SEVEN

DAY ELEVEN – EMPTY WETSUIT

20 SEPTEMBER 2018
Distance: 457.8 km (284 miles)
Start: Gervenai, Lithuania
Finish: Burachki, Russia
Weather: 25°C, sunny

Momentous Day 11. We had to cross Lithuania and Latvia, exchange motorhomes and cross the Russian border. Hitting strategic milestones was the reason picking up my game yesterday had been so important – everything had to work like clockwork today. We started 278 km (173 miles) from the border with Latvia, where the motorhome would be swapped. It was then another 178 km (111 miles) to Russia. Eleven days into the attempt, it was a big ask of every member of the team and sponsors. On a day like this, it all comes down to your preparations. Collective deep breath.

Day Ten's heroic effort to get me out of a psychological slump and performing at my best continued into the morning. I set off in a fresh 7°C with the sun already up in front of me, lifting the low-lying fog that hovered over fields on either side of the major road. Jem had written new motivational quotes for me and stuck them on the aero extensions. On the left, in capital letters the word "RUSSIA" and an arrow pointing straight ahead. On the right, "FUCK YEAH!" The team was pumped and I felt good. This was the day when it was all going to happen. I danced on the pedals up climbs and glided down descents in harmony with the landscapes. It was one of those mornings when riding a bike is poetry.

I sped through small dusty hamlets of large wooden farmhouses, where fruits and vegetables grew in front gardens and open barn doors hung from their hinges, revealing pitchforks, horse-drawn ploughs and traditional farming tools. North from the village of Butrimonys, the roads suddenly deteriorated to corrugated gravel and I stopped at the roadside, where Jem pulled up beside me.

"Really?" I asked, looking at the sandpit ahead.

"You've got two options," he replied, "ten kilometres like this, or a detour that adds about a hundred. Your choice."

The road ahead looked horrendous but it was a better option than adding 100 km (62 miles) to an already long day. *Screw it. I can't control what lies ahead, only my reaction to it.* Jem dropped the pressure in my tyres, I changed down into a small gear and spun the pedals. The aggressive corrugation jolted the highly tuned bike around like a fairground bucking bronco as the alternate ridges and grooves picked up the front and rear wheels out of time with each other. Standing on the pedals, more like a mountain biker than a roadie, I cycled the best line I could find to avoid deep sections of sand. The front wheel slid when I turned, the rear wheel spun when I put the power down. Every few hundred metres, when the bike sank into a patch of sand, I was on my feet, finding a firm patch to start cycling on and going through the whole thing again. It took just under 40 minutes to cover the 10-km (6-mile) off-road stretch, averaging an agricultural 15.4 kph (9.6 mph). The previous 10 km had taken 20 minutes. I cursed every metre of that gravel track and Jem knew it.

I got to the tarmac road at the end, where he waited with a track-pump beside the motorhome.

"That wasn't so bad, was it? I told you *you* could do it," he mocked.

I looked at him in silence, my legs and bike covered in white dust. I clipped in, changed up into a big gear and accelerated down the perfect road I'd rejoined.

"This is better," I shouted back and pushed on towards our important milestones.

In the first block of cycling, I covered 95 km (59 miles). At a crossroads, surrounded by lakes in the wilderness of Lithuania, we rattled through the break and on with the second block. We threaded through Neries Regioninis Parkas, a huge forest to the north-west of Vilnius, the capital, before turning and heading due north to skirt Labanoras, another regional park. After 8 hours on the bike, we had 214 km (133 miles) in the bank. Jem organized the upcoming logistics while Kerr and Jahna worked through the break routine in a bus stop on the major road to Utena, the next city.

The Russian motorhome was at the border of Lithuania and Latvia. Jon, the owner of ACE Sameday Couriers, was waiting for us. As I set off on the third block, the team would drive 60 km (40 miles) ahead to rendezvous with Jon and transfer everything we needed into the Russian vehicle for the final leg of the challenge. It was a time-sensitive operation, and everything needed to run to plan.

After 2 hours alone on the road, the two vehicles came into view as arranged, in a layby opposite a large lake. Frantic activity surrounded the vehicles, with their doors and windows open, the team running back and forth with boxes and equipment scattered on the road all around. Every cupboard was emptied, every list double-checked, equipment and food boxed and referenced. Jon's plan had become reality and every aspect of preparation, from science to logistics to sponsorship, worked together to make the most difficult task appear effortless. I turned off the road, where Jon and his wife Marina were waiting for me at the roadside.

"Hello, mate! You don't look like you've been on the bike five minutes, let alone across a continent!" Jon exclaimed.

I looked down at my leathery skin, crisp tan lines and the cuts down my dusty legs, wondering if he was being serious or sarcastic. "It's so good to see you, Jon! Thanks so much for this," I replied.

"You wouldn't believe the adventure we've been on to get here," he continued.

Jem looked over at me, arms fully loaded with boxes, gesturing with his head for me to get back on the road. It didn't stop Jon.

"Well, we arrived at the hotel, if you can call it a hotel – ah, you don't need to know about that. The rental place, though, it's in the basement of this enormous building! We were wandering around for ages trying to find the office. So, I show this guy our booking and he points us the way down this long, dark corridor. We get to the end and there are security guards. With Kalashnikov AK-47s! Well, I wasn't going to turn back…"

Jem had packed the boxes by this point and stood, looking at me, pointing at his watch and the road.

"I've got to get going, mate," I told Jon.

"Of course you have, you're breaking a world record, aren't you? But before you go, I better tell you about customs. Marina wanted to bring a couple of cartons of fags back to England with her, well, they've got limits on that kinda thing haven't they, so we had to share them between our allowances. Make sure you separate out the cigarettes and alcohol…"

I put fresh bottles on the bike as Jon was talking and set off.

"Thanks Jon, I've gotta go. You're a legend Jon! Thanks again. See you on the other side!"

The vehicle swap was slick. We were now reduced to basics; anything that we took from this point, including the bike, had to be taken home as luggage on the plane or thrown away in Ufa. Basic tools, a pump and nutrition supplements were kept, together with a stockpile of foods the team had been topping up across Western Europe, mitigating any potential risk of unreliable sources in Russia. Ruth's physio couch, the generator, my tent, camping gear and everything else that could be spared, including the fags and alcohol, were going back to the UK in Jerry's motorhome with Jon and Marina.

At the end of the third block, the major logistical challenge of the project was complete. The team caught up with me and there was a positive buzz in the air; they loved the new vehicle. It was newer than Jerry's, the layout was more spacious and the modern facilities enabled them to do more. I hadn't considered that a working space would lift team spirits so much. It helped me, too – there was a sleeping area that was isolated enough for me to get better sleep in the motorhome rather than sleeping in the tent.

In the lounge area of the vehicle, the team and I chatted about the last block of the day. The scientists had been analyzing the data and the challenges that lay ahead. We needed to pull an exceptional day out of the bag. It was going to be tough. The final 2-hour block of the day needed to be extended so we could cross the Russian border in the middle of the night. If we left it until the busy hours of the following day, it could potentially take 8 hours to clear immigration. It was already 6.35 p.m. by my body clock, and having crossed another time zone it was now 8.35 p.m. local time. We were still 140 km (90 miles) away. It was going to be a testing night.

Jem and I made the video evidence just outside the city of Daugavpils, Latvia, and I set off into the night. The far reaches of eastern Europe felt empty – not the wonderful emptiness of Portugal on that first morning, but an unwelcoming emptiness. I didn't see another town all night, I rarely even saw a streetlight. On their highest output, my lights ate through batteries on the roads that were free of traffic, undulating through woodland and around a national park. On the map it appeared to be a beautiful area, dotted with lakes, but sightseeing wasn't going to happen tonight. The ethereal air changed as I cycled through it, pockets of warmth then cold, clarity then mist. The environment had an eeriness that had me constantly wondering what might be watching me from the darkness of the trees, I never felt comfortable as I cycled towards the Russian border.

Following the arrow that Jem had drawn on the aerobar, I pressed on into the longest day. I was cycling beyond my own expectations and for 90 minutes I averaged 31 kph

(19.3 mph) – outstanding after 12 hours on the bike on the eleventh day of cycling. However, at 10 p.m. it was as though every system in my body began to shut down. As it had been in my first training session in the HPU, no matter how hard I wanted to push, my legs were like jelly. My shoulders slumped and my gaze drifted down towards my front wheel. I struggled to cycle, I struggled just lifting my head. The last 70 km (43 miles) of the day were torture, infinite pedalling in an empty world. My average speed dropped dramatically and there was nothing I could do about it. I kept checking the GPS, believing I must have been going uphill, but it continued to read low speeds on the flat. The road widened to become a dual carriageway as I approached the border, and even the short distances between the posts of the Armco barrier started to take a lifetime to traverse. The incessant final block of the day lasted almost 6 hours.

At 2.30 a.m. local time, I cycled up to the window of a small hut under saturated, bright yellow lighting and showed my passport. Not a word was said by the stern-faced Latvian policewoman and a barrier lifted. I went under, stopped, and watched the team follow me through. So far, so good. We passed another control gate and approached the looming blue signs and floodlights of Terehova border control. Beneath a long, corrugated metal roof, lanes split to take drivers either side of immigration officers in kiosks. Cars and trucks were backed up in queues hundreds of metres long, the drivers asleep in their seats, faces melting down the inside of their windows. It looked as though we would be waiting all night. I should have been filled with nerves – this moment could set back the record by hours – but all I felt was exhausted.

A woman in a hi-viz vest walked with conviction towards the motorhome, shouting at us in Russian.

"English?" I shouted back.

"But... Russian vehicle, yes?"

I explained what we were doing as best I could in simple English before Jem showed her a paragraph about the attempt that he'd Google-translated. She ushered us to an empty lane. I leaned the bike between the kiosk and the motorhome as the border officer took her seat at the desk and began looking over our passports.

"Leigh Timmis?"

"Yeah."

"Jahna Drunis?"

"That's me."

"Anthony Jemmett?"

"Howay!"

"Kerr Mechanical?"

"Hahahaha!" Jem laughed a huge belly laugh. "Mechanical! Mechanical? There's nothing mechanical about him, hahaha!"

"McNicoll," Kerr answered.

The border official's mistake had Jem in stitches. Our

passports were stamped and the motorhome was searched. We were through customs in 45 minutes.

I got off the bike next to the motorhome, parked between rows of articulated trucks on the Russian side of border control. Wow. Achieving every single part of the day, with the fatigue we were all feeling was something very special. We'd nailed it. Day 11 had been epic; 458 km (285 miles) cycled in 17 hours, two more countries off the list, and in swapping the motorhome and clearing Russian border control, we'd completed the two most difficult logistical challenges of the whole attempt. All the effort through preparation, the dedication of ACE and the communications of the road and science teams had paid off.

"How's that, man? What a day!" Jem bellowed. "Look at the state of you, total threaders! You're an empty wetsuit, man!"

I looked up and gave him an exhausted smile.

TWENTY-EIGHT

DAY TWELVE – IT'S OK NOT TO BE OK

21 SEPTEMBER 2018
Distance: 281 km (174 miles)
Start: Burachki, Russia
Finish: Nelidovo, Russia
Weather: 25°C, sunny

Every one of us was exhausted after yesterday's efforts but morale was high in the motorhome. From here, it was a straight shot to the finish line. Jahna stood in front of the hob, cooking oats and heating coffee, Jem made sure the bike was ready for another day, Kerr checked his camera batteries had enough charge. I sat at the table, spooning as much breakfast into my mouth as possible, considering the day ahead and where I had got to.

Throughout training, I'd been watching my own data and knew that, physically, I was capable of cycling across Europe in 14 days. Although the team and I had put together a best-case target of 16 days, which accommodated for traffic and delays, I secretly had a great surprise planned. I was going to pull the extraordinary out of the bag and become the first man to cycle across the continent in under two weeks. I'd imagined the larger-than-life media headlines and the praise that would surround such an astonishing feat. It would be like Mark Beaumont's *Around the World in 80 Days.*

How incredible that would be! How incredible I would be! But as I sat there eating breakfast, that dream came crashing down around me. I had seen myself missing the daily target required for 14 days almost every day through Europe but I didn't let myself believe it, I couldn't let go of those delusions. Russia was the tenth country out of ten and, in my mixed-up head, I was in the last 10 per cent of the record. That morning, I realized how far I still had to go to the finish line and I was faced with the undeniable fact that Russia is very big. I still had 25 per cent of the challenge to go. I was consumed by the knowledge that today was a short 10 hours on the bike. I needed a long day. *Those last slow hours yesterday were a waste.* It was a massive blow to my motivation.

I stepped out of the vehicle and Jem recorded our evidence video as I took hold of the bike. Before I made a start to the day's cycling, I muttered the only thing I'd say to the team that morning. "I'm never going to do anything that impresses me."

The long shadows of tall pine trees cut the mist that hung over the highway. The wilderness I cycled through was so dense, I wondered whether I would ever be seen again if I walked just 100 m away from the road. *I could lose myself forever, truly into the wild.* I was emotionally fragile, at breaking point. It was the fourth hour of the White Wall Test all over again. Every contact point hurt. My shorts were uncomfortable after 12 days of only being rinsed in the motorhome shower. Comparisons drove me crazy. *What will people think of me? I can do better. Other cyclists can do better than this. I'm not good enough.* Every regret from the previous days' mistakes replayed in my mind.

I cycled the tightrope of tarmac, between the white line at the edge of the traffic and the metal roadside barrier; between who I was and who I wanted to be. Physically and mentally, I'd been broken down as far as possible. The challenges I'd faced over the previous 11 days had stripped away all layers of Phil's psychological onion, beyond my *why*, beyond where the world record attempt should have taken me. With infinite time and space for thought, the last sentence I'd said to the team kept spinning through my mind. I couldn't shake it. *I'm never going to do anything that impresses me.*

After an hour on the road, I stopped pedalling, got off the bike and removed my helmet and gloves. I flagged down the support team, asked them to turn off the engine and get out of the vehicle. I told Kerr to bring his camera – I had something to tell them.

"I'm not filming anything until I know what you're saying," he replied. From the look in their eyes and the way they turned to each other, I'm certain they thought I was finished, the record attempt was over. The four of us stood at the roadside, in the shade of the motorhome, as trucks sped towards Moscow behind us.

"I've been thinking about what I said this morning and it's not about the record attempt, it's about my whole life. For as long as I know, I've been living up to something, trying to impress myself or somebody else and I just don't know why. I'm tired of it. I'm so tired of it. We're never going to get the chance to do this again and I just want to enjoy it." Tears welled in my eyes. "I want to stop all the psychology and be surrounded with jokes and laughter. I want to tear down the motivational quotes. I want this to be a party bus and to play loud music and to have fun all the way across Russia. I don't want to be a lab rat anymore; I want to stop being analyzed. I want to be human." I concluded with a lump in my throat. It struck me that all I actually wanted was to be seen for me, as a human being, and to be accepted.

I hugged Jem, then Jahna, then Kerr and got back on the bike. It was the first time I acknowledged what was *really* important in my life. I knew the team were touched by the moment – Jahna had tears in her eyes and Jem's hug was caring rather than his usual motivational pat on the back. Although we could have taken time to change things there and then, to spend some time as friends, we all knew I had to ride on. I'd set myself this challenge and the strategy couldn't stop – I knew it and so did the team.

On the break that followed, Jem handed me a bottle of alcohol-free beer that the team had bought for me in Germany.

"We were saving this for a special occasion but we thought it might cheer you up," he said. I sat on the step of the motorhome, drinking it with a childlike smile, so emotionally drained I felt drunk. I checked inside the motorhome; the team had kept the motivational quotes on the walls. Psychological analysis was still conducted at every break, and we continued to implement our tactics on the road. For the first time, I couldn't bring myself to answer Phil's psychological analysis. Jem later told me that when Phil asked what my mood profile looked like from that morning, he'd said, "Leigh's not in the mood to tell us about his mood."

The camera rolled as Kerr asked me about the success of yesterday. Nothing was mentioned about the morning. It was as though the team knew an emotional moment had been coming. I had no doubt that Phil had been prompting them from the other end of the phone. I opened another random envelope from Clare, ate the chocolate and read her note, "It's OK not to be OK."

Although the team had my back in that moment, it didn't change the long game. We had to keep moving, we still had a challenge to complete. We had a strategy for success and we stuck to it. I had set this challenge for myself and when the team told me to continue, they were only telling me my own words. The perfect athlete is a robot, programmed to perform at its limit. But behind every athlete is a human.

Back in England, it was Mark's wedding day. On the third break I chatted to Phil on the phone and asked him to pass on my congratulations. When asked, I told him about my emotional crash at the realization that I wouldn't hit my aim of 14 days. He reminded me that we were still on track to hit our best-case result. It was true and I wanted to recalibrate my mind to believe his words, but it was hard to do. An element of doubt remained as to whether I was good enough. Still, I covered that up and our banter continued about the wedding.

I was now on the extreme rollercoaster. One minute I hated everything I was doing, the next I loved it. One minute I struggled, the next I was performing well. One minute I was robotic, the next I was emotional. Up then down, that's how the day became. At times I must have seemed out of control, on the edge, emotionally unstable. Sometimes, as Jem read out the emotions on Phil's psychology questionnaire, he would pause or look at Jahna in a way that suggested I was answering in complete contradiction to the way I'd behaved only minutes before. He would be right to think that – I was all over the place.

Limits are subjective. I'd seen the same 100 times before on the Cycle Mickleover club ride. Riders push themselves, it hurts, they swear, they want to give up, but they push on and at the end they wonder if they could have just gone that little bit harder. I had stretched my capacity over the course of a year, through physical and psychological training, so that it took back-to-back 250-mile days of cycling to reach my limit, but I was now finding it.

It never gets easier, you just get faster.

TWENTY-NINE

DAY THIRTEEN –
A SLICE OF SWISS CHEESE

22 SEPTEMBER 2018
Distance: 359.4 km (223.3 miles)
Start: Nelidovo, Russia
Finish: Reutov, Russia
Weather: 25°C, sunny

In bike racing, number 13 is always pinned to the jersey upside down to combat the number's unlucky traditional curse. Today, Day 13 on the road, we needed all the luck we could find. Every number 13 around the motorhome was turned, or written, upside down. I'd come through the toughest days of the attempt, but I'd gained something from it – three people who I knew were there for me as both my team and as friends. We chatted over breakfast before I took to the saddle. I was far from fresh and my body felt heavy but psychologically I was in a more positive place today.

"Righto buddy, Moscow here we come!" Jem enthused as I stepped out of the motorhome into a layby on the edge of a major road in an uninhabited world. Still surrounded by the wilderness that hadn't changed in a whole day's cycling, it seemed outrageous that I was only 200 km (124 miles) from a megacity, home to over 16 million people.

It was the most dangerous day of the world record attempt; the day we planned to traverse Moscow. The capital of Russia is the most congested city in the world, a vortex of four- and five-lane motorways that swirl around the metropolis, and I would have to cross it without the team. To drive the motorhome from A to B in a similar time to the bike, the only option was for them to circumnavigate the city, while I headed straight through the centre. This would have been a big risk on any normal day but, to make things worse, I was again struggling with incredible tiredness.

When I'm in love with cycling, I make it look effortless and light; I bunny-hop over potholes, track stand at traffic lights and choose the racing line through fast turns. When the fun is gone, I look heavy. On this day, I cycled like a sack of potatoes. No matter what we tried, I could not shake a deep fatigue. My legs felt hollow. That dream of cycling across Europe in 14 days was completely off the cards now, I'd have to cycle an impossible 848 km (527 miles) a day to achieve it. Having let go of that target, I struggled to find the motivation to squeeze out the extra effort, to sit with the discomfort that makes the difference of a couple of miles per hour. When the roads were empty, the team drove past, Jahna holding her Bluetooth speaker out the window and the whole team dancing to our "No Brainer" soundtrack at full volume. I laughed with them but was soon alone again and the tiredness returned.

Through the first block of cycling, the team tried everything – energy drinks, water, food, power naps and caffeine pills – but in 4 hours I only managed to ride 87 km (54 miles). On the break when I spoke to Kerr, I was vacant. Unshaven for two weeks, with glazed eyes barely open, I talked about my single focus of simply needing to get through Moscow.

"And in between now and then it's just…?" Kerr asked.

"Get to Moscow, just get through it," I exhaled, unable to look him in the eye.

Back home, friends and family who saw the social media video from the day could tell I was in a bad place.

Jahna held a mobile phone towards me. "It's Phil, he wants to speak to you," she said.

"I'll only speak to him if he's got a solution to this," I replied. I wanted a quick fix, to become fresh, to feel energized and motivated. I wanted someone to wash this cloudiness from my brain and to fit me a new pair of legs. I knew that Phil would want me to think back over work that we'd done in training and I didn't have that mental energy to spare. I was frustrated, feeling that everyone had a demand but nobody had an answer. The phone remained in Jahna's hand as I turned away and got back on the bike.

Jem shouted his encouragement at me as I returned to the road, "Go kill it, go kill iiiiit!" I went back out and gave it my best shot but the same story repeated; I just couldn't energize myself. I cycled tragically slow. In my deteriorating state, Jem was unwilling to let me cycle headlong into Moscow's traffic and was concerned whether we would even make it across the metropolis that day.

At the end of the second block, 110 km (68 miles) from the edge of Moscow, I cycled towards the motorhome for what seemed an eternity – in view but never getting closer. In the endless wilderness, the characterless filling stations in their blankets of diesel fumes were my only connection with Russian civilization. My ride through this final country became the Tour de Forecourts. We stopped to take the morning break on the brick-paved concourse of one of those outdated blue and red concrete buildings that stood out from the ploughed fields surrounding it. Physio didn't seem necessary; I wasn't working my legs hard enough to need it. I sat at the table and struggled to force my large bowl of satay peanut pasta down before lumbering slowly across the forecourt to use the toilet behind the bare-shelved shop. On the way back, Jem took me aside to speak one-to-one under the shade of the canopy. He looked at me and put his arm around my shoulder.

"Mate, I'm running out of ideas here and I can't let you cross Moscow in this condition – it's too much of a risk," he said. "We've tried everything we can think of to pick you up this morning and nothing's worked. What can we do to get you through this? You've got a team behind you who will do anything for you but you're gonna have to tell us, what can we do?"

It was a wake-up call. Jem's words made me realize I didn't need anything more. This wasn't just about me; the project was bigger than a bike ride. It may have been my idea but the project had infected everyone involved. Since the beginning, Steve had been invested, he'd been messaging me through the attempt and it was his *no compromise* that rang out in my head. I had a road team with me who were giving everything they could and tolerating difficult conditions to push towards *our* goal. There was a team of scientists in the UK crunching numbers to keep *us* on track and there were sponsors who believed in what *we* were doing.

"I've got this, Jem," I said and firmly took the bike.

"Okay dude. 'Av it!"

Head down, thumbs up, focused and determined, I tucked into the aero position and increased the tempo. For the penultimate block I was buzzing. *I don't need to get myself across Moscow, I need to get all of us across. Suck it up, and let's do this!*

My newfound motivation that I was not only doing this for myself fuelled me through the following 4 hours on the bike. The roads grew wider, one lane expanded to two then three, and the landscapes became industrialized. From endless forests, I emerged into concrete and scaffolding, telegraph poles and streetlights. The world got funnelled in, between factories and then high fencing either side of the road, and I was swept along averaging 32.5 kph (20.2 mph).

For the third break of the day we rendezvoused under neon lights that reflected off polished chrome, in a built-up area on the western edge of the capital. From this point, I would be alone. Jem changed the notes on my handlebars to read "Video Evidence" as he wouldn't be there to film me. As I rode off, Jem shouted, "Boss it!"

"Like a boss!" I shouted back.

The major roads of Moscow were terrifying. Out of the slip road, I was sucked into the fast-flowing four lanes of traffic like a twig caught in torrents of white water. The hard shoulder was punctuated by on and off ramps, tributaries of cars and trucks accelerating to find space in the busy traffic. I was vulnerable. Without the protection of the support vehicle, I felt truly at the bottom of the food chain. I pushed through the outskirts, under bright road signs in Cyrillic script, along 5 m-high fencing that channelled the surging traffic into a blur of tunnel vision. Nerves, fear and adrenaline mixed in a heady cocktail of exhilaration.

Busy roads diluted in the city centre and sedately crossed ornate arches of iron bridges, under decorative streetlights that reflected onto the enormous River Moskva. I stopped beside the entrance to Gorky Park, imitating Jem's mannerisms and catchphrases, as I recorded the video evidence. The haunting whistle of the Scorpions' "Winds Of

Change" echoed in my thoughts as I navigated through the lights, noise and smells of a cosmopolitan Saturday night and out of the city.

Two hours after leaving him, I looked up as a familiar Geordie voice shouted my name. Jem, Jahna and Kerr stood above the road, like a Formula One pit crew watching their driver pass the chequered flag. I hadn't felt the wrinkling crow's feet of a genuine smile in too long, it was wonderful. I punched the air and they cheered; we had cleared the final logistical challenge of the attempt.

I asked Jem what had inspired his speech on the forecourt that turned my performance around that day. Surely, they were the words that every human being wanted and needed to hear. *You've got a team behind you who will do anything for you. What can we do to get you through this?*

Jem described his motivation; he wasn't driven by achievement, he was concerned with the process. Jem saw each role on the world record attempt as a slice of Swiss cheese with holes through it. His job was to arrange them so that the holes lined up and he could drive the motorhome through to the finish line. I might have been the cyclist who was aiming to break a world record but, to Jem, I was just a slice of cheese that needed lining up. To do that, Jem knew he couldn't force me to be better through anger or frustration, he needed to be empathic, he needed to ask me what it would take.

"Oh, and hey!" Jem continued. "Remember when Beaumont said I couldn't do this?"

"Yeah," I replied.

"I'm gonna prove him wrong."

THIRTY

DAY FOURTEEN – THE STORM

23 SEPTEMBER 2018
Distance: 387.4 km (240.7 miles)
Start: Reutov, Russia
Finish: Gorbatovka, Russia
Weather: 15°C, storms

On 19 September, Storm Ali had hit the UK with torrential rain and gusts of 100 mph, killing two, causing major disruptions to transport and leaving 300,000 people without electricity. Since landing in Portugal, we had been treated to near perfect weather. On Day 14 the storm caught up with us.

I woke to the sound of rain on the metal roof of the motorhome. Water ran down the inside of the wall, soaking the end of my mattress. The storm brought colder weather than my research had predicted. I layered up with the clothes that Jem's mates had brought for me in Germany. I was so grateful; I don't know what I would have done without them, I'd probably have frozen. As I pulled on my cycling shorts, it felt as though I'd sat on something sharp, I pulled it and tore a layer of skin off; saddle sores. I crammed as much food as I could into my body even though I had no appetite and looked out the doorway, sipping fresh coffee from a metal travel mug. A sky of thick grey clouds that reflected in the puddles across the car park was accompanied by the hiss of fast-moving tyres on the carriageway. It was everything that Phil had prophesied when he had asked me months ago what would get me back on the bike and stay on it all day.

"Now, if I tell you I'll give you a certificate to do that, you'll tell me to get lost." Phil's words rang clear in my mind. "And you won't care about the respect of other people because they don't understand the pain that you are going through." All that time ago, he knew exactly what he was preparing me for.

I put my hand in the plastic wallet, dug out one of Clare's envelopes and read the note aloud. "To be outstanding, get comfortable with being uncomfortable."

Jem and Kerr stood outside in the rain with me.

"Start of Day 14, GPS started, zero six forty one, we're on the outskirts of Russia and ready to roll ou—" I stopped Jem as he recorded his evidence video.

"Russia? Moscow? We're definitely still in Russia, haha!" I laughed. Jem never made a mistake.

"Moscow, *of* Russia," he replied.

"Hahaha," I pedalled away, into the stream of traffic.

We turned our back on the palaces, factories and tourists in the streets of the city, and returned to forests dotted with red and white radio masts. East of Moscow, three cities were all that stood between me and the finish line; Nizhny Novgorod, Kazan and Ufa. The first two names now started to appear on the blue signs at the roadside. Beside them were massive numbers representing the distance to each, numbers that never seemed to get any smaller.

The roads reduced to dual and then single carriageways and the traffic became denser. The luxury of space disappeared, the tightrope I cycled was now narrower and hung between fast-moving trucks and a deep gravel shoulder, either of which could easily take me down. Strong winds pummelled me in the gaps between vehicles. The light rain of the morning increased through the day and by the afternoon I was riding through a deluge. Water hit me from every direction – down from the clouds, up from my wheels and sideways from the passing vehicles. It poured through my helmet and down my back, absorbed into my gloves and crept into shoe covers. Cold rain plastered my jersey to my body and the cold seeped into my bones. Waterproofs, too, have their limit and I'd found it.

The team began a battle to keep a set of clothes dry for me. On every break, I peeled off sodden apparel to be draped over the dashboard and dried over the heaters as the team drove. Four hours later, they went back into rotation and were replaced. Operating the motorhome as a launderette was added to the duties carried out by the team and I was hugely grateful for their sacrifice. They created a level of comfort for me in an environment that was incredibly challenging. They could see the difficulty that Phil had explained I would be going through and gave up their own comfort, travelling in a dank motorhome to keep me keep cycling.

By early evening, the temperature had dropped to 2°C. With the windchill, it felt more like zero.

"Riding in this weather, you're officially badass. You got this," Jem encouraged me.

"Thanks, mate," I replied, reluctantly pointing the bike back into the thick of it.

"Go kill it, bro. 'Av it, let's 'av it!"

I turned and smiled at him. Wearing seven layers to keep warm, I looked like a rigid Michelin man and I could barely bend. Just like Day Two when I was bloated, it became impossible to get my body into the aerodynamic position. I felt uncomfortable and slow. Conditions were horrendous. If ever there was a time to give up, this was it. The daylight faded and I cycled blindly into darkness. The bright beam of light from the front of the bike was filled with surface spray, obscuring any view of the tarmac. Water ran across the outside of my cycling glasses and the inside steamed up. Wearing them, all I saw was a kaleidoscope of headlights but if I took them off, I had to squint my eyes almost closed to avoid them filling with grit. Still, against everything Russia could throw at us, we pushed on. The team supported me with every motivation they could provide and I persevered, knowing that even when I could do nothing else, I could just keep pedalling.

It was the most vulnerable I felt on the whole ride. I knew how dangerous this was and for the first time I worried, not about finishing, but about surviving. I cringed with every diesel engine that screamed past followed by the sssssssshshshshshshsh and the crashing waves of gritty, black water breaking over me. *An unseen pothole or brick in the road could have me off the bike at any moment.* I spent a lot of time that evening wondering what kind of a smudge a cyclist would make if squashed between a lorry and a roadside barrier, and whether a truck driver would even notice if I rag-dolled underneath his wheels.

In spite of the storm, that day I cycled the same distance I'd been covering on the metronomic days before we reached Russia. We'd already made it to Gorbatovka on the outskirts of Nizhny Novgorod, the first of the remaining cities on the way to Ufa. We bedded down for the night in the forecourt of a closed petrol station, where security dogs barked and rattled their chains in the gravel yard behind the shop. I lay in my bunk, reflecting on the day which had only been made possible with the help of others. The team launderette, Jem's mates' clothes and Phil's psychology work had got me through the day.

I found myself questioning whether real-world conditions with the potential to kill me slowed me down less than the psychological whirlpool in my mind. I could deal with external problems; they distracted me from myself. I wondered whether I was slowing myself down more than anything else. Had my greatest torment been self-inflicted? Or did I just have a tailwind?

Whatever the reason, we were making good progress again. I was optimistic and I knew the team were there for me. We were focused on reaching the finish line.

THIRTY-ONE

DAY FIFTEEN – THE LIGHT AT THE END OF THE TUNNEL

24 SEPTEMBER 2018
Distance: 338.4 km (210.3 miles)
Start: Gorbatovka, Russia
Finish: Yemetkino, Russia
Weather: 15°C, rain

The storm relented a little but the days of good weather were over. The air was cold and cycling between rain showers, I continued to wear all that I had. As with the "Beast From the East" earlier in the year, the season changed overnight. The backdrop of dense green wilderness turned to gold and brown. I'd ridden into autumn. Similarly, the smooth black tarmac that had flowed out of Moscow turned into a patchwork of potholes, roadworks and contraflow. I swerved on the road, avoiding mounds of concrete and ruts that threatened to grab my wheels and throw me off the bike.

The hard shoulder was lined with construction vehicles. There was no doubt that the road needed upgrading, but it couldn't have been worse timing for us. Fast-moving traffic funnelled through road cones into a single lane and crossed the central reservation. I was forced to go the same way and, stuck in the narrow lanes of contraflow, traffic impatiently pushed past me, leaving millimetres either side of the handlebars. It was a horrible day on the bike.

At the end of the first block, I cycled towards the motorhome as the persistent stream of trucks rumbled on. I was tired – not even alert to the most apparent obstacles – and, as I turned into the layby, I misjudged the change in surfaces. The front wheel caught a kerb and, for the second time in the attempt, I was thrown to the ground. I fell heavily. Too surprised and fatigued to put my hands out, my head, elbow and hip struck the concrete and I bounced to a standstill on my side. The crash shredded another pair of shorts as well as the jersey and waterproof. Road rash showed through the holes. It was a much harder fall than the one on Day Ten and it hurt.

I picked up the bike and wheeled it towards the support vehicle as the team ran over to me. Something was wrong with the bike – it didn't feel right as I wheeled it and the tired gremlin in the back of my mind hoped that it was damaged enough to give me some respite while Jem replaced some parts. I showered and cleaned the grit out of my cuts and Jahna dressed my wounds for the second time on the attempt. I'd taken a good amount of skin off my hip, my elbow was swollen and my helmet had taken the impact. I was lucky – if I'd fallen in the other direction, I would have been under the trucks.

I spoke to Kerr with ice packs taped over my injuries as I warmed up with coffee and paracetamol in the back of the motorhome. I took the second fall in much better humour than the first. In the five days that had passed since then, a lot had changed within me and my motivation. I had wavered but I hadn't given up on achieving my best and I now understood that it meant something different to my original expectations. My best didn't mean always being ten out of ten. Sometimes I was only a four but, on those days, if I could give my best four then I had nothing to regret. My best meant carrying on, no matter how slowly, when I didn't feel I had anything left to give. My best meant being friends and appreciating that I was taking the belief of those who supported me across the continent. The old me wouldn't accept those thoughts but when Day 12 had broken me, I accepted that I was human after all. I was allowing myself to accept these things and with the freedom it gave me, I was becoming more and more positive.

"Are you feeling confident?" Kerr asked.

"Yeah, if I can keep the bike on two wheels, that'd be great!" I laughed.

That morning I'd read the word "Ufa" on a road sign for the first time and beside it was a three-digit number. The target that had been 6,500 km (4,000 miles) away at the start line was now less than 900 km (560 miles).

It alleviated a pressure I'd been feeling and it quantified a distance that for so long had felt insurmountable. I'd felt responsible to sponsors and friends for a promise that I was uncertain I could deliver on, but I knew I could deliver on 560 miles. As I cycled that morning, I had chunked the distance down into blocks and realized that I only needed to average 25 kph (16 mph) to cover 100 km (62 miles) in each block. Mathematically, Ufa was only nine blocks away. That sounded good, achievable. I felt happy, confident this challenge would soon be ending and it would all be worth it. As I described my new reasoning to Kerr, Jahna turned and smiled. There was a lift in spirits of the whole team as I began to see the proverbial light at the end of the tunnel.

Half an hour later, I was back on the bike. The right-hand shifter was broken and the handlebar was cracked on the same side, the drop hanging by a thread. The bike would be limping home and, covered in cuts and bruises, so would I, but it felt as though we were finally getting there. I ignored the pain and focused on pushing the pedals. Having done the calculations for myself I eventually believed Phil; I was going to hit our best-case scenario of 16 days. The roads changed, the seasons changed and my outlook changed.

THIRTY-TWO

DAY SIXTEEN – TWO WOLVES

---

25 SEPTEMBER 2018
Distance: 336.1 km (208.8 miles)
Start: Yemetkino, Russia
Finish: Togayevo, Russia
Weather: 15°C, rain

On a bike, it's not the long climbs that hurt. You can pace them, you can break them down and you gradually work your way to the top. It's the undulations that hurt. Each climb is short but one by one they knock you back and steal your momentum. Picking yourself up time and time again, that's what makes a champion.

I stood on the crest of a hill, in the gravel car park of a workman's café where we slept the night before. The sun rose as a line of pink under a blanket of cloud. We filmed an evidence video just before the heavens opened and Jem took a photo of me, wearing full winter gear, beneath a rainbow. Even in uncomfortable times, there was beauty.

Undulating climbs at 9 per cent gradient continued all day long. Every ascent was painful. I stood on the pedals and pushed all my body weight through the bike to keep it moving forwards, hoping that the top would bring me to a stretch of flat road. But when I reached the summit of each climb, I looked ahead at another descent followed by an equal climb. The descents lasted seconds and the climbs felt as though they took hours. Every success was rewarded with another challenge and frustration built within me as the little things began mounting up.

An hour into the day, I descended to a steel bridge that spanned an enormous valley where the murky torrents of the Sviyaga and Volga rivers meet and dominate the landscape. The eastbound lane of the bridge was closed for resurfacing and, as I waited at the temporary traffic lights, I looked out at the magnitude of the waters it crossed. I'd seen similar in Alaska. I wondered whether bears lived on the large islands in the middle of the river or fished in the strong currents. I imagined camping on the banks and washing in the water at the end of a long day's cycling, boiling it to cook rice and whatever vegetables I'd bought from the people I would have met that day. I considered how small and free I would feel, sat down there at sunset beside a campfire, watching the traffic rushing to reach its destination on the bridge above.

The motorhome had crossed and was driving away on the far side of the river but the traffic lights stayed red in front of me and the traffic behind me built and built. That descent through the Pyrenees on Day Three had taught me early on that stoppages cost more than slow cycling and my impatience mounted as the clock continued ticking. I caught the attention of the road workers, leaning on their shovels in their orange hi-viz overalls who waved me through their construction site. I eagerly clipped into the pedals and cycled down the ramp and onto the bridge, where my wheels immediately sunk into liquid tar. Not wanting to put my feet down and with nowhere else to go, I cycled all the way through it. Sticky black sludge covered the bike, and as I rejoined the road, sand, stones and dirt clung to it. Efficiency disappeared in one fell swoop; wheels stuck to the road, the chain crunched, and outer layers of winter clothing flapped around in the turbulent dregs of the storm. As the hours passed, things didn't get any easier. In the second block of the day, the battery died in the GPS watch and, not long after, in the electronic gear system.

I was mentally and physically wrecked and the temptation grew to stop cycling. When the day got warmer, I pulled over at the side of the road, took off my gloves, a waterproof, a thermal top and a long-sleeve jersey, just so I could take off my arm warmers from underneath. Then I took a load of time putting every other layer back on. Jem watched from the motorhome behind me.

"What made ya think it was yer arms that were hot?" he laughed as I handed him my discarded clothing. I hadn't stopped with the intention of such a prolonged striptease but perhaps my weakened mind was looking for any break from pedalling.

On the second break, I wrapped up warm and sat in the back of the motorhome eating cornflakes with Kerr. Phil's laminated quote, taped on the window beside me, read, "Not many people in the world, when they have given everything, can put their left foot in front of their right foot and continue on."

We discussed the difficulties I was going through on the road, the obstacles in my path and the negative thoughts that I struggled to fight out there alone. There were hundreds of times when I had wanted to get off the bike and, in those moments, nobody would have known if I just stood in a bus shelter and waited for the hardship to pass. But through everything, I persisted – left, right, left, right. I shared with Kerr the analogy that Phil had told me, of two wolves competing for attention in my mind, and only I could decide which one I fed. The negative wolf was now going for all the food, and it was becoming increasingly difficult for me to feed the positive one.

"So, what are the positive thoughts that get you through?" asked Kerr.

I told him the first thing that came to mind – how privileged I felt to be there at all. I was grateful just to travel through these wonderful places. Simply standing on a bridge that morning, overlooking the incredible wilderness below and appreciating all that I'd experienced in this world record attempt and in cycling around the world; that was a huge positive for me. But as I cycled into another block with Kerr's question in my mind, I was embarrassed by how shallow my answer had sounded. *If I was honest with myself, what did truly get me through?*

Music. For the best part of 14 hours a day, the three playlists that Phil had asked me to create beat in my ears. For me, there were times when it was more than just a beat or a lyric. Music evoked something and transported me to another place. It had the ability to pick me up. "The Eye of the Tiger" had been key to getting the best out of myself after the fall on Day Ten. At times when I felt genuinely downtrodden, I sang songs out loud, letting the lyrics put positive words in my mouth and mind. Construction workers and commuters across Europe heard me murder Journey's "Don't Stop Believin'" and Elton John's "I'm Still Standing". When I'd rather be anywhere than spending another monotonous day pedalling, songs transported me to a better place. The Jackson Five's "ABC" and the *Guardians of the Galaxy* soundtrack carried me back to the previous summer with Steve's family, "Rings Around The World" by the Super Furry Animals morphed into the last day of cycling the world, and Green Day, Nirvana and the Foo Fighters time-warped to summer days of mountain biking with my teenage friends. Music hooked into memories that had brought me to this point and reasons to keep going.

The team. They were a special group of people and I was so lucky to have them with me. Not only experts in their fields but also incredible individuals. I don't think there is another group of people in the world who would have committed themselves so completely to this project. Whether covering me in sun cream, cheering me on at each border, passing me coffee through the night, or playing that infuriating Justin Bieber song, the road team were always there, delivering well-honed strategies and desperately trying anything and everything to keep me on track. Living in the back of a motorhome with relative strangers, 24 hours a day for over two weeks, was intense and still they surrounded me with positive energy. The same went for the science team in the UK. Mark, Phil, Nicky and Ruth had become my extended family over the year that it took to prepare the project. Although I rarely spoke to them on the road, they were still with me in their decisions and tactics that influenced my actions. When Jem shouted, "What's the view like from the balcony?" they were Phil's words, delivered perfectly.

Even on his wedding day, when Mark hugged Phil at the church, he was thinking of me as well. "So, how's Leigh doing today?" he whispered into Phil's ear.

"You're not allowed to be thinking that, this is your wedding day. But he's doing good, he's doing really good, brother," Phil whispered back.

There were seven people beside me who, through rain or shine, for better or for worse, were prepared to give everything to get the best out of me.

Friends and family. The loneliness of riding a bike for 14 hours a day, pushing myself to keep going with only my own thoughts for company, was at times a dark and difficult place to be. When I got off the bike and read messages or watched videos from friends and family, I remembered who I was, why I was doing this and that I was not alone. Loved ones at home waited for the 1-minute social media videos that Kerr uploaded daily from the road to see how I was doing. Mum sent brief text messages, saying "I love you" and "thinking of you". She always said it was hard to find the right words but she didn't need to say more. I knew that Mum would be worrying about me, hoping her son wasn't hurt from falling off his bike and that I was all right in my mind. She would want me to enjoy what I was doing.

When Steve saw me fall off the bike on Day Ten, he got my friends together from Cycle Mickleover and sent a video of them all lying on the grass with their legs and arms wrapped around their bikes as though they'd fallen off, shouting, "Are we nearly there yet?!" It was silly but it was perfect and when I received it later that week, it brought a smile to an otherwise difficult day. Steve made dozens of videos with his family and Cycle Mickleover, which he uploaded for Jem to show me when I needed them. Steve's wife, Gill, made a heartfelt video that brought tears to my eyes about meeting me and the difference that it had made to their family. His daughters, Hayleigh and Shelley, videoed themselves singing a song that we'd sung together but they changed the words so it was about breaking world records. Steve took the camera to a charity cycling event and recorded messages from friends as they sat on static bikes. The same friends that had joined me on my last day of cycling around the world and who had shared my difficult times in training, were there for me when I fell off my bike and when they saw my lowest times. Unlike when I pushed everyone away in my 20s, I embraced it. This wasn't just a bike ride or a world record attempt. Everything I was doing impacted those around me and their actions affected me too.

When we stopped for the last break of the day I was, in Jem's words, "threaders". My condition made 3 a.m. at the Russian border seem fresh. All I wanted was to get into bed. "You're not going to like what Phil's got to say," Jahna told me as she handed the phone over for a chat with him. The science team had calculated that with an extra-long push into the night, we would finish at a good time tomorrow.

After a gruelling day, my whole body was heavy, my eyes would barely stay open and I could hardly push the pedals. All I wanted was sleep but I went back out into the night, took the bike and pedalled on. Each one of us was tired but we didn't stop. I cycled and, catching their eyes as they urged me on, I smiled knowing right there and then that this was a team to really be proud of. They waited for me on every corner, they filled my bottles with coffee, they topped me up with sweets and they played terrible music at full volume. At that time, nothing else mattered but cranking through the remaining distance, metre by metre if that's what it took. It was torturous and slow but together we got through it. Every pedal rotation completed today was one less for tomorrow. My tar-covered body collapsed into the motorhome in the middle of the night, having left everything on the road.

We were 275 km (171 miles) from the finish line.

THIRTY-THREE

DAY SEVENTEEN – THE FINAL DAY

26 SEPTEMBER 2018
Distance: 275.7 km (171.3 miles)
Start: Togayevo, Russia
Finish: Ufa, Russia
Weather: 10°C, rain

Jahna handed me two plastic packets of immaculate, unused kit that she'd saved for the last day of the record. The other five sets of kit were ruined; torn, stretched and stained, ready to be incinerated. The last one was crisp, it fitted perfectly and the chamois was fresh. I beamed a smile and thanked her. This simple gesture meant everything; I'd be comfortable for the day. I got dressed and stepped out of the motorhome into a sprawling, dirty car park filled with trucks, under a grey sky of diesel fumes.

I thought back to getting on the bike at the lighthouse in Cabo da Roca, wearing the first pristine kit, with the breeze blowing in from the ocean. The last day on the road could not be a greater contrast to the first. I had tackled the continent from west to east, from the Atlantic to the edge of Siberia. The peaks and plateaux had ingrained themselves in my wounds and my heart. The fresh cyclist who had danced his bike uphill into the Portuguese sunrise had gradually unravelled and now cycled as if dragging an anvil behind him. The final day was a big ask of all of us. We had already given this record everything.

The wind continued to blow heavy rain clouds across the sky. The backdrop of autumnal wilderness was replaced by dirty agriculture as it had been on the outskirts of every Russian city. We were now approaching the final one. Every time I passed the support vehicle they banged on the doors and shouted encouragement but still the first 4 hours were slow. Where 120 km (75 miles) had been a standard block for so long, I struggled to hit 100 km (62 miles). At the end of the first break, the whole team got out of the motorhome to urge me onward. Only a short distance remained until we joined the final GPS track that would navigate me to the finish line. Jem gave me his military version of a pep talk.

"One hundred and sixteen kilometres to the end of the map, see if we can do that, eh? That's your target. Got it?"

"I can't, I've only got ninety watts coming out my legs, you don't understand, it's —" He cut me off before I finished complaining.

"Can't means won't, won't means jail. That's what we used to say. You *can* do that. You the man. Let's do it.

Let's get double busy. Think of that sauna tonight. Think of it! Get your arse there. *Schnell machen.* Go go goooo!"

I couldn't bring myself to appreciate where we were in the grand scheme of things, what we'd overcome, or acknowledge the magnitude of what I was achieving at the time. I couldn't smile or laugh with the team or get back on the bike enthusiastically. I was so focused on how painful every second had become that I just complained. In my mind, I argued with Jem. *There's no sauna tonight. Why would you say that to me? We haven't got the budget for that.* Jem was a superhero. He still had the belief and enthusiasm to push me on, even when my own was wavering.

I hit Jem's target and, after 8 hours, the remaining distance was down to double digits. Only 85 km (53 miles) stood between us and realizing the world record.

The team went ahead to wait for me at the finish line and I cycled alone for the last few hours. In that time, my eyes and my mind changed and with them so did the world around me. I knew I was going to make it. If the bike broke, I would carry it. If my legs stopped working, I would drag my body along the ground using my lips. No matter what happened, I was going to cross the finish line and the record was mine. I would achieve what I'd set out to do.

In solitude, my mind rewound through a mixtape of memories. I thought back to a year before, when I first saw the record and decided to ride a borrowed bike from Derby to Skegness and back, to see if I could do it. I remembered my first meeting with Mark, and then Phil. The testing, training and workshops I'd gone through to be ready for this attempt in June, only for it to be deferred because of sponsorship. I recalled my elation at getting the main sponsors on board and breathing new life into this dream. And I reflected on everything the team and I had been through in the last 4,000 miles on the road, across a continent. I was overwhelmed by what I had nurtured into reality, from the spark of an idea that I'd had when I wondered what to do with my life.

Every emotion I hoped I would feel surged through my body – happiness, joy and pride. My heart beat hard and fast as it had with anxiety but this time with excitement at the completion, achievement and success. I pedalled hard, uplifted. The streetlights in the dusky sky twinkled through the tears in my eyes. Few people take the first step towards accomplishing their ambition and here I was, close to completing my second.

"Oh my god, this life is amazing!" I shouted into the foreign black and orange nighttime roads.

From the bridge across the Belaya River, I looked down on the city of Ufa and saw the domed roof of the railway station, where the chequered flag on the GPS route marked the finish point.

"There it is, there it is!" I hammered on the handlebar that was falling apart beneath me, euphoric.

Butterflies filled my stomach with that inertia just before the free fall from the highest point of the roller coaster. I cycled in a stream of car lights, through the sssssssshshshshshsh of tyres on wet roads, until I saw the support team and the familiar motorhome. I rode towards them, flashing the front light, before lifting the front wheel on to the concourse outside the building, the finish line.

Jem was already at the kerbside, waiting for me. He put out his hand and I grabbed it before he leaned over and hugged me. Jahna and Kerr came over to where we stood and hugged me too.

Wow! We did it! I laughed with each "congratulations" and thanked them.

In an instant, every difficulty, every pain, every frustration disappeared. Overwhelmed in the moment, feelings of completion, fulfilment, contentment washed over me. *How on earth has this possibly happened?* Again, I'd had a wild dream and here I was, 12 months later, a record breaker. *Normal me, a record breaker!*

The team from ACE Sameday Couriers had arranged for a local bike club to greet us at the end. They ran over to us though the rain, cheering and congratulating me with a jar of local honey and a handwritten poster that read, "Leigh Timmis, you are the champion!" I laughed with them too, shocked and touched that they'd gone to such lengths. How wonderful!

Kerr walked me to the side of the commotion and asked me to do a piece to camera about the accomplishment. Exhausted and emotional, I didn't even know what time we had finished in. For once, my mind was silent. I yelled the question to Jem, who sat in the driver's seat uploading data and figuring out time zones.

"Hold on, mucka..." he shouted over the traffic. "Okay, here you go..."

"SIXTEEN DAYS, TEN HOURS AND FORTY-FIVE MINUTES."

THIRTY-FOUR

THE SPICIEST DISH

The team and I checked into an enormous Russian hotel. Our excited energy overflowed into the warm, cavernous reception, where businessmen in suits congregated after dinner. Dirty rainwater dripped from my cycling clothes into puddles as we organized ourselves at the check-in desk. Our jokes and conversation with the receptionists were lost in translation but, from the filthy, exhausted state of me, I doubt they had trouble believing I'd cycled there from Portugal. Jem arranged the rooms and handed me the key to an executive suite they'd booked from the road. I went ahead of the others, carrying my grab bag and backpack down a long corridor, and pushed open the door into a large room. I peeled off my cycling clothes and indulged in the luxurious comfort of the shower. Warm water washed 16 days' worth of grime from my skin and, for the first time in a year, I relaxed.

It was done.

I'd broken the world record by eight days and 17 hours.

I smiled. For a whole year I'd worked towards this moment of "completion" and here it was; I was a round-the-world cyclist *and* I'd broken a world record. It was everything I'd wanted to achieve, I'd proven myself and I was on top of the world. Yet, it was strange. If I looked at anybody else in this situation, I'd expect them to be jumping for joy but I had a weird sense that something was missing.

When I got out the shower, my mobile phone was ringing. It was the BBC. Wrapped in a towel, I sat on the enormous, soft bed and gave an enthusiastic interview, speaking exuberantly about what we'd achieved and how elated I was about it. I described all the wonderful emotions I'd felt cycling towards the finish line but when the call was over, I couldn't understand why I sat with this strange, juxtaposing sensation.

I called Phil.

"All right there, brother! You did it! Congratulations!" he answered, positive as always.

"Haha! Thanks, mate! And thank *you*, it wouldn't have been possible without you," I replied.

"How's it going? How are you feeling about it all?"

"Honestly, mate, I'm good, it's all good but I'm a bit confused. It's like, I worked towards this moment for the whole year, and now it's all come together, you know, we've absolutely smashed the record and that's fantastic. But. I dunno, it's hard to describe."

"Go on."

"I think part of me expected an incredible finish line fanfare and elephant parades, but it was just a cold, wet train station in the dark, ha! And, internally, I expected that extravagant moment for myself too – like, I expected to change, become a better person. But it was just me, normal me, who broke the record and that's strangely disappointing."

"What do you mean, it was just *normal you*?"

"It's like, deep inside, I didn't believe that *I* was the person who deserved to break records, you know?"

"It's too early for the magnitude of it all to sink in, buddy. It'll take time to realize what you've achieved. For now, go and enjoy the moment." Phil reassured me that we'd go through everything in a debrief when I returned home.

I dressed and hunted the hotel for the team. I wanted to be around them even more, to share in the team buzz, whatever they were doing. Jem stood in the middle of his busy room with black, oily hands, having stripped down the bike, while Jahna and Kerr packed the remaining equipment from the motorhome. Each one of us was exhausted; four empty wetsuits in the Middle-of-Nowhere, Russia.

Among a pile of folders and documents stacked on the floor, I noticed the plastic wallet containing Clare's daily motivational notes. Of the 20 that she'd prepared for me, three envelopes remained sealed. I opened each one and read the quotes aloud.

"Be strong... You never know who you are inspiring," read the final one.

"Look!" Jahna smiled and pointed to the desk under a mirror at the end of the room. "We bought you a drink from every country we passed through." Lined up were ten bottles of various colours and shapes, all with indecipherable labels. Close to midnight, we ordered burgers and fries through room service and, in an alcoholic game of Russian roulette, we chose a bottle each and toasted the end of the record attempt. Without the pressure to analyze or strategize, we sat around laughing at what we'd been through and chatted about what we had planned for the last weeks of the summer when we got home.

In sharing our experiences, I started easing into a feeling of fulfilment. It was the quality time I'd wished to share with them when we were on the road. They were a great team but even better human beings.

After a couple of hours' sleep, Jem, Jahna, Kerr and I woke before sunrise one last time and boarded the first flight out of Russia. We slept non-stop, Ufa to Heathrow, before disembarking into a sweaty London afternoon on 27 September, with bags under our eyes bigger than the ones in our hands. The relationships we'd built over those 17 days together seemed too intense, too meaningful to just end in an airport. We'd shared more than just a journey across a continent; we'd overcome so many challenges, tolerated so much and dug deeper for each other than any other circumstance would ever demand of anybody. I thanked them for everything they'd brought to the project. At that moment, we were the very best in the world at what we did. We promised to stay in contact and hugged before picking up our bags to leave.

Kerr and I turned and walked through the arrivals lounge. Outside, Jon pulled up in an ACE courier van. He'd safely arrived home in Jerry's motorhome, with his fags and booze, a couple of days before we did. Kerr and I threw our bags, a bike and a skateboard into the back and hauled our bodies into the cab. On the drive home, Jon told us that his wife, Marina, had never been abroad before. Their adventure with armed Russian guards, choreographing world record border logistics and a road trip from Moscow to Derby had been her first foreign holiday. She'd loved it. Of course, he told us every detail.

———

Two days later it was the Bustler Market, the monthly street food party that I loved. The last time I was there, my diet was under strict control and I'd left without saying goodbye. This time, I walked in through the warm, smoky barbecue air, filled with music and conversation, between the food trucks and around a corner into a sea of familiar faces. Everybody I knew was there – Steve and his family, Ruth, Cycle Mickleover, school friends and people I'd met over the year. It was great to be back. I was embraced by the group of loved ones. I ate whatever I wanted from the food trucks and I was never without a drink in my hand. I stood among my friends, holding a pulled pork burger in one hand and a beer in the other, with a beaming smile across my face. We laughed and chatted under the fairy lights and my head was adorned with an illuminated pink tiara that I kept on all evening.

Friends laughed with me about the days when I'd fallen off, asked about the highlights and the hardest times, and gave me kudos for what I'd achieved. They'd been inspired to wake up every day and see how far my icon had moved across the map, showing off about me to their colleagues at work. I was so happy to hear that I'd been on their minds and that I'd done something that impacted them, too.

As I stood with a good friend from the cycling club, waiting to get the next round of drinks in, she told me, "We're so proud of what you did but, you know, it wasn't about you breaking the world record. You gave us something to believe in, you gave us hope." That sentence moved me more than the finish line itself. I felt full, complete, joyful, tearful. It meant so much to me but I had no words, I just smiled and hugged her. I was filled with a happiness that lasted throughout one of the best nights I'd shared with friends.

The group of us drank long into the night. When the Bustler Market closed, we went to a gin bar around the corner. When that closed, I went back to Steve's. My achievement had given something back to the people that cared about me, I was a part of a community. I was loved.

"What's that I smell?" Phil laughed as I walked towards him. "Ah, yes, the fragrant whiff of bullshit bingo!" We sat in the coffee shop above the Human Performance Unit, where the sound of squash balls ricocheting off walls echoed up the stairs and the glass wall looked outside onto the AstroTurf courts.

The attempt had been verified. The story was broadcast on TV, in newspapers, across social media and it was published in *Guinness World Records*. It helped raise the profile of mental health and thousands of pounds for the charity, MQ. I resumed speaking at events with new lessons to share and I returned to the University of Derby, where Phil and I debriefed. It was good to be back in the familiar setting but, as I honestly told Phil, I wasn't bothered about examining our outcomes. In my mind, the record was over and it was time to move on. When I began my pursuit of the record, all I had seen was the challenge. I never thought of the day after its completion or what would happen next. Phil assured me that these were equally as important as the attempt itself; I had to understand what I had been through and learn from it.

We talked about how I felt when I called him from Ufa and Phil explained two interpretations of success. *Ego-based success* relied on the prestige of recognition and praise from others. It was a success that I couldn't control and if I based my outcome on it, I would never find fulfilment. He told me to define myself instead by *task-based success*, for which I was my own indicator. I had to look back at what I had set out to achieve and mark myself against my own criteria.

Phil set me three questions that I had to answer when I reflected on the attempt. *Did I achieve my best? Did I reach my limits and push through them? And, what did I learn?*

"So, do you think you achieved your best then, pal?" Phil asked.

"My best? Ah mate, I don't know about that."

I reacted to Phil's question in the same way that I had after the first incremental test, when I got off Excalibur and asked myself, even after all that I'd given, *could I have pushed on a bit longer?* On the attempt, I'd been aiming for 14 days and I hadn't achieved that. I'd made mistakes with the route, with weather preparations and I'd let my motivation slip. I could have done better with all of those aspects. I wish I'd had the ability to acknowledge the magnitude of what I was achieving at the time, appreciate what we'd overcome and be more grateful for every second. Phil reminded me that *we* had never set the goal of 14 days – it was an unrealistic expectation that I should never have put upon myself. He also reiterated that this was always going to be our worst ultra-endurance event because things were going to happen that we couldn't plan for.

"You'd never done anything like that in your life and, in those difficult moments, you reacted in the best way that you could with the experience you had. You're looking back at what you did with different eyes to those that saw the road at the time," Phil reassured me. "There's no point ruminating on what you would have done differently. You need to reflect and look at the takeaways."

Phil must have heard himself tell me those words time and time again over the previous year. He reminded me that thinking about the past was only useful if I was going to learn from it. I could make changes and act differently when similar situations came up in the future. I had to accept what I did right and what I did wrong and be okay with it. Win or learn.

"We all make mistakes," Phil told me. "No regrets."

Phil's prompts helped me reframe what I defined as "my best". Rather than evaluating myself based on the result, I judged myself by the effort I'd put into achieving it. I'd brought together every expert and resource necessary and, for an entire year, I'd dedicated every aspect of my life to the pursuit of the world record. It was a year without compromise. Every single decision I'd made had been based on riding a bike across Europe as quickly as possible.

I never limited myself with my goals; I went beyond just beating the record and aimed for the very best I could achieve. The time on the clock when I arrived at the finish line was the result of a great amount of hard work, and from that came great reward – we hit the top end of our target and raised the bar on any attempt that had gone before.

Standing on the metaphoric balcony, I looked back and stubbornly admitted that I genuinely had achieved my best. A smile crept across my face.

"Buddy, what you achieved was incredible, and that was your first time!" Phil encouraged. "So, do you think you hit your—"

"Did I hit my limit?!" I interrupted him. That was one thing I was certain I'd done.

We'd all seen it happen; I'd reached breaking point so many times throughout the attempt. Achieving my best demanded hitting my limit. Phil had always known that; it was why he'd forced it upon me in the White Wall Test. The improvement in how I dealt with those crisis situations was one of the outcomes I was most proud of and I put it all down to the work he'd put into developing my psychology. Inevitably, the way I reacted in those moments and whether I could summon the energy to continue determined the result.

Retrospectively, it's difficult to believe I originally thought the attempt would purely be about physical strength. The motivations, self-awareness, positive thought process and psychological interventions Phil taught me through the project were key to our achievement. As Mark had said before I even met Phil, I could be the fastest cyclist in the world on the start line, but it meant nothing if my mind wasn't strong enough to get me to the finish line. I was incredibly indebted to Mark, Phil and the rest of the team for seeing the bigger picture in terms of both the project and my personal strengths and weaknesses. They weren't just there to support me; they challenged me, changed my perspective and opened my eyes to opportunities using better methods. The project was never about *me*, it was about *us*.

As I chatted with Phil, I admitted that, even after all the work we'd done, his positive thought processes still hadn't become natural to me. When calm, I knew exactly how I was supposed to act but when stressed and under pressure, it was easy to fall back into old reactions. I felt like my head knew what to do but it hadn't become automatic; it wasn't in my heart. He told me that changing thought processes took time and practice but by building habits like centring into my everyday routine, I could continue building my control and working towards the mindset I desired.

"So," Phil continued, "let's talk about what you learned."

Since meeting Steve, I'd probably heard him say, "Every day's a school day," a million times and, mostly, it was in relation to the world record. From a project management point of view, I'd learned everything from scratch. I'd assessed what was needed, found the best solution, coordinated a team of experts, financed the project and tied all the elements together with people skills. During that time, I also became an elite athlete, learning cutting-edge scientific approaches and dedicating myself to training practices across physiology, psychology, nutrition and physiotherapy. I'd gone from wondering what to do with my life to leading a team of expert scientists and breaking a world record, in just 18 months. I learned that, with a *no compromise* approach, I could achieve anything. I owed a lot to Steve's guidance, which informed my rapid progress.

It was easy to account for the skills I'd learned, however, it took much longer for me to step back and fully understand that the personal outcome of the project was more than holding a record. The fulfilment that I was hoping for at the finish line was never to be found there. The entire project had come down to innovation; a change in approach to the record attempt and, ultimately, a change in me. It was a year of enormous personal transformation and what I learned about myself was profound.

My challenge wasn't exclusively a cycling contest against a rival or against the clock. The real battle had been with myself and I brought my *whole* self to the project. The scientists' approach forced me to confront the issues I'd been running away from ten years before and address what I should have done in counselling. I realized that the quick solution to the mental health issues that I was looking for in my mid-20s didn't exist and I couldn't run away from them, either. I had to face uncomfortable truths about my character, develop tools to help me through difficult situations, and put in the hard work necessary to change myself. Ultimately, this transformation came down to a change in lifestyle through the implementation of simple habits that demanded commitment and practice.

"No doubt, you're at your best with structure," Phil agreed. "Now, I want you to look back at your *why*. You told me you wanted to define yourself; to find out how you react when everything is going against you. So, what did you find?"

The time trial is called "The Race of Truth" because there is nowhere to hide; it's just a cyclist against the clock. You give all you've got and the consequences are exposed for all to see.

On Day 12, when my physical and mental strength had been stripped away and my expectations fell apart, I faced my own truth. I accepted who I was and who I wanted to be. At the side of a dual carriageway in Russia, holding back the tears as I spoke to the team, I stopped defining myself by the statistics I was delivering or by the time that I would eventually finish in. I realized that I was chasing much more than a record and, instead, I defined myself as a human being who wanted to be accepted.

In that moment, I'd realized that I would never be breaking the record again and I had to appreciate what we were doing. No achievement I could ever aim for would be good enough and I had to allow myself to be happy with who I was.

I am defined not by the achievement, but by the process that takes me there. That process is built on the decisions I make, the morals I live by and the habits I form. I had wanted to become the best in the world when, actually, all I had to become was *my* best. It was mine all along. Success isn't a result; it's a mindset.

As it had been at our first ever meeting, winter approached and I sat with Mark in the corner of Blends, catching up over coffee. This time we discussed his wedding day, what we'd achieved on the record, and our future dreams.

"Did anyone show you the data we collected from the project?" he asked.

"No, mate. Have you got it here?" I replied.

Mark opened his laptop, scanned across the neatly organized folders on his desktop and opened a spreadsheet. He clicked through tab after tab of data from every hour of the record attempt, colour-coded and cross-referenced. Speeds, distances and durations. Heart rate, power and RPE. Calories consumed against energy expenditure. Sleep analysis and psychological profiles. Graphs of my development through training. No stone left unturned. Nowhere to hide. Every variable was quantified and documented.

"Beautiful, isn't it?!" Mark beamed. "From this data, we now know exactly how you react and what to expect from you. We can analyze this and adapt our approach when we do it again. We're in an incredibly powerful position for another attempt."

"No way, that's insane!" I said in awe. "I don't think any other ultra-endurance cyclist in the world has this kind of breakdown. This is massive. Imagine what a head start this gives us over anyone else!"

"Exactly. So, what's next?"

ACKNOWLEDGEMENTS

Breaking the world record and capturing the story on paper were only possible with the support of a great number of people. I'm incredibly grateful to everyone who stood beside me throughout both challenges, with special thanks to the following.

James Spackman at The BKS Agency and the team at Summersdale – Debbie Chapman, Rebecca Haydon and Jasmin Burkitt – and Ross Dickinson and Miranda Moore. Thanks also to Phil Lynam for the incredible cover photo.

My family, especially Mum, Dad, Emma and Al, for your love, support and belief that underpin everything I have achieved. And the family that embraced me when I returned to Derby, Steve, Gill, Hayleigh and Shelley Reynolds.

The world record team. Mark Faghy, Phil Clarke, Ruth Anness and Nicky Gilbert for having my back from the beginning. The specialists that joined us through preparation, Phil Woodbridge, Andy Brooke, Dan Bigham and Dean Jackson. And the road team for digging deep for 17 days across Europe to get me to the finish line, Anthony Jemmett, Jahna Drunis and Kerr McNicoll.

Sponsors of the fastest cycle across Europe. Jon Jenkinson, Edd Cunliffe, Chris Scothern and the team at ACE Sameday Couriers. The University of Derby, especially Bev Crighton, Nikki Davis and everybody at the Human Performance Unit. Rob Hallam at Unit 27 and Marty Bowler at Wattzone. Mark

Smith and the team at Cycle Derby. Paul Wright at Accrofab. Felix and Luke Frixou at Benz Bavarian. Sean Price and Hajre Hyseni at Kosbit. Robin Sibson, Colin Adams and the team at Mount Cook Adventure Centre. Jack Williams at Archer Hampson. Mark Swift and Sam Hanson at Exposure Lights. Scott Knowles at East Midlands Chamber of Commerce. PKF Cooper Parry. Tom Mawhood at Fuel For Sport. Tim Ward at Schwalbe Tyres. Mike Copestake at Freeths. Kieran Harrod Brand Design and Consultancy. Hayleigh Reynolds at Wondersmith. Anthony Goddard at ZeroSixZero maps. Pádraic Quinn at Velotec. Document Network Services. John Forkin, Lindsay Hatfield and the team at Marketing Derby. And to everyone who donated to the crowdfund campaign.

Jerry Clark, Richard Oakes, Clare Thompson, Nick Britten, Andrew Edmondson, Andy Ramsdale and Cycle Mickleover for your time, effort and borrowed equipment.

Elizabeth Fothergill CBE, William Burlington, Jenny Romeo, Steve Price, Kate Gadsby, Keith Howard, Andrew Cowen, John Kimberley, Alice King, Pete and Lizzie Roe, and Charlie Walker for your invaluable advice that shaped the book in its early stages.

To my colleagues on the Derby Wellbeing project, at Community Action Derby and the NHS Community Mental Health team, for the crucial work you do every day.

And finally, to Gill Reynolds for joining me on this writing adventure. I'm forever grateful for your patience, commitment and confidence. Thank you.

ABOUT THE AUTHOR

On the 26th of September 2018, Leigh Timmis pedalled into the record books, becoming the fastest person to cycle across Europe in a time of 16 days 10 hours and 45 minutes. Leading a team of sports science experts, he pioneered an innovative "no compromise" approach to ultra-endurance cycling to break the previous world record by an astonishing eight days and 17 hours. In November 2022, Leigh became a double world record holder, riding 2,230 miles – the greatest distance cycled in seven days.

These incredible achievements were built upon a unique and inspirational journey of self-discovery. In 2010, Leigh left the UK to cycle around the world on his epic solo expedition of 44,000 miles over seven years, across 51 countries, and on a budget of only £5 per day. Pushing the limits of cycling and human endurance, he rode his bicycle in some of the most inhospitable places on Earth but also to some of the most magnificent.

Leigh's life-changing experiences have instilled within him a deep belief in the goodness and strength of humanity. Since returning from his first epic adventure in April 2017, Leigh has focused on helping others to become better versions of themselves through motivational speeches for business and education audiences across the UK. Leigh is an ambassador for MQ Mental Health Research and is the Honorary Colonel of the Derbyshire Army Cadet Force.

Leigh's exciting and moving stories of aspiration, self-motivation and survival have been published in the international and national press. Leigh has also made appearances on BBC television and radio as well as delivering talks for TEDx and National Geographic.

For more information or to book Leigh for a speaking event, visit www.leightimmis.com.

RESOURCES

In the UK
Samaritans
Samaritans offer a free, 24-hour, confidential helpline and online chat to support whatever you're going through.
Call: 116 123
Email: jo@samaritans.org
Visit: www.samaritans.org

In the USA
988 National Suicide & Crisis Lifeline
The 988 Suicide & Crisis Lifeline offers free, 24/7 call, text and chat access to trained crisis counsellors who can help people experiencing suicidal, substance use, and/or mental health crisis, or any other kind of emotional distress.
Call: 1-800-273-8255 or 988
Visit: www.988lifeline.org

Donate
MQ Mental Health Research
Leigh is an ambassador for MQ, the UK's leading mental health research charity. MQ strive to create a world where mental illness is better understood, diagnosed, treated and, maybe someday, prevented. For further information or to donate, please visit www.mqmentalhealth.org

Have you enjoyed this book?

If so, why not write a review on your favourite website?

If you're interested in finding out more
about our books, find us on Facebook at
Summersdale Publishers, on Twitter at **@Summersdale**
and on Instagram and TikTok at **@summersdalebooks**
and get in touch. We'd love to hear from you!

Thanks very much for buying this Summersdale book.

www.summersdale.com